192308

956
.7
043
092
Franc

Francis, Susan.
    Nowhere to hide : a mother's ordeal in the killing
fields of Iraq and Kurdistan / Susan Francis with
Andrew Crofts. -- London : Weidenfeld and Nicolson,
1993.
    vii, 240 p. : ill. ; 23 cm.

06845355   ISBN:0297812890

1. Francis, Susan. 2. Persian Gulf War, 1991 -
Personal narratives. 3. Iran-Iraq War, 1980-1988 -
Personal narratives. 4. Refugees - Iraq - Biography. I.
                    (SEE NEXT CARD)

80   94MAY30   fc/kc   1-00605368

NOWHERE TO HIDE

NOWHERE
TO HIDE

A Mother's Ordeal
in the Killing Fields of
Iraq and Kurdistan

**Susan Francis
with Andrew Crofts**

**Weidenfeld and Nicolson
London**

First published in 1993 by Weidenfeld and Nicolson
An imprint of the Orion Publishing Group, Orion House,
5 Upper St Martin's Lane, London WC2H 9EA

A catalogue record for this book
is available from the British Library

ISBN 0 297 81289 0

Filmset by Selwood Systems, Midsomer Norton
Printed in Great Britain by
Butler & Tanner Ltd, Frome and London

'Susan Francis' is a pseudonym.
Other names have also been changed to
protect her family still living in Iraq.

Illustrations

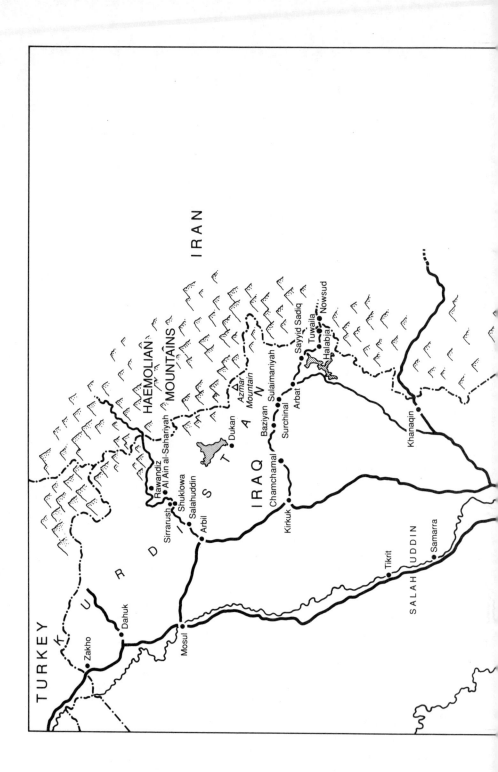

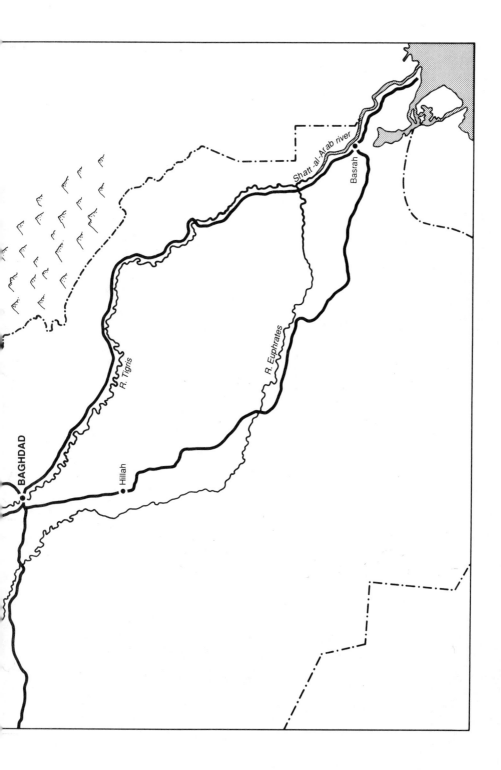

ONE

IT was our wedding anniversary, and it seemed as if we were now going to die together, slow, agonising deaths with our grandsons in our arms. Or, worse still, Azziz would go first, leaving me alone to look after the children on the mountain, a task I was now too weak to manage on my own. I walked outside in the chilly dawn rain, while Azziz and the two boys, too feeble to rouse themselves, slept in the car, which had run out of petrol days before. I didn't even have enough supplies left to make a pot of tea to warm their sick stomachs. Hunger and thirst were gnawing at our insides, the pain mixing with the diseases and poisons which were now gripping us all.

I wandered around for a while, my clothes which had almost dried during the night becoming sodden and heavy once more. I picked my way through the sick, the dying and the exhausted who littered the roadsides, avoiding people's stares but watching out of the corners of my eyes to see if anyone had anything I could beg to eat or drink. I had no pride left now, I would do anything to get nourishment for my husband and the boys. The stink of sewage and rotting bodies filled my nostrils, making me retch, but I had nothing in my stomach to vomit. A few people had managed to get fires going with the damp, green sticks which were all that was available, and were boiling water or trying to heat scraps of food. Some who still had enough strength and anger would shout at me, or spit at me for being a foreigner, but I no longer cared. I had lost the rest of my family and I believed they had all been killed. As far as we knew our home in Baghdad had been destroyed by the Allied bombings, but there was no way we could find out. I had gone from being the centre of a large, happy family, to being a helpless refugee statistic, a husk of my former self, with no control over my situation.

Every direction I looked there were crowds, hundreds of thousands of people slumped in grey heaps in the mud, huddled beneath piles of clothes and blankets which were soaked through by the constant rains and which, despite layers of filth, still couldn't keep out the cold winds of the mountain nights. It was as if life was ebbing away from the entire crowd, and no one had the strength to fight to hold on to it. There was no hope in any direction. No one was coming to save us. We were just waiting until our bodies were unable to take any more suffering and released us.

The poisoned water which cascaded down the mountain streams, mixing with the rainwater and turning everything to mud, had infected thousands of people. Everywhere you walked you stepped in pools of orange and yellow faeces left by people too weak to move away from the crowds or to bury their own diseased excrement. Some families no longer had the strength to bury their dead, just leaving them where they fell or perished in their chilled sleep. Both Azziz and the boys were suffering terrible dysentery from the poison, and probably the only reason I wasn't was because I had barely eaten since we had fled from Sulaimaniyah a week before. I had eaten nothing nourishing for several months before that.

I was beginning to believe that Azziz was going to die within a very few hours. The thought of losing him was unbearable, but I had no tears left to cry. All seemed lost. I was shivering and feverish and I didn't think I had the strength to keep going any more. But there was no alternative. From those who had left after us we heard tales of how Saddam Hussein's advancing army was killing and torturing everyone who turned back, marching unstoppably after us, wiping out towns and villages as they came.

All his life Azziz had prayed three times a day, but that day, which was a Holy Friday, he stopped praying. He had lost his faith, and without it I couldn't see what there was to keep him going. People with strong faith can withstand a great deal of physical suffering, and achieve great feats of endurance. Once that faith has gone you are just left with the suffering.

'How can I believe in a God when such terrible things are happening?' he asked me. 'Perhaps if we ever get back to Baghdad I shall start to believe again, but I can't pray up here.'

When Azziz and I married in England nearly forty years ago I was just twenty and he was twenty-two. It all seemed so exciting to me, as if I was fulfilling my destiny in some way, following a path which I had subconsciously known about ever since I was a schoolgirl.

'So,' my teacher, Miss Reed, had sat down opposite me and smiled kindly, 'what do you think you would like to do when you leave school, Susan?'

'I would like to marry the Sheik of Baghdad,' I answered. It was simply the most exotic thing I could think of. I couldn't have dreamt that one day I would actually fall in love with and marry the son of a Baghdad landowner and local sheriff. I knew nothing about Baghdad, or even where it was, but it seemed like a place where you could have wonderful adventures and discover some of the mysteries of the universe. It sounded like it was about as far from Bournemouth as it was possible to get, which was all I was interested in then.

Miss Reed was kind enough to smile at my joke, but she didn't waste more time discussing my future with me. There were plenty of other girls who knew what they wanted and whom she could help with advice and information. She gave me my allotted time and then politely said goodbye. A few years later I was able to return with my Arab husband and introduce her.

'So,' she laughed, 'you got what you wanted after all.'

It had seemed like it at the time, even though everyone warned me against marrying a man from such a different culture. Nothing seemed to matter except that I had someone of my very own, someone who needed me and cared for me, and whom I had promised never to leave. I must have known instinctively that he was a man worth fighting for, despite my naivety and lack of experience. If something inside me hadn't been sure that he was the only man for me, I would have let all those doom-merchants put me off with their predictions of disaster, and I would never have endured the treatment I received in my early years in Iraq.

I was a student nurse when we first met, enjoying the freedom of being away from home, living with girls of my own age. I had never even been to a dance before I left home, and so it was with considerable trepidation that I set out for my first one at the Guildhall in Southampton. In 1953 young people were still doing the formal ballroom dances, with the girls sitting around the edges in semi-darkness on plush red seats, waiting to be asked. I sat, pretending to smoke cigarettes and trying not to choke, and chattered nervously with my friends, so that anyone watching would see how sophisticated I was and what a good time I was having.

A student from the university asked me to dance. With my heart crashing in my ears I tried to follow his lead, stumbling over his feet, hardly daring to touch him as my friends tried to shout instructions from the sidelines.

'Step, one, two, three . . .'

'Move closer . . .'

'Relax!'

In the end the poor boy pushed me away – 'Hopeless!' – and I returned to my friends, mortified.

I didn't even see Azziz at first, until he was standing at my shoulder. I looked up and saw he was foreign. 'Would you like to dance?' he asked, with a heavy accent.

'Jane,' I shouted to my friend, 'do you want to dance with this bloke?' Jane shook her head. 'All right then,' I agreed, not wanting to hurt his feelings. I was relieved that he was even worse at dancing than I was. We shuffled stiffly around the dance floor together. He was wearing a brown suit and scruffy brown shoes, an outfit which I thought was particularly unflattering, but he was very good-looking with huge, liquid brown eyes and a clear, olive-coloured skin. He tried hard to make conversation in broken English and I tried to sneak looks at him without appearing too forward. Being completely ignorant of the world outside my own, I assumed he was Italian or Greek, and when he said he was from Iraq I had no idea where that might be. I certainly didn't connect it with the magical city of Baghdad. He told me his name was Azziz.

He was a kind, gentle man. To begin with I thought he was a little effeminate. He had lovely hands and a strong face which was always creased up in a smile. He told me how beautiful I was and how he loved my blonde hair, and that was wonderful to hear as no one had ever told me things like that before. Over the following weeks we drifted into a calm relationship. He became my first real boyfriend and lover, but I had no idea of making plans for the future. It didn't occur to me that this man and I would spend our lives together, enjoying and enduring so much. I was just living from day to day, my mind more on my work than on my personal life.

He was at the university in Southampton to learn English and to qualify in civil engineering. He had been sent by his government and he was obviously very clever. He told me tales of his home in Baghdad, of his father's many wives and their lives behind the walls of their huge house, and I took him shopping for clothes that would suit him better. Some of the other Iraqi boys filled their girlfriends' heads with tales which could have come straight from the Arabian Nights. They talked about the gold plates their families ate off, and of flying carpets if they were willing to believe in them. Azziz was very honest. He showed me photographs of the family house, of his mother shrouded in black and his father in flowing ceremonial robes. He explained that although they weren't a poor family by any means, life in Iraq was very hard compared to Britain.

'It doesn't matter,' I assured him, 'whether you live in a tent or a palace, you are enough for me.'

The world he described was so far away. I couldn't really imagine what it was like, and I didn't try all that hard to understand what he was telling me. I suppose my mind was too full of all the other things which occupy teenage girls, like my nursing friends and the things I was learning at the hospital. I think he could tell that I wasn't taking it in, and after a while he stopped talking about Iraq. We concentrated on our day-to-day lives in England, both of us working hard at our studies and seeing one another whenever we could. Because our studies forced us to spend so much time apart, it made our time together all the more precious. I longed to be able to be with him all the time.

One hot day in August I called round to his house, to be told that he had gone away to Scotland for a few days. He had left me a note to say that his beloved half-brother had been killed doing stunts on a motorbike. I knew he was close to this wild young man who had been down to visit a few weeks before, and I could imagine how devastated he would be by the news. The body had to be dispatched home from Heathrow Airport, sent off by a milling crowd of Iraqi students.

When Azziz eventually got home a week later he was heartbroken, and clung onto me as if he was drowning. 'I suppose now,' he said, 'you will leave me, just like my brother.'

'No,' I said quietly, 'I won't leave you.' It was a careless promise, given just to console him at the time, but it was a promise I never went back on.

Looking back on that time from the nightmare of the Kurdish mountains, after all we had been through in the last thirty-seven years, it looked as if death was going to tear us apart just when we needed each other most. It was as if we had arrived in hell together, and had brought our family with us. Was this our punishment for defying our families and all the other people who had said we should never marry?

From the corner of my eye I saw a woman making tea on a small fire built from a few sticks, which she was managing to keep going despite the steady rain. I shuffled over to her. 'May I have a glass of that?' I asked. 'It is my wedding anniversary today.' I waited for her response. Would she spit at me or take pity?

She stood up from where she was crouched over the pot. She was thin and bent with weariness; she was probably only in her thirties but she looked twice that age. She stared into my face, her expression hostile at first at the sight of a foreign woman, then tears welled up in her eyes and she put her arms out to me. 'Oh you poor creature,' she hugged me to her and we both began to cry, 'how can you bear to be here on such a day?'

TWO

'I HAVE been ordered to go back,' Azziz said, his large, soulful eyes watching anxiously to see my reaction.

'Back where?' I asked, stupidly. I had been so busy thinking about the immediate problems of my day-to-day existence as a new mother with no money that I had hardly given any consideration to what I would do when he wanted to return to Iraq. We had only been married a year and I now had baby John, who took up all my waking hours and totally enchanted me, seeming to me to be the most beautiful creature in the world. Azziz had been busy with his studies most of the time, leaving me to my own devices. I don't suppose I was paying him enough attention. He was always very patient with me. I think perhaps he felt guilty that he was not able to support me better while he was studying, and so he did not complain when I did not look after him as well as a young wife should. Something told me, however, that this was a serious matter.

'Home, to Baghdad.' He gave me the letter, which was in Arabic. It meant nothing to me.

'But you still have a few months before your exams,' I reasoned, 'that gives us plenty of time to plan.'

'No,' he shook his head, 'they want me back now.'

'But why? That doesn't make sense. Why would they call you back a few months before you qualify, after spending so much money on you?'

'It's not just me. Everyone has had these letters. The government must have a good reason.'

I couldn't believe his unquestioning acceptance of the order. He was always such an independent person, so happy to argue and debate any point with his friends, so sure of his opinions and so strong in his convictions. It made no sense to me at all and the sudden announcement that I had to uproot myself and my new baby to a completely foreign country, where I didn't speak the language and knew no one, was a shock. I suppose I had realised all along that I would go to meet his family eventually, but I had been so busy coping with each problem as it came up that I hadn't prepared myself. It had seemed a long way in the future, but now I had to face it.

It wasn't until many years later that we discovered why the letter had arrived. In those days the British were still running Iraq, and they kept all the best positions for themselves. Although they were supposed to be training local Iraqis to take over, they had no wish to give up their comfortable expatriate lives, with their houses, clubs, servants and easy jobs. Therefore they found every excuse they could to recall Iraqi students early so that they never qualified and could be kept in the secondary jobs. This situation was soon to change, when the British were sent home in 1958, but not soon enough to help us.

Azziz seemed in a way to be relieved. He had been away for three years and now he had an excuse to return to his family. 'Don't worry, love,' he comforted me, 'I can always return and finish my studies later, or perhaps I can finish them in Iraq. It will all work out.'

I couldn't argue with him because I knew nothing about it, but it seemed a very foolish decision to me. As it turned out not all his friends made the same mistake. Many refused to go back until they had qualified, but we were the first of the fools. Looking at it from his point of view, he was still little more than a boy himself, and he had been swept into a marriage in a strange land with a woman whose ways were completely foreign to him. Brought up to believe that women should be silent and compliant, there simply to serve the needs of their men, it must have been a great strain to find himself married to someone who stuck up for herself and argued about things. We had squabbled a lot in the first year, but that never matters when you are young and in love. Now the thought of returning to a country and people that he understood and was comfortable with was very tempting for him.

To begin with he suggested that he should go back first, and then I could follow with John once he had organised us somewhere to live and I had grown accustomed to the idea. I liked that suggestion. But after a few days he changed his mind, and insisted that I should go out with him.

'Why have you changed your mind?' I wanted to know.

'Because if you stay here with John on your own, you will never follow me,' he said, 'and I could not bear to be without you both.'

'Please,' I pleaded, 'just stall them a few months until you finish, please just do that, so that you have your qualifications and I have time to organise myself.'

'No.' He was adamant. 'My country wants me back. I must do my duty.'

I knew it was hopeless to try to change his mind once he had set it on something. I already understood how stubborn he was, especially when he was in the wrong. It was one of the things I loved most about him, even though it infuriated me sometimes. 'Oh well,' I tried to look on the bright side, 'at least I'll be leaving freezing old England. It will be warm out there, won't it?'

'Oh yes,' he looked so relieved and hugged me, 'I promise it will be beautiful weather.'

Mum was horrified by the news, mainly because it meant she would be losing baby John, who was by then the most important thing in her life. He was the most beautiful baby, like a little monkey with big brown eyes and a shock of black hair. 'You can't go,' she insisted, 'it's uncivilised. Arabs are filthy people. They still live in straw huts. There are flies and diseases everywhere. You can't take a baby to a country like that.'

'Oh Mum, it's not like that, not really,' I wasn't at all convinced of the case I was arguing, remembering the photographs which Azziz had shown me of his home. 'Azziz will be there to look after us. They aren't an uncivilised people, they're just like us.'

'You won't find things any better out there than they are here, that's for sure,' she ranted on. 'What happens if you hate it and he won't let you come back?'

'No one has ever stopped me doing what I want.' That wasn't quite true; I hadn't wanted to give up my nursing course, but having a baby had forced my hand. I was so thrilled with John that I didn't mind now that I had him, but I was very disappointed at the time. It is something which I have regretted ever since, and the main reason why I wanted Azziz to finish his training while he had the chance.

'Maybe they'll kill you, and bury you in the desert and none of us will ever be any the wiser. Things like that have been known to happen, you know.'

'Mum! Do you think Azziz could kill anyone, let alone the mother of his son?'

'It'll be different when you get out there, he'll be different.' She changed her tack. 'Leave John with me, I'll take care of him. You don't know what you are taking him into. Later you can come back and get him, once you've got a home ready for him.'

'It's no good, Mum, we're going and we're taking John with us, so you might as well wish us luck.' Her warnings did alarm me, even though I didn't believe that they were founded on truth. But I was set on a course from which I would not be deflected, and by taking the stand she did I think she made me even more determined to do as my husband wanted. I don't know which of us was the most stubborn, Azziz, Mum or me.

I had become pregnant very soon after we were married. I decided not to tell anyone at the hospital, just to continue my work. I was embarrassed and I truly believed that no one would notice and I could have the baby in secret without interrupting my training. It is hard to believe that I could ever have been so naive. But I soon began to feel ill. I went to see a doctor and she was very angry with me for not looking after myself better. She told me that I had developed an infection in one of my kidneys and would almost certainly have to go into hospital before the baby was due. Azziz was so busy with his studies that I didn't want to worry him. I found it embarrassing to talk about such details with any man, even with him, so I tried to continue in silence. I wanted so much to finish my course, but the pain from my kidney eventually became unbearable. Azziz realised that I was in no fit state to make my own decisions and took charge of the situation. But he was just a young man and he knew nothing of women's problems, so he took me down to Mum's so that I could see another doctor. The doctor came to the same conclusions as the one in Southampton. By now I was too ill to argue with them all, but I insisted that Azziz go back to college, leaving me at Mum's. The next day I found myself with a suitcase in my hand, going by bus from Mum's house to Boscombe Hospital alone, leaving all my dreams of becoming a nurse behind. My rash decision to get married had changed my life.

As we prepared to leave for Iraq, frantically working out what we would need and trying to pack everything for John, I began to become excited. I was, after all, about to fulfil my childhood fantasy and travel to the exotic Baghdad. After a few days we were ready. We had one large trunk and baskets full of baby milk, bottles, teats, nappies, food, a thermos of hot tea and just enough money to afford a black cab to take us from Mum's house to Bournemouth Station on the first leg of this great adventure. I had grown used to the idea and it all seemed such fun to me then. Oh, how stupid we were and what risks we were running with the life of our baby!

THREE

I HAD never been to London before, which heightened the excitement for me, and on the train we met Mary from the university, who was on her way up to the city to visit some friends.

Mary was one of a group of girls who were going out with Iraqi students at Southampton University, and we had become good friends. She was a short, round, happy person, always laughing and interested in everything that went on around her. She was from Ireland originally, one of a large family. She had been very kind, welcoming me into the group, rather like a mother hen. Her boyfriend, Abdul, was Azziz's best friend, a very clever man who was studying electrical engineering. He seemed a lot older and wiser than Azziz, although they were the same age. Perhaps it was because he was the eldest boy in his family, not the youngest as Azziz was, or perhaps it was to do with the way he looked. He was very tall, thin and imposing, which made him and Mary an odd couple, but they were very happy together. Sometimes Azziz would go to him for advice, rather like an older brother, and it nearly always seemed right.

All Azziz's Iraqi friends at university had British girlfriends whom they planned to marry, and many of them remained close to us throughout our time in Iraq. Mary and Abdul were my favourites.

Mary and I used to laugh together all the time and Abdul and Azziz used to talk for hours about the state of the world, and about what they would do with their lives. Later I was to find out just how much talking men in that part of the world go in for, leaving much of the 'action' to their womenfolk, but then it was exciting because they seemed so full of ideas and opinions that were new to me. We all used to meet in the refectory at the university and the conversation was lively, intelligent and funny. I loved their company and felt that I fitted in.

Nearly all those men married their British girlfriends, yet all of them must have known how unpopular their decisions would be with their families back in Iraq. I don't know whether they genuinely fell in love with us all, or whether it was the only way they could get sex in those inhibited days. Perhaps they saw us as 'trophies' which they could take back home and then abandon when they grew tired of us. Perhaps they were attracted by the differences between us and the women they had grown up with. Sometimes Azziz would grow very quiet and thoughtful, and would refuse to tell me what was worrying him. Then I put it down to worries about his studies, but thinking back I'm sure that he was concerned about how his family would deal with his marriage.

In Iraq they were used to women being completely dominated by the men in their families; in England we did things very differently. All the Iraqi men I knew were attracted to intelligent and headstrong women, none of whom was likely to take easily to the traditional role of the Arab wife. Perhaps they were rebelling against their families, or perhaps they were just swept away by their adolescent passions. Most likely they were acting as spontaneously as we were, living for the present and heedless of the future.

I doubt if the other girls had any more idea of what they were letting themselves in for than I did. All we knew was that we enjoyed the company of these men, and that they seemed as nice as any others. We couldn't know anything about the darker shadows of their backgrounds which would bring such unhappiness to so many of the girls they married, or which would make us outcasts in the unseen families which we were joining. We were young and unworldly and such subjects as the history of the Arab world or the teachings of Mohammed were beyond our experience.

The train journey to London passed very happily as we chatted and laughed and picnicked, but I noticed John was beginning to cough a little and seemed to have a temperature. I hoped he wouldn't develop a cold on his last night in England.

'What's the matter with the baby?' Mary asked.

'I don't know.' I put my hand on his head, 'I think he's a little feverish.'

'He's all right,' Azziz insisted, 'don't fuss with him so. He just needs to get to a warm climate.'

'Yes,' I agreed doubtfully, 'some sunshine will do him good. When will you be coming out to join us, Mary?'

'Oh, not long,' she said, 'once Abdul has finished his exams and got his qualifications.'

I looked across at Azziz, but he was staring out the window at the passing countryside, avoiding my gaze. He looked distant, so handsome and so lost in thoughts I couldn't guess at. I felt a surge of love for him as I cuddled John to me and went on gossiping with Mary.

What a shock London was to me; so busy and noisy and full of cars and people, walking, driving, cycling, everywhere a roaring babble. We dragged our trunk out of the station and loaded it into a taxi, keeping John bundled up against the cold. We were booked into an hotel in Queensway, a run-down area to the west of the centre. It was owned by an Iraqi and all the guests were Iraqis too. My heart sank as we walked through the door. It was my first taste of Iraq, and it wasn't the flavour I had been expecting. Azziz saw that I was unnerved and put his arm around my shoulders. I noticed other men staring at us. Some of them looked angry at this public show of affection, others leered lasciviously, but Azziz did not flinch.

There was a worn piece of carpeting on the floor and the dirty paper was peeling from the walls. Bare, dim light bulbs hung from the ceilings and the smoky dining-room was full of people jabbering loudly in Arabic. Our room was a pokey little hole with the wind whistling through the grimy windows, making them rattle in their frames. There was a smell of stale cooking and old bedclothes in the air, and all the noises of the hotel came through the thin walls of our bedroom, mingling with the street noises outside. I felt lost and alone. I wanted to run back to Bournemouth and the safety of my mother's house, but I told myself it was only for one night and there was nothing else we could do now. We had just enough money to get us to the airport and buy a meal. We couldn't possibly move to more expensive accommodation, or even get a train back to Bournemouth. I was tired from the train journey and needed a good night's sleep before the next leg of our adventure. We sat for ages on the bed together, just holding hands and watching the baby sleep.

As the evening wore on in this dingy, smelly place, John's cough and fever grew worse and I started to worry. He would cry pitifully and then be unable to catch his breath. He was going bright red in the face and I was frightened there might be something wrong with his lungs. As darkness fell in the strange city I began to panic.

'We have to get this baby to see a doctor,' I said.

'How can we do that? How can we find a doctor in this city, where we don't know anyone?' Azziz looked worried and unable to decide what to do. He seemed so vulnerable. I put my arm round him and we held each other close as we watched John. I didn't know the answer, but my baby seemed to be suffocating.

'We'll ask the hotel manager,' I said.

I carried John downstairs and the hotel manager very kindly agreed to take us to the nearest hospital. I held John close to my chest, anxious about the cold night air on his lungs. The car was old and noisy and the manager swung it round the corners with gay abandon, talking all the time to Azziz in Arabic. The streets looked hostile and strange, and I was relieved to breathe the familiar smell of Dettol as we went into the hospital. We waited anxiously while a young doctor examined poor little John.

'I'm sorry,' he said to us eventually, 'your baby has pneumonia. He will have to be hospitalised.'

We stood staring at him, stunned. We had no money to get back home – we could barely afford to get back to the hotel. We were in a strange city, embarking on a long journey and suddenly our baby's life was in danger. I felt so young and alone and lost, all I wanted was someone to tell me what to do next. I looked at Azziz, but he was as lost and helpless as me.

They rushed John away to an oxygen tent, and we sat for several hours waiting for news. The hospital grew quiet as the patients slept, the visitors went home and the staff went about their night duties. Azziz lay down on one of the benches, using his coat as a pillow, and tried to sleep.

'Typical,' I exploded, 'your baby is dying and all you can think of is your beauty sleep!' I was so tired and so frightened, it made me very nasty.

'How can this happen?' Azziz had his head in his hands now. 'We have to catch the plane tomorrow morning or we will never get the money for another ticket.'

'I don't understand how he became so ill so quickly,' I said, putting my arms around him. 'I'm sorry, I didn't mean to be so angry. It's all so frightening.'

'It'll be all right,' he tried to comfort me, but he didn't sound confident of his own words. We fell silent, holding onto each other, both lost in our own worries. After several hours they came to tell us that John's condition had improved and he was in a ward. I was allowed to sit by his bed, but Azziz had to stay in the waiting room. I was quite relieved to be able to be on my own with John; at least then I didn't have to worry about my husband as well.

I sat in the darkened ward, listening to John's wheezing breaths and the moans and snores of the other children, my thoughts going down into deeper and darker places as the night wore on. Suddenly, like a shaft of light, I remembered something from one of my lectures during training. A doctor had been discussing asthma and he had said something about patients never coming to any harm in aeroplanes because the cabins were oxygenised and pressurised. When the doctor came back onto the ward in the morning I asked his opinion. Would it be all right to take our baby on the plane as arranged?

'Don't be so damned stupid,' he snapped. 'You are a mother! Do you want to kill your baby?'

I tried to explain our dilemma but the tears were coming and I couldn't get the words out through my tightened throat. He wouldn't listen. 'Okay,' I said finally, desperately trying to keep my voice calm. 'I'm taking my baby out of this hospital. Could you please have the release papers signed for me.'

An hour later, the doctor's insults still ringing in my ears, we left, armed with medications, injections and syringes, and with John wrapped up like a tiny mummy. We had to go back to the hotel and pay for the room we had never used – no discount of course – and by 9.30 a.m. we were using our last cash to get a taxi to Heathrow Airport. We checked our trunk in and found a warm place to wait until we boarded the plane – my first flight ever.

The plane seemed so big, and the seats so narrow and uncomfortable. John was behaving like an angel, strapped onto my lap. Once we were up in the air and had all been fed, John in a clean nappy and asleep in a makeshift cot, I began to relax and enjoy myself. I sat holding hands with Azziz and chatting to our neighbours. Our first stop was Cairo, and as we descended through the clouds I peered out the window. All I could see was mile upon mile of sand.

'Where are the buildings?' I asked.

'The airport is outside the city,' Azziz explained. 'You will see the airport buildings in a minute.'

Stepping out into the sunshine, excited by my first experience of being abroad, we were greeted with jeers and glares from the Egyptian workers on the tarmac. One of them spat at me as I passed. Unknown to us the Suez Crisis was blowing up between the British and the Egyptians. I was hurt and frightened by this unexpected reaction and stayed close to Azziz.

We were left outside on the tarmac in the hot sun, waiting for the smaller plane which would take us on to Iraq. There was some shade, but as soon as we got out of the sun it was too cold to stand around. I began to feel faint with tiredness when I heard a quiet voice speaking to us, 'Would you like a meal?'

'We have no money,' my husband said.

'That's all right. Bring the baby in out of the sun.'

The man was a waiter in the airport canteen who had seen us through the window and taken pity. He brought us food and drink and allowed us to sit in the cool for a little while. There are so many kind people in the world. They are nearly always the most ordinary ones, the ones who have the least to give. In years to come I would have to rely on such kindness many times for the survival of my family.

I was so relieved by how well John seemed, and glad to have got him out of the cold and damp of England. 'So much for medical opinion,' I said to Azziz as John gurgled happily on my lap.

'Doctors are just people,' Azziz smiled, 'they can't know everything.' He was always far more understanding and tolerant of other people than I was.

By the time we took off it was evening and we arrived in Basrah, the city which was to be our first home, at midnight. The stop-over in Cairo had been like a brief period in no man's land. Now I was entering a different world, one which was completely alien to me. The first thing I noticed was what Shakespeare called 'all the perfumes of Arabia'. It is a smell like hot urine mixed with smoky fires and animal dung, very distinctive and very strong to nostrils more used to disinfectant. The night air was bitterly cold, the wind whipping round us as we walked from the plane to the buildings. I clung onto Azziz's arm.

He squeezed me reassuringly, but he seemed very eager to get into the buildings, hauling us along in his wake.

'I thought you said it would be warm,' I grumbled, worried again about John's chest.

'It will be,' Azziz laughed. 'This is the middle of a winter's night.' He seemed so happy to be home.

Hugging John tightly to me I allowed myself to be swept into the airport building on a tide of activity. Now I realised that I really had married into a family of influence. Until then I had assumed that Azziz was exaggerating in order to impress me when he talked about how important his family was, and how many relations he had. The head of Customs – a friend of the family – ushered us away from the queues into the safety of his small office, beaming with smiles. We were honoured: no waiting in queues, no checking of luggage. Whoever we were, a friend of the family, a friend of a friend, a bribe, everything seemed to be so easy for us. I did not even try to understand what was happening that night, I was too tired. Azziz was the confident one, greeting people, chatting, shaking hands, hugging and kissing people. He seemed very different from the quiet, diffident young boy I had met in the dance hall. I soon learnt that when the strings were not being pulled, which was most of the time, life was a great deal harder. You could often wait hours or even days to complete a simple piece of business – 'in sha Allah', God willing.

Everyone seemed to be some sort of relative of Azziz's, so many of them, all poking their heads round the door of the Customs office; endless men's faces, most of which I would never see again, each one eager to get a look at the foreign wife of the son of Khaled. Everyone kissed and hugged Azziz, so pleased to see him home, and looked me up and down with a mixture of curiosity and disdain. I knew that Azziz was afraid of these people, his strong, domineering family, afraid of how they would react to his marrying a foreign woman. But then he was the hero of the hour, the young man being welcomed back from his travels into the bosom of the family.

On the few occasions that Azziz had spoken of his fears of his father's disapproval or his brother's scorn, I had always dismissed them. 'It'll be all right,' I assured him. 'I'll win them over, you'll see.' Now I was here I wasn't so confident. How do you win people over when you can't communicate a single word, and you can't understand their expressions, their gestures or even who they are? None of them spent more than a few seconds weighing me up, before turning their backs and getting on with their lives. I began to feel that I was fading into invisibility, but I was too tired to care.

Hustled through the main doors into the night air I was urged into a big, yellow, wooden cattle truck, followed by other shadowy figures. Azziz and his brother sat in front with the driver. Seated on a hard, splintery seat, I clutched the front seat with one hand and my baby with the other as we took off like a bullet from a gun, hitting bumps and potholes and bouncing into the air. I soon learned that in Iraq a man who drives slowly is not a real man.

I would become familiar with this mode of travel. The 'taxis' were used for carrying people or animals, dozens squashed inside, others clinging onto the roof in the burning sun or driving rain, heads, arms and legs sticking out in all directions. You often came across a dead animal which had fallen off one of these speeding trucks, bang in the middle of the highway. Packs of stray dogs would wait patiently for the road to clear before dashing in to grab chunks of the unfortunate creatures, snarling viciously at each other. The biggest, meanest dogs usually won and ran off, chased by the smaller ones hoping to get a bite before the fresh meat was swallowed.

The lights from the truck swept over shabby shacks and dwellings, lighting up these packs of mangy dogs as they scavenged in the rubbish. Black, unlit alleys ran off in all directions. We were on the main highway, but it was little more than a mud track, the thin layer of asphalt potted with holes. There were trenches everywhere which had been dug for some utility or other and then abandoned.

'Oh my God, Azziz, look at that!' I was horrified to see a man, with what looked like his nightshirt (I discovered this garment was called a *dishdasha*), hitched up, urinating against a wall and over his legs, his naked bottom presented to the world.

'You shouldn't be looking,' Azziz answered sharply, and I kept quiet for the rest of the drive while the men jabbered on.

FOUR

AFTER driving for about half an hour we arrived at Azziz's brother's house, a tiny roadside hovel made of wattle and sticks, crouched amongst other, stone buildings which seemed to emit a pungent, night-time odour that made me feel queasy. We were met by four witches. The old women were shrouded in black, eyes glaring at me over their veils. I tried to smile politely and greet them, but they simply ignored me, seeming to look through me once they had sized me up. I was so tired I asked if I could go straight to bed and I was shown into a small room with carpets all over the walls. In one corner was a high, hard bed, which I needed steps to reach. The bed was covered in a tra-ditional *ilhaf*, which was like a cotton duvet, only much heavier than the ones which later became fashionable in the West. The Iraqi women go to great trouble to embroider the *ilhafs* in wonderful colours, and to line them with materials like white satin for special occasions such as weddings.

I tucked John in on the side of the bed nearest the wall, so that he couldn't fall out in the night, and climbed in beside him. 'Tomorrow,' I thought to myself, 'I will start to get to know them and soon we will all be the best of friends.' It still seemed like an adventure to me, despite the hostility of the women outside. In the past I had always been able to get on with everyone I came into contact with, and I saw no reason why I shouldn't be able to get on with these people if I put enough effort into it. I had no idea how deeply rooted their hatred of women like me was.

Despite the babble of excited voices, I fell into a deep sleep. I didn't even hear Azziz coming to bed. When I woke up it was still pitch dark, with no sign of dawn. I could just make out the contours of the room in the moonlight and I could hear Azziz sleeping beside me. My bladder was aching to be emptied.

'Azziz,' I whispered in his ear, stroking his bristly face.

'What!' He sat up with a start.

'Sssh, you'll wake the baby. I need the toilet, where is it?'

'Outside the house, round to the building at the back, up the stairs opposite and onto the roof. You'll see it on the other side. Be careful you don't fall over the side.' He turned over and went back to sleep as I climbed over him, clambered out of bed and tried to remember his instructions.

It was silent and chilly outside and my heart was beating in my ears. What if I bumped into someone else on their way to the same place? I managed to find my way onto the flat, mud roof he had described. I saw a door set in the side of the roof and investigated, but there was no toilet. I went back to Azziz and woke him again. I told him that I had found the roof and a door but there was no sign of a toilet.

'That was the toilet, you idiot,' he grumbled.

Muttering to himself, he got out of bed and came with me outside and up the staircase. 'There,' he said, pointing to a hole in the floor inside the little door.

'That's the toilet?' I was aghast. 'So where do I wash?'

'There should be a tap around here somewhere,' he mumbled, feeling around outside the door until he found it. 'Fill this *ibriq* and take it into the toilet with you to wash yourself.'

'*Ibriq?*'

'This jug,' he waved it at me impatiently and went back to bed.

On my next visit to this facility it was daylight and I was horrified to see that the walls were crawling with huge black lizards. I went back to find my husband again. 'Azziz,' I said firmly, 'I am not using that toilet until you clear away those lizards.'

He laughed. 'You need the geckos,' he explained, 'to eat the bugs and mosquitoes. They won't do you any harm.' I had a lot to get used to.

The room we had been given was my brother-in-law's bedroom,

the best in the house, and the old women were furious that I had been accorded this honour, even if I was Azziz's wife. To them any Western woman must be a *jahabah* – a prostitute – particularly one who worked as a nurse. In Iraq at that time only women from very low backgrounds became nurses, because women from decent families were never expected to work outside the home. As a result, hospitals were terribly badly run places, as I was to find out to my cost in years to come, and nurses were thought to be there solely for the sexual pleasure of the doctors. That was how they viewed me. I didn't realise all this at the time, but I could see that they didn't like me and there was no way I could change their opinion since they wouldn't allow me to communicate with them, and Azziz seemed reluctant to act as my interpreter.

Their contempt made me very uncomfortable, but I thought if I ignored it they would get used to me. I had believed we would only be in that house for one night, but I soon realised that Azziz did not intend to move on yet and after a few days I became uneasy.

'How long do we have to stay here?' I asked every day. 'We have to get a home of our own, darling, so that we can start our life out here properly.'

'Wait until my job is sorted out,' he begged me. 'I'm going to get a job for the government and they will house us, but you have to be patient. They say I have broken my contract with them by marrying a foreign wife. It will take time to sort out.'

So it was partly my fault that he couldn't get a job, or so I was told. Perhaps that was one of the reasons that the old women hated me. Or perhaps that was just an excuse to shut me up. I had no way of knowing what the truth was since I had neither friend nor ally in the country apart from my husband, so I tried to keep quiet, but I couldn't be patient. Azziz seemed to be treating me differently now we were in Iraq. He was more offhand and seemed to confide less in me, preferring to talk to the other men. I began to feel very isolated. I loved him so much but I felt he was drifting away from me. I didn't want to keep pestering him with my questions and requests, but I had no one else to turn to. He was doing his best to be patient with me, but the strain was telling on him. I could feel the hatred of the women burning into me all the time, growing in intensity as I refused to become a doormat for them to walk on. They never seemed to do anything but sit around the house jabbering to one another, waiting for their men to return so that they could serve them. I concentrated on looking after John and hoped that things would settle down on their own.

Once I had the temerity to take a tomato from the fridge because I was hungry, and the women screamed abuse at me for the rest of the day. I was told that I should never have taken food that had not first been offered to the men. The moment Azziz came home the women ambushed him at the door and regaled him with hysterical tales of my misdemeanours. He calmed them down and then tried to explain to me what I had done to offend them.

'But I live here too,' I protested, 'I have to eat.'

'I know,' he tried to soothe me, 'but you must understand their customs as well.'

Months passed like this, and finally things reached a climax. We had fish for supper that evening, and the old woman who hated me the most had made it. She offered me the first slice, and she insisted on cutting it for me from a very particular part of the fish – supposedly the best part. I noticed that everyone else was given other parts. Perhaps at last she had decided to accept me, and show me some kindness. The old woman made a gesture to me with her hands which I didn't understand. I assumed it meant 'bon appetit', but later I discovered that it wished me a speedy death. None of the others appeared to notice or care as I tucked into the fish. Soon after the meal I started to vomit and pain seared through my body. I wanted to die.

My agony continued late into the night and Azziz, frightened, called a lady doctor. She came into the room and saw me retching, my stomach still heaving even though it had nothing in it to bring up.

'I will be back in a moment,' she said to me in English, giving me a reassuring smile, and she walked straight out again. She returned a few minutes later with two policemen and they escorted me to a taxi. Everyone was jabbering at one another and Azziz was persuaded to stay with the baby while one of the men from the house came in his place. In the taxi he seemed to be haggling with the policemen as we drove to the hospital, but I was too ill to care. The doctor seemed angry and was shouting at the men, pointing at me. When we arrived she pumped out my stomach and put me on a drip. Next morning she came to see me.

'You nearly died last night,' she said.

'What was it?'

'Arsenic poisoning.'

'Can't be,' I said quickly. 'You must be mistaken.' It is hard to believe that someone has tried to murder you, especially a member of your family.

'No,' she said, 'I am not mistaken. I have seen it before, in circumstances very like yours. Do you want to press charges against these people? You could have them arrested. They should not be allowed to get away with it.' She seemed to understand exactly what must have happened.

'No,' I said quickly, 'I just want to get back to take my baby out of the house.' Involving the police would not help me get on with my new family, nor would it make me any safer from future attempts on my life. How did I know if I could trust the police any more than my in-laws? I didn't even know if I could believe this doctor, although she seemed to be the nearest thing to a friend I had met since arriving.

'Yes,' she nodded, 'that would be a wise thing to do.'

Mum's warning was ringing in my ears – 'They could kill you and bury you in the desert and we'd never know.' The thought of running back home to England was very tempting, but I didn't want to be beaten so easily, nor did I want to leave Azziz or take John away from his father. As long as I was able to get away from the old women I was sure I could start to build a proper life in Iraq.

Azziz was waiting for me when I got home. He put his arm round me and helped me up to the bedroom. The women's eyes were watching through the open door of the sitting room; they were whispering amongst themselves.

'Shut the door, darling,' I said once I was lying on the bed. He did as I asked and came back, sitting at my side and stroking my brow and hand, his eyes deeply troubled. 'We can't stay here any longer,' I said softly, 'they hate me too much.' He tried to protest but I put my finger to his lips. 'I know it. If I stay here they will kill me, or drive me mad. We have to find somewhere of our own.'

He looked at me for a few moments, his eyes filling with tears. 'I know,' he spoke so quietly I could hardly hear him, 'I'm sorry. I will arrange something.' He kissed me gently and left me. While I slept he went to one of his uncles and asked if we could stay with his family for a while, until we were on our feet. The uncle was kind and agreed. He had a self-contained flat at the top of his house which we could have, so I could be separate from the rest of the family when I wanted to be. This made my life a great deal easier as we waited to be housed in a home of our own. The flat had large, airy rooms and a view out over the roofs of the city. It was hard work climbing the stairs with John, who was growing into a heavy toddler by now, but it was worth it. I felt that we had a private sanctuary, the three of us, where we could hide together against the world. The first time we were left alone in our new home I threw myself into Azziz's arms and covered him with kisses. I was so relieved to get away from the others and to have him to myself again. He laughed, obviously pleased to have been able to make me so happy, and proud of himself for putting his foot down with his family.

The attitude of Iraqi families to the foreign girls who married their young men was much the same everywhere. In the years to come I would talk to many foreign wives about their experiences in Iraq, and many had a far more difficult time than I did. Although Azziz was in awe of his family, he understood my problems. Some of the women I talked to were more in danger of being killed by their husbands than by anyone else. So my mother's imaginings hadn't been quite so wild as I thought. Many of the women gave up the struggle and went home, which no doubt was exactly what their husbands' families had hoped for, but it always seemed sad for the couples who must have started with such high hopes. I have always believed that marriage is a commitment which must be honoured, however trying the circumstances. I had made a commitment to stay with Azziz as his wife and I could not allow other people to make me go back on my word. They tried so hard to make my life intolerable, but they couldn't stop me from loving my husband.

Because in those early days I didn't understand Arabic, I was spared some of the humiliation being heaped on me. Some things I only came to understand later. One afternoon, for instance, I was taken to a room with all the other women and they brought in a pretty young girl, who must have been about fifteen. They dressed her up as a bride and had her parade around the room. Everyone was making a fuss of her and ignoring me, but I didn't mind. I just sat in the corner, watching. Later I discovered that the girl, who was the daughter of a local government minister, had been promised to Azziz as a wife before he left for England. Now they wanted to persuade him to marry her as well as me and put us in separate houses. I can't imagine how they thought he would do that, since he couldn't afford to house even one wife. Perhaps his family would have been willing to help him financially if he was married to a local girl. The fact that he had chosen to marry a foreign 'prostitute' instead of this lovely girl was more than his family could stand. All I could do was endure their hatred.

'She's very pretty,' I said to Azziz when I found out the truth, 'she would have made a lovely wife.'

'Yes, she's very pretty,' he teased me, 'but not as pretty as you.' He held me in his arms and kissed me, whispering in my ear, 'You are the only wife I want, and you are better than all of them rolled into one.' How I loved to listen to such flattery when he was holding me tight. I would feel a warm glow of happiness in my stomach and I was sure that any amount of discomfort was worthwhile if it meant I could be with him.

The girl's father later became a good friend of mine; he thought I was fun and had spirit. He used to come to our house to eat and drink and he used to tease Azziz, telling him that he should do more for me, like buy a bigger house. But his wife could never forgive me for stealing her potential son-in-law.

Many Iraqi men married more than one woman. As soon as their first wife began to grow old, or became weighed down with children, or simply found enough confidence to refuse to be completely dominated, they would bring in someone younger, more willing to be manipulated. It wasn't unusual to find that even a teenage boy already had three or four wives. All of the men held this threat over their women. Even my dear husband wasn't above shouting threats at me when I had annoyed him.

'I can always marry someone else, you know!'

Right from the beginning, I decided to call his bluff on that one. 'Okay,' I would say, 'there's the door, you go out and marry someone else, but don't ever expect to come back here, because once you've gone that's it.' Even then, when I was still so young and innocent, I knew that unless I stood up to him from the start our relationship would not last. However strong our passion for one another was then, it was bound to fade with the years, and it had to be replaced with a mutual respect. It was important that we always knew where we stood with one another.

My attitudes would infuriate him sometimes and we would argue fiercely, but we always ended up hugging one another, both apologising and asking the other's forgiveness. I hated fighting with him, but I was so afraid of being submerged into the culture and of allowing him to become like the other men, changing from the kind, thoughtful man I had fallen in love with, that I resolved never to appear to weaken.

Some of the foreign wives simply give in and let their husbands marry again. Perhaps they were relieved to have other women to share the burdens of marriage. One German woman actually allowed her husband to banish her to a shed at the bottom of the garden while he went on to marry two younger women.

'Never for a minute think that you are superior to me just because you are a man,' I told Azziz in the heat of one argument. 'I am your equal, and I will never believe that you are better than me.' Those words, which seemed so simple and obvious to a Western woman, must have sounded very threatening and disorientating to a man brought up from the cradle to believe that his gender is unquestionably superior.

He was quite possessive of me, which I enjoyed. Once, when we had been in Iraq a couple of years, I took little John down to the cinema with me, and in the queue I met a man who worked with Azziz. He started talking to me and then began to touch my bottom. I was taken completely by surprise. Grabbing John's hand I rushed straight home and told Azziz what had happened. He was furious, and stormed down to the open-air café where he knew he would find this man. Dragging him off his chair, Azziz laid into him like a man possessed. I was pleased to see him react so passionately, even though I realised it was as much his own pride he was protecting as my honour.

In the beginning I found it hard to eat any of the local food. The women cooked mainly greasy stews with fatty meat and vegetables, heavily laced with a mixture of curry powders. There were always mountains of rice which smelt unwashed, and which would take the women hours to clean of bugs and tiny black seeds. The men always had the best of the food and what was left would go to the children next and finally the women. At breakfast, for instance, the women were only allowed dry bread and tea, whilst the men were allowed milk and sugar, eggs and all the other good things.

Baby John lived on rice and thinned-out soup, but seemed to adapt to it and became quite healthy. His favourite treat was a fish which was baked over charcoal. I had no idea how to cook any of the local dishes and none of the women in the family had any intention of teaching me. When we were finally living alone poor Azziz had to survive on egg and chips for years, the only dish I knew how to cook.

Azziz wasn't around much in the early days, always out looking for work or on family business, meeting the other men of the family and arranging things for the future. I soon discovered that Iraqi men in general are very lazy, preferring to leave their wives to do all the hard jobs of running the house and bringing up the children. They like nothing better than to sit around in cafés, or outside one another's houses, talking. Mostly they gossiped endlessly about politics, arguing furiously with one another. Sometimes they talked about business, or about family matters.

'My son is coming of age now, perhaps we should arrange a marriage with your daughter . . .' They would spin these discussions out forever, occasionally shouting to their wives to bring them tea or coffee. The women were just as bad, and often they were match-making for the children while they were still toddlers. I'm sure Azziz was trying his hardest to establish himself in a career at that stage, but everything moves so slowly in that part of the world – who wants to rush around in such heat?

I didn't mind him going out with the men, but when he brought them to our home, I was not willing to be treated like a servant. I would be hospitable, but if they started ordering me around without a 'please' or a 'thank you' I would tell them to do it themselves. The men grew used to my ways and would laugh, but I think the women found them very offensive. Azziz may have been embarrassed to have such a disobedient wife, because I wouldn't let him order me around in front of his friends either, but he didn't try to change me.

The men had a lot of habits which I found hard to get used to. Apart from the robes they wore which looked like nightshirts (and the pyjamas which they were quite happy to wear outside in the street), they all carried worry beads, each made of some, to me, new and exotic material like amber or crystal or ebony. They were continually spinning these toys around and fiddling with them until the clicking nearly drove me mad. They also had very different personal habits, happily picking their noses in front of me, using the extra long nails which they grew on the little fingers of their left hands, rolling up the results and flicking them onto the floor. I got used to the toothpicks which they would use after every meal, but I never got used to the spitting in private places, and peeing against walls.

I grew adept at recognising all the different men's headdresses, each colour denoting a different tribe or area, and the style of wearing it demonstrating the status and profession of the wearer. Only the older women in town would wear the full black *abaya*; most women were now content to wear skirts of modest length, and although Azziz had warned me that I should cover my arms at all times, I soon noticed that other young women were wearing short sleeves and quickly followed suit because of the heat. I had an *abaya* of my own which I would wear if I was visiting a mosque or attending some formal event like a funeral. Some of the older women had beautiful ones with black lace sewn into them. The poor country women had old, worn ones which had turned brown with age.

I spent a lot of time on my own while Azziz was out looking for work, but I didn't mind too much. I was happy to look after my baby on my own, always trying to make sure that John was asleep and didn't annoy Azziz when he came home, and I took to walking with John to pass the time during the day. The women of the family didn't approve of me going out on my own, but since they didn't want to come with me there wasn't much they could do. They tried to make Azziz stop me, but he told them that I needed some freedom and fresh air. I think he was quite proud of my independence at times. I always made sure that I was dressed respectably in a long *dishdasha* or skirt, and I would cover my blonde hair so as not to attract too much attention.

I was fascinated by everything I saw, and often shocked by the primitiveness of the people's lives. Everywhere in Basrah were narrow lanes of wooden-fronted buildings, the women seemingly imprisoned behind their barred windows as they worked away inside, chattering to one another while the men were out of the way. Brick-built houses were beginning to take over in towns, but many of the two-room homes were still built of mud and sticks, with roofs made of bamboos holding up straw mats which the women made, and then sealed in mud. The roads were all unmade and covered with potholes which filled with water whenever it rained. Dogs were forever rummaging among the refuse which lay in trenches down the centre of the roads. Life was hard and uncomfortable for everyone, but particularly for the women, who seemed to be working all the time. There were no public toilets, so if I was caught short, as I often was when I was pregnant, I would simply knock on someone's door and ask to use theirs. They were always overwhelmingly welcoming, pressing me to a cup of tea and something to eat. I think they were all bored and tired of their own company and family gossip. Later, when I began to make friends with Iraqi couples, I always found them wonderfully hospitable. If I went to visit a family they would always insist on killing a chicken or a lamb in my honour, even if it was their last one. They are the most generous of people in that way.

I was frightened of the street dogs, which always hunted in packs of a dozen or so. They were mangy, yellow, wolf-like curs, their coats as matted and tattered as camels'. If you caught their eye they would bare their teeth at you, cringing down as if ready to pounce. Left to their own devices they would snap and snarl at one another, fighting over every scrap of food or dead carcass they came across. There weren't too many of them in the city centres because the police would go out shooting them at night, but as soon as you got to the suburbs they were lurking on every corner, and no one went out walking without a heavy stick. In the country they terrorised lone travellers with impunity, and anyone who walked outside at night was in grave danger of being attacked and killed. In later years we went out into the countryside in cars for picnics and were sometimes unable to get out because packs of dogs would come jumping and snapping at the doors and windows.

Many of these wild dogs were rabid, and the government encouraged people to kill them. At one stage they actually offered money to anyone bringing in the body of a dog or a cat, and the numbers went down dramatically. No Iraqi would think of having a dog as a pet, and any European seen in the street with a dog on a lead was likely to be ridiculed.

I liked to go down to the Corniche along the Shatt-al-Arab river, sitting under the tall palm trees in a beautiful garden which the British had planted, and watching the swift waters flowing past, not daring to put my feet in in case there were sharks – how did I know? Sometimes Azziz would come down with us in the evening and we would share a bottle of Pepsi in a riverside café, because that was all we could afford, chew sunflower seeds and listen to the soft sounds of reed pipes floating over the waters. At those moments I felt completely content with my life in Iraq. As long as I had Azziz and John with me, and everything was peaceful, I was happy. The periods of peace and togetherness, however, became fewer as the years progressed.

'Why does everything smell of cow dung?' I wanted to know.

'The women mix it with straw and mud,' Azziz explained, 'and leave the pats out in the sun to dry. Then they use them as fuel to bake bread. Also the mud which they use to plaster the houses is made from a mixture of dung and river mud.'

'And the smell of burnt urine?'

'The men relieve themselves against the walls,' he shrugged, 'and then the sun evaporates it. It is part of the mixture for building houses too.'

'My God, what a place,' was all I could think to say, but I was growing used to it all, especially the slow pace of life. In the West everyone is always in such a hurry to get things done, but in Iraq there would always be another day, and life would continue whether you rushed or not, so why bother?

By the time high summer had arrived I was beginning to find the heat difficult to take, which was a surprise to me since I had always thought that as long as I was warm I would be happy. It would be many years before we could afford air-conditioning, so we were reliant on ceiling fans and cold showers. The Iraqis used to create a primitive sort of air-conditioning by taking the scrubby little camel thorn bushes which grew in the desert, pressing them in frames and putting them in the windows. They would then allow water to drip down them from hosepipes and if there was a breeze it was supposed to blow cool air into the rooms – I don't think it had any effect at all. The thorns on these bushes were so sharp that when women went out to collect brushwood they wrapped their legs in white bandage-like material to protect themselves.

I would rely mainly on cold showers, but the moment I stepped out of a shower, I would be bathed in perspiration again. The loss of body salts led to dehydration and I started to develop 'elephant's skin', going grey and scabby and needing constant supplies of skin creams. I took to wearing a thin *dishdasha* around the house with nothing underneath it, but I still couldn't keep cool. If those women had known how little I was wearing, I dare say it would have confirmed all their suspicions about my morals. Everything about the climate was so violent, the summer days so hot and the winter nights so bitterly cold, it wore you down. Very soon I began to understand why the women in that part of the world grew to look so hardened and old. Their lives seemed to consist of endless toil and discomfort, and mine was no different.

FIVE

FINALLY Azziz came home with good news. He had a job in one of the government's civil engineering offices, building roads and bridges, and a flat was being prepared for us. While we were waiting we could move into some brand new labourers' houses. I was delighted, until I discovered that my brother-in-law Ahmad and his wife Nadera were coming too. I was growing to hate this huge elephant of a man, mainly because he beat poor Nadera continually (I didn't understand then that almost all Arab wives have to put up with abuse from their husbands). I also thought he was a bad influence on Azziz, always trying to turn him against me.

Although the thought of taking Ahmad and Nadera with us depressed me, I agreed because I knew we were in their debt for letting us stay in their house when we first arrived – however much I might have hated being there, and however much they may have despised me. I was so relieved to move into a place of my own, especially as I knew that I was pregnant again, that I would have accepted almost any conditions. The flat had been very comfortable, but I had still felt that I was a guest in someone else's home, my every movement being watched and disapproved of.

The new house was very basic with unplastered walls, concrete floors and ceilings. The familiar, tiny, prison-like barred windows

perspective for me. 'Don't worry so much, Susan,' she would say, 'in a hundred years time, who'll care about any of it?'

Nearly a year had passed by the time Azziz found a job and a home for us. Only then did he announce that he wanted to take me to visit his parents in Baghdad. I could tell that he was frightened at the prospect of having to face his father, but I was looking forward to meeting them.

'How will we get there?' I asked.

'By train, we will travel overnight.'

A few days later we climbed into a first-class carriage on an old-fashioned British steam train. There were wooden shutters on the windows and shiny wooden seats to lie on – if we had gone second or third class we would have travelled in windowless cattle trucks. They gave us bedclothes and in the morning they brought us bacon and eggs for breakfast – another hangover from the days when the British had organised everything. It was an uncomfortable night, but exciting for me despite having little John to look after and another baby kicking me in the stomach every few hours.

'When you meet my father,' Azziz told me as we clanked through the night, 'you must kiss his hand.'

'I'm not kissing his hand!' For some reason the thought filled me with horror. 'You never kissed my father's hand, why should I kiss your father's?'

Azziz fell into a sad and thoughtful silence at my outburst and I felt sorry for all the trouble I caused him, but I didn't intend to climb down. Perhaps it was a silly thing to make a stand about, but it seemed like a matter of principle to me.

Baghdad station was a sea of people. There were hundreds of beggars moving amongst the families who had set up camp around the building, cooking meals on portable charcoal stoves, sleeping, drinking, chatting and behaving as if they were in their own homes. The noise and stench were overpowering as we fought our way through the crowds. I felt dizzy from the powerful mixture of sensations.

'What are all these people doing here?' I shouted to Azziz over the din.

'They came in last night or the night before and they are waiting for their connections tonight or later this week,' Azziz explained. 'The trains in Iraq only travel at night because the heat in the day makes the rails expand. It means journeys take a long time.'

Once out of the station we took a jolting ride through Baghdad in a wooden bus until we reached my husband's family home. It was a very modern city even then, and the wide boulevards were an exciting contrast to the mean streets of Basrah. There still weren't many cars – it was the mid-1950s – and most people used buses or donkeys to get around. Camels strolled elegantly along the streets, often laden with merchandise for the markets. There were more people in Western clothes and tall modern buildings were beginning to appear on the skyline, amongst the domes of the mosques.

The house was surrounded by a high, ancient wall which was pierced by one giant, iron door. Azziz knocked on the door, and it was opened by two men whom I guessed were more of his brothers. They greeted him with hugs and kisses and then they all disappeared into the house, leaving me standing in a courtyard of lush trees with John and my unborn child.

Their voices faded to silence and I stood waiting in the tranquillity of this strange no man's land, puzzled and wondering what I was supposed to do. Nobody came. I pushed my head tentatively through one door and called out 'Hello', but all I heard was my own echo. There was an archway leading through into another courtyard with an oasis of palm trees and an area where the women washed the men, but it was just as silent and empty through there. I must have waited outside for over an hour before another of the brothers came past.

'What are you doing here?' he asked in English.

'No one has invited me in,' I said. 'My husband has disappeared.'

'He has gone to eat with our father.'

'What am I supposed to do?' I controlled my anger as best I could, 'my son is hungry too.'

'Come in, we will find you something.'

He led me across yet another courtyard to where he lived with his wife and children. It was a huge, cavernous room hung with Persian carpets and with a few ancient wooden seats pushed back against the walls. It had a calm feel to it, a sense of age and quiet which dwarfed the people who lived in it, imbuing them with some of its dignity. Their sleeping area was divided off by screens. I later discovered that each of the brothers had a room like this within the house. The father had his own room, which was the biggest and finest, into which only men could go, and usually only family members or important religious leaders. At the back of the house were some tiny, dark rooms which they used as kitchens, and there were stables for the livestock. His wife kindly fed John and me while we waited for Azziz, who eventually appeared.

'Where have you been?' I demanded.

'To see my father,' he seemed surprised that I should even ask.

'But you just left me . . .'

He shrugged, 'I have to do as my father tells me.'

'Why?' I smiled at him. 'Well, can I meet this father of yours now?'

'No, he has retired to his room.'

I was perhaps less shocked than many might have been by the way I was treated in Iraq, because I had experienced the same prejudice in reverse in England. When I started to go out with Azziz I was horrified by other people's reactions. The authorities at the nurses' home forbade me to invite a 'wog' to any staff dances. Normally they thought that students were suitable partners for us, but apparently not foreign ones.

This was nothing compared to Mum's initial reaction. She was beside herself when she heard the news. 'How can you marry an Arab?' she shouted. 'Your children will be coloured. How can I take them out? People will look at us!'

'I'm only going out with him, Mum,' I tried to calm her down, 'I haven't said anything about marrying him.' I was hurt by these reactions, but they made me all the more determined to do as I pleased. I certainly wasn't going to stop seeing Azziz just because they all thought there was something wicked in it. He was a good deal more courteous and considerate than many of the English boys I had met. Even if I did have children with him, I reasoned, I couldn't imagine Mum would want to have anything to do with them, whatever colour they were – after all, she had never shown any interest in us when we were children. As it turned out I was misjudging her on that point as much as she was misjudging Azziz.

When they actually met, Mum was instantly won over by him and became his most ardent fan. I don't think she had ever met anyone so polite and charming, so willing to hang on her every word and to fetch and carry for her with such good grace.

By the time we decided to get married I knew I had a real 'catch' and I was very proud of him. I made my way down to my local church of St Clements. The Reverend White was a kind man, always pleased to see me. 'I'm planning to get married, Mr White,' I told him, 'and I'd really like to do it at St Clements.'

'Wonderful, wonderful,' I thought he was going to hug me.

'My boyfriend is from Iraq, he's a Muslim.'

Shutters seemed to fall across the vicar's face. He sat, grave and silent for a few seconds before answering. When he did speak his tone was cool and brusque. 'If you wish to marry this young man, then so be it, but not in this church, young lady.' He went on to lecture me on the reasons for not marrying someone from another faith. I felt myself becoming hotter and hotter with anger. Eventually I stood up to leave, and I imagine my face was flaming red by then.

'I believe, Mr White,' I kept my voice as polite as possible, 'that there is only one God. Or is there a special one for Christians, or Jews or Arabs?' I turned on my heel and left. I went to my Gran to cry on her shoulder. She hugged me to her. 'I did warn you, dear,' she said softly, 'that the Church wouldn't like it. But you don't need their blessing to be happy. If you know he's a good man that's all that matters.'

My troubles didn't end there. We decided we would marry in the same building as the ballroom where we first met. When I got back to Southampton I went down to the beautiful white Guildhall to register our intention to marry.

'Wait in here,' I was told, 'someone will be along to see you.' I sat alone in the musty room, listening to the bustle of officials going about their business in the corridor outside, until a white-haired gentleman came in. I later found out that his name was Judge Avery.

'What can I do for you, young lady?' He looked at me without smiling.

'I want to marry my boyfriend Azziz, he's from Iraq, he's a student at the university . . .' I could hear my words tumbling out, out of control under the disapproving gaze of the old man. When I finally ran dry he shook his head sadly and began to lecture me on the foolishness of my decision, on the problems we would face due to our differences, and on the dangers of marrying someone from a culture which was so different to my own. I sat, silent, waiting for him to finish. He finally sat back, obviously confident that he had put his case convincingly.

'I would still like to register our intention to marry,' I said finally.

He stood up, slamming his hand down on the desk. 'Come back in a month with a letter of permission from your parents, and I very much hope you will change your mind in the meantime!' With that he stalked out of the room, leaving me boiling with rage once more.

All these memories came back to me as I lay awake in the house in Baghdad that night. I never did meet my father-in-law on that visit.

The family obviously wanted me to be left in no doubt as to how they viewed Azziz's 'bad' marriage. Many years later I was finally allowed to meet the revered head of the family, and I found out a great deal more about him from his wives. He had three of them living in the house, including Azziz's mother who was a kind, sweet woman. My father-in-law was a vain old man who liked to have all his clothes made for him from the finest English cloth and had never even washed his own face let alone worked for a living. He owned a lot of land and the farmers had to pay him rent every year.

When he wanted female company at night he would send for one of the wives to be brought to his room. Once he had satisfied his appetites he would literally kick her out of the bed and order her back to her own quarters. My mother-in-law, to whom I would later become very close, told me all this. I don't think there was ever much hope that my father-in-law and I would like each other.

Several years later one of Azziz's sisters-in-law was due to have a baby in Basrah. I went round to help. When I got there I was told that my father-in-law was due to come to see the baby as soon as it was born. I went about the chores as usual, and I was sitting on a low stool washing clothes in a metal bowl on the floor when he arrived. He greeted everyone, but I kept working because I had still not been introduced to him. After a while he asked who this woman was and he was told that I was Azziz's wife.

'This is the English woman?' He was obviously astounded. Apparently he had been expecting a cabaret dancer or nightclub hostess, not a simple mother and wife. He came over, took my hands and guided me to my feet. 'I'm sorry,' he said, 'I am ashamed. I can see my son was right and you are a good woman,' and he kissed me on the cheeks.

Because of the tradition of the men eating all the best food, my mother-in-law used to weave baskets and mats and sell them for extra money. She and the other women would spend the money on fruit and other treats which they kept hidden under their mattresses to eat when they were alone, and to give to the children.

At the same time as I was in Baghdad in 1957, a man a couple of years younger than me was quietly entering the political arena as a low-ranking member of the Baath Party. His name was Saddam Hussein and that year he started his slow, sure ascent of the Iraqi power structure. None of us knew anything about him then, or the chaos he would bring to all our lives.

SIX

LIFE in Iraq was very peaceful in those days of King Faisal's rule, and a peaceful life was exactly what I wanted. While everyone always talked politics, especially the men, we were not aware of any serious unrest. We certainly weren't aware that a rebellion was brewing. I suppose we were a long way from the centre of power in those days. We used to see members of the royal family fishing in Basrah sometimes, without bodyguards, and no one bothered them. As long as people have enough to eat and are left to get on with their lives they are usually willing to put up with whoever is governing them. It is always the minorities who take the action for change on behalf of the rest of us, and most of the time we don't even know that we need change.

Food was plentiful in Iraq at that time, for those who could afford it, and people managed as they had for hundreds of years. Modern conveniences were beginning to creep into the country, but slowly, and only for those who could afford them. Personally, I was quite ambitious to improve our lifestyle. I wanted to be able to own a decent house, and to have enough money to buy the children shoes and give them a good diet. I could see that in the long run I would have to work again in order to have these things, but that was impossible as long as I had small children. I certainly didn't want to leave them to be brought up by someone else. That meant that I had to budget very carefully. For the first six years that we were in Iraq I wasn't able to buy myself a pair of shoes, having to manage with slippers. It was twelve years before we could afford to buy luxuries like butter. The most expensive item for us was milk for the children, and we always managed to find enough for that, even though it meant that we had nothing left for pleasures of our own. Each day Azziz would go down to the markets and would buy a sliver of meat, four eggs, some small loaves of bread and vegetables for soup. Occasionally the camel-sellers would come in from the countryside selling filthy salt from sacks on the camels' backs, which was the only salt we could afford. There was only one supermarket, which was used mainly by the expatriates, where I bought the children's milk. Our poor diet meant that we both lost a lot of weight, and I became particularly thin and weak. The doctor told me that I had become anaemic. He said that I must have injections, daily at first and then becoming less frequent, to boost my red blood cells. We couldn't afford to pay a nurse to give me these injections, so I taught Azziz how to do it.

Because he was working so hard just to keep us afloat, I didn't see much of Azziz in those early days. During the day he worked for the government and in the evenings he went down into Basrah with Abdul to earn extra money wherever he could. He was under a lot of pressure and I knew that he was finding it hard to suppress his instincts, which told him that he should keep his outspoken wife in line, with physical violence if necessary. But I was determined never to allow myself to be crushed like all the other women I saw. I kept reminding myself, 'I am not inferior just because I am a woman. I am the equal of all these men and better than many of them.' I wanted so much to keep our relationship as good as it was in the beginning and not allow other people and worries to drive us apart.

I admired the way Azziz stood up to his family in my defence, and the way he refused to behave as they wanted. I tried to understand when sometimes he became angry with me. The heat and the pressure of bringing up small children made me difficult to live with sometimes, but we never ended the day angry with each other, we both made sure that by the time we went to sleep we were friends again. I knew I was lucky to have found such a good man and I believe that he felt he was lucky to have me too. He certainly told me so often enough. Looking back on those days now I can see that they were hard, but on the whole we were a very happy family, and perhaps the difficulties we faced in those early days helped to strengthen us for the ordeals which we would have to undergo later in our lives.

My second baby began to arrive in the middle of a cold winter's evening while we were living in the squalid little workman's house. Azziz was down in the town working. I went next door and asked Abdul to find him and bring him back, and to ask Azziz to get a bowl and some disinfectant on the way home so that I could deliver the baby safely. Abdul agreed but returned without Azziz a few hours later.

'He was angry,' Abdul told me. 'He says, where is he supposed to get the money to go shopping for you? He says you are imagining it, that the baby isn't due yet. Don't worry, it won't come tonight.'

'I'm a nurse, Abdul,' I answered angrily. 'I know when a baby is arriving.'

Some expatriate Englishmen living on the other side of the internal gardens from us were throwing a party. They were nice people, and I liked them a lot. I could hear the music, the laughter and the voices as I went about the house doing my chores with my contractions growing increasingly painful. I didn't feel like going over to join them. At midnight Azziz returned from his work.

'Help me,' I pleaded. 'Fetch a midwife.'

'Don't be stupid, if you are still walking around the baby can't be coming yet,' he seemed tired and irritable. 'I'm going across to the party.'

'Please get someone to help,' I held onto his arm.

'Get off me,' he shouted, pushing me backwards so that I fell painfully against a table. I crumpled onto the floor and he stormed off to join the party. I pulled myself up, shaken and surprised by the sudden violence. I knew I would have to do something to stop him behaving like that towards me, but my first priority was to get the baby born.

After a while my friend and neighbour Bernadette came round to sit with me. Mary was away at the time, visiting her relatives, otherwise I would have asked her to come as well. I missed her terribly when she wasn't there, she always managed to make the time pass quickly with her laughter. Bernadette looked very frightened at the prospect of having to help me give birth without any professional assistance. She was younger than me and hadn't yet had any children. She was a highly strung, nervous girl, married to Nizar, who was a large, powerful man, very pompous and bombastic, but surprisingly gentle and understanding with his fragile wife. His family owned a trading business, and he had had an air of prosperity about him even when he was a student in England. Nizar liked Azziz and was always trying to find ways to help him and I was fond of Bernadette, but didn't have much faith in her ability to help me if anything went wrong.

Azziz must have started to feel guilty about me once he got across the road because a few hours later he came back with a midwife, a filthy old crone with dirty hands. The two women helped me up to my bed and Azziz went to sleep in the other room. Bernadette and the midwife fell asleep on the bed with me as I dozed between the contractions, trying to bite back the cries of pain so that I wouldn't wake them. Just before dawn I knew that we had started for real and I woke them up. The cold was intense but we had no hot water except what we could heat on the oil burner, which filled the house with acrid black smoke.

When my baby April finally arrived the midwife had nowhere to put her, except on the floor, while she tried to prepare some water. As soon as I could, I got up to help her look after the tiny thing and try to keep her warm. Azziz rose at his normal time, pleased to find that his second child had arrived while he slept. I busied myself getting John up and feeding him, ignoring Azziz. When Bernadette and the midwife had left I turned on him.

'If you ever lay a hand on me again,' I said quietly, 'I am going straight back to England with my children. I love you more than anything in the world, Azziz, you know that, and I do understand the pressures you are under, but you must understand that I cannot live in fear of what you will do to me next. Violence can become a habit so easily. Don't think this is an idle threat, because you know I mean it.' He just nodded, leaving the house without saying anything. John and I sat together on the bed watching the new arrival sleeping. John was the most beautiful, sweet-natured boy. Everyone who saw him commented on his wonderful eyes, even strangers in the street. He was so pleased with April, he couldn't stop stroking the soft down on the top of her head with his fingers, and brushing his lips against it.

That evening Azziz came home with a piece of cloth for me to make the baby some clothes, and apologised for the way he had behaved. I cannot understand why so many Arab women bring up their sons to believe that they are superior to their sisters, and that they will become heads of their households over their widowed mothers. If they continue to do that they can't complain when they and their daughters-in-law are treated like virtual slaves.

It was soon time for John to start at nursery school. 'We need to see a copy of your marriage certificate,' the teacher told me when I went to enrol him. 'Without that we can't take him.'

'Fine,' I said, 'I have the certificate at home. We brought it with us from England.'

'England?' she said, 'it was a Christian ceremony?'

'Yes, of course.'

'I'm afraid that is no good here. You will have to remarry your husband under our laws.'

Azziz wasn't too bothered by this news and we went together to the Shi'ite mosque to see the *imam*. This wise, elderly man with his white beard and many years of religious study was in no doubt. 'Under no circumstances,' he told Azziz, 'can you marry this woman.'

'It seems to me,' I said as we left, 'that religious people are the same all over the world.'

Azziz didn't answer and I didn't go on because I knew that he was a religious man, always praying to Mecca three times a day and following the teachings of Mohammed.

We went next to the Sinna, a rival religious group, and asked the priest if he would marry us. 'Certainly,' he agreed, 'come to a room behind my mosque and we will do it there.' He advised Azziz not to tell his family what we were doing. They were a well-known Shi'ite family and would have been scandalised at the thought of us going to the opposition to be married. The three of us went through to the cool, tranquil room and the ceremony was duly performed. Then it came to the signing, which would make the whole thing legal. 'So, how much money are you going to pay for this woman?' the priest asked.

'Money?' I knew nothing about this. 'What does he mean, money?'

'It is the custom,' Azziz explained. 'I pledge a sum of money to you to equip the marital home and to be given to you should we ever divorce.'

'I'm not a cow,' I don't know why but something about the whole thing annoyed me, 'you don't buy and sell me. I'm not signing that form.' I strode outside and waited for Azziz to follow me. Eventually he came out to take me home. I was already feeling rather foolish, but I couldn't face climbing down now that I had taken a stand. 'How much did you put down?' I asked.

'One pound, seventeen shillings and sixpence,' he said, 'the price of the English licence.'

As we walked home I remembered our first wedding in England. The parental permission hadn't proved to be as great an obstacle as I had feared. Azziz had charmed Mum sufficiently and she agreed, somewhat reluctantly, to sign the papers. I went back to the Guildhall in Southampton a month after my first visit, my mind full of carefully rehearsed responses should the judge start lecturing me again. This time he said nothing and merely completed the paperwork. I suppose he thought that he had done his best to save me from myself, and now it was up to me to face the consequences of my rash decision.

The wedding was on a spring day in 1954 and I was twenty years old. We didn't tell anyone at the university or hospital about our plans. Mum and Len, my stepfather, agreed to be witnesses. The night before the ceremony I went home to Mum so that I could travel up with them on the train the following day. I had no special wedding dress, just an old beige suit, some new beige shoes and a buttonhole which I pinched from someone's garden on the way to the station. The weather was beautiful, but all the way to Southampton Mum kept saying, 'You don't have to go through with this if you don't want to, you know. It's not too late to change your mind.' I stared silently out of the window, frightened that I was making a mistake and wishing she would be quiet. 'Oh well,' she said eventually, 'I suppose you can always get divorced if it doesn't work out.' I didn't answer, but that was one thing I was determined never to do. I didn't want any children of mine to lose their father in the way I had.

Azziz was waiting nervously for us on the steps of the Guildhall, and we all walked in only to come face to face with Judge Avery. There were no fanfares, no good wishes, no loving family members around us, just a mouthful of words from a reluctant judge, a signing of the register and back outside into a lovely day. Five minutes, no more, and a promise to be kept for life.

As we were about to step outside I felt someone take my arm. I turned round to see the judge, his face suddenly full of compassion for me. 'Come back one day, my dear,' he said quietly, 'and let me know how your life is going.'

'Yes,' I said, 'I will.' But I never did.

It was all over by 11.30 in the morning, too early to have a meal really, and Mum was insisting she wanted to get back before my brothers came home from school.

'You must have something to eat before you go,' Azziz insisted. 'We must celebrate the wedding.'

She protested, but he was adamant and led us down the High Street, past the bombed-out buildings and piles of rubble from the houses being demolished to make way for ambitious new building schemes, carefully avoiding the holes in the road from which workers stuck their dusty heads to watch the legs of passing women. Azziz bought us a meal upstairs at the virtually deserted Odeon Cinema dining-room, but none of us was hungry. Then we walked Mum and Len back to the station. As we watched the train carry them away, I clung desperately onto Azziz's hand, all the false bravado that had got me through the day draining away. I was committed now. I was on my own with this man I barely knew, with no idea of what the future might hold. I felt empty and frightened.

Without my signature on the certificate we were still not married in the eyes of Iraq. The school continued to insist on seeing a copy of the certificate and I continued to dig my heels in. Having made the stand I didn't know how to get out of it without appearing even more foolish. Finally Azziz threw his hands in the air. 'Okay. I give up. I'll marry you another way.'

I had no idea what he meant, but that night he came home with the necessary certificate. I later discovered that he had married me by proxy with one of his workmates standing in for me. I didn't mind at all, in fact I thought it was very funny. I had saved face and managed to get John into his school as well. I was also able to tease the kind workmate who had volunteered for the job, who was known from then on as 'Mrs Azziz'.

It's hard being poor, but you get used to it and I was happy just to have my husband and children, and our growing band of friends. All Azziz's friends from the university were now coming back to Iraq with their British wives and we started to meet many more couples in the same situation. In all there were about a thousand foreign girls married to Iraqis, not just from Britain but from all over Europe and America, wherever the boys had been sent to study. We were given a new flat with a spacious garden, which we moved into straight away. Once again Mary and Abdul were able to move in next door to us, and other flats were allocated to other acquaintances of ours with mixed marriages, including Nizar and Bernadette.

It was a tight-knit community amongst the women and we were always in one another's houses for coffee and tea, or going for walks with the children in the cool evenings before we put them to bed. Mary would always be the loudest one, singing and cracking jokes and drawing disapproving glances from the locals. Her antics used to horrify Bernadette, who wanted nothing better than to disappear into the background. 'Please keep your voice down,' she would beg Mary, 'stop drawing attention to us!' But Mary would just laugh and continue to tease her. I would usually end up having to make peace between them, persuading Mary that Bernadette did have a point, and assuring Bernadette that Mary meant well, however boisterous she might seem.

Mary was also better at asserting her independence from her husband's family. She was the first of us to start working, even when Abdul begged her not to for fear of what his family would think. 'They think I'm mad anyway,' she would say, 'so I've nothing to lose.' She was only doing menial office work, which was well below her capabilities, but it inspired the rest of us to believe that we would be able to follow her eventually. Bernadette found the whole prospect of going out into the world terrifying, and swore that she was quite happy to allow Nizar to protect and keep her.

There were about a dozen of us who became close during that period. Together we shared the births of our babies and helped one another to learn to cook, sew, bring up children and all the other skills which women are expected to master but are seldom taught formally. We learnt to make furniture from orange boxes, turning the discarded packing cases into wardrobes and kitchen tables. By sticking together we were able to keep the outside world at bay.

These people would become Azziz's and my closest friends over the next twenty years. It was here that I learned the true value of friendship; the kindness, the help and the laughter which still consoles me to this day, when so much has happened to disillusion me about the human race. Without these friendships to support us, I don't know how any of us would have been able to put up with the heat, the poverty and the demands of the men. We sometimes used to go on outings together with our husbands, perhaps taking picnics to islands in the Shatt-al-Arab river. No one had any money, not even Nizar in those days, but we still managed to enjoy ourselves.

The American girls seemed to find it hardest to accept the Arab way of doing things. I suppose they were just that little bit more liberated and opinionated than the European women in the 1950s and the gulf between the two cultures often proved too wide to be bridged. Most of us, however, found that with support from one another we could adapt to our new lives.

Many of the wives found that the men they had married in America or Europe behaved very differently in Iraq. Nearly all the marriage problems stemmed from the men's need to dominate their families, and their wives in particular. If they weren't clever enough to do so with their tongues – and the constant verbal bullying was bad enough – then they would use their fists. The same attitudes went with them into the bedroom. Many of the wives complained about how violent their husbands were in bed, and many had miscarriages because of the treatment their husbands dealt out to them. Some of them were horrible men, but many were very good friends who appeared not to understand that there was a better way to treat women than the one they had learnt at their fathers' knees. Whenever I heard some poor woman telling a fearful story, I thanked God for my luck in finding a kind and gentle man who tried so hard to understand my needs and fears.

As far as the British expatriates were concerned, anyone who married an Arab was a second-class citizen. I was registered at the consulate, so I would occasionally get invitations to the events which they held there. I loved to wander around the old-fashioned building and gardens, and I met some charming people there. But if I was with Azziz I would be ignored, and if we were seen together in the street by the stalwarts of the expatriate community they would cross to the other side to avoid us. These foolish people had been living off the fat of Iraq for so long that they had come to believe that they were superior to the native population. Such arrogance was to be their undoing. Although the Iraqi people admired the British for their brains – 'Ah,' they would say to me, '*al-ajnabiyah shatrah*,' (the foreigner is clever) – they were heartily sick of the expatriates who 'behaved like gods'. It was because of these insensitive people that Britain lost so much influence abroad.

As a foreigner married to an Iraqi there was also a risk that you would be jeered at or spat at by the locals. I think they resented the fact that we had been given nice housing when we were considered to be 'Western whores', the lowest of the low. Still, we grew used to the treatment, and managed to make many friends amongst Iraqis as well as amongst ourselves.

Azziz and I had somewhere nice to live and just enough to eat, but there was certainly no money left over. To get wool to knit clothes for the children I had to unravel my old jumpers. I cut down a pair of Azziz's old trousers for John to run around in, and I made something for April out of the lining of one of her father's jackets.

Because April had green eyes and bright red hair some of the women of Azziz's family said that she must be the daughter of another man.

I was so impatient with their stupidity that I told them she was the daughter of the local baker, a hideous, dirty old man whose bread none of us would buy for fear of catching some dreadful disease. They seemed delighted to believe this. It made no difference to me what they believed any more. They only ever came to visit us if they felt ill and wanted me to give them medical advice.

It became known locally that I had trained as a nurse in England, and Iraqis were always coming to the house asking for help. I was happy to oblige them if I knew what to do. I delivered babies and injected the drugs which they got from the doctors and chemists. Sometimes I might even suggest that a doctor's advice should be adjusted. Many Iraqis seemed to believe that the more medicine you took the better you would be, and I would often have to cut down dangerously high dosages, especially when they had been prescribed for children. As we made more friends, I learnt to speak Arabic fluently and grew very contented with our life. I now felt that I was a member of the community, that I had roots. I came to think of Iraq as my home, particularly as my children were Iraqis.

Many of the local women would start to have babies when they were twelve or thirteen, and would still be fertile in their fifties, although they would have trouble breastfeeding. My mother-in-law was well into her fifties when she had Azziz, but he had been breastfed by his sister as his mother had no milk by then. Perhaps this long period of fertility was nature's way of compensating for the many miscarriages the women had, and the many babies they lost through childhood diseases. I noticed that grown-up twins were rare in Iraq, and a friend explained to me that a mother who had two or more babies would deliberately let the weaker ones die in order to give the stronger one a better chance. They were very philosophical about the whole business of childbirth. The long period of fertility also meant that brothers and sisters could be forty years apart in age, and half-brothers and sisters even more. A man with a string of young wives could continue to father children well into his seventies, having started at thirteen. As a result the families were all enormous, each one a cobweb of different generations.

Although I was enjoying my role as an unpaid medical adviser and midwife, I decided that if I was going to earn a living in the future I would have to give myself some skills other than an unfinished nursing course. If possible I wanted to get a better job than Mary's, which didn't seem to be leading her anywhere. Azziz managed to borrow a typewriter for me from his office and I sent off for a correspondence course in shorthand and typing which provided a certificate at the end. I felt that I was starting to gain some control over my life again. Azziz did not earn much money in those years but he was gradually working his way up in his career.

The quiet days of the kingdom ended dramatically on 14 July 1958.

SEVEN

'THE king is dead,' we were told, 'they have killed the king.' Everywhere people were anxiously discussing what was happening. Radios were blaring out from every house and shop, and the Koran was ringing out from the mosques day and night. Everyone was agitated and worried, no one really knew what to do other than go to work and hope it wasn't true. But it was true. The young boy king had been shot on the steps of his home in Baghdad; the Prince Regent, Abdul al-Ilah, and the Prime Minister, Nuri Sa'id, were dragged through the streets by angry crowds, their bodies mutilated and their heads hung on the gates of the Ministry of Defence. The whole Hashemite dynasty, which had ruled Iraq since it had been established by the British in 1921, had been wiped out overnight.

Word came to us that as foreigners we should not go out onto the streets with the children, and we were met with glares of hatred by any locals who saw us. They had had enough of foreigners in general, and the British in particular. From now on they wanted to run their own affairs, and who could blame them? It was very alarming for those of us who had no knowledge of politics and couldn't predict what would come next.

Then a quiet calm seemed to descend on the country. Martial music was played on the radio and we heard the official news from England that a coup had taken place and our new leader was General Abdul Al Karim Qassem. He came on the radio himself ordering that no foreigners in Iraq were to be harmed. Life was to go on as normal. In Baghdad times were changing, but for us in Basrah life went on much the same for many years.

Bad feeling against the British continued to simmer, despite the orders from the new leader not to harm us. If we went out for walks in the evenings we were met by hostile stares, and everywhere we heard the chant 'Throw out the Brits'. The Iraqis wanted access to the better jobs; justifiably, they felt they had been held back too long. Many of the Iraqi families who had befriended us over the last few years were now closing their doors in our faces, afraid to be seen talking to us. That hurt. Invitations to other people's houses dried up. We still had our own community, but we didn't feel welcome in the country as a whole.

Soon the British who were not married to Iraqis were sent home, many of them without notice. We were not sorry to see the backs of those silly, snobbish people. It also meant that people like Azziz suddenly had far more responsibility at work, responsibility for which many of them were inadequately trained. They had to work twice as hard in order to make up for their lack of experience. Often he would be at work until the small hours of the morning, but we felt it was our duty to work hard in order to help Iraq stand on its own feet.

'Once the expatriates are gone,' we assured one another, 'things will get better for us; the Iraqis will be able to accept us as equals.'

Although things were calm on the surface, my political awareness became sharper. I realised that there was a current of violence beneath the surface in Iraq which had previously been hidden from me, a current which could erupt at any time, and which would later wash our lives away in a lava of horror and misery. Any country which could destroy its rulers so radically and ruthlessly was very different from anything I had been brought up to understand. My mind was never really at peace from then on, even though actual incidents were few and far between for many years. I sensed how close to anarchy the country was, and how even a small political shift could lead to terrible cruelty and bloodshed.

I had another baby boy, whom I called Peter. Having babies no longer seemed difficult. I got up straight away, had a cup of tea, cleared up the mess, washed the clothes, cooked the dinner, saw to the other children and carried on with my life. My little family thrived on home-made soups and stews, thrown together and usually tasting all right in the end. I still couldn't cook rice, but my babies never suffered from lack of food. Azziz was still eating mainly egg and chips and I existed on boiled eggs. He was very patient with me, but I could see from his face when he was eating that he was longing for something a little more varied. I vowed to try harder, but somehow there were always other things to do. I continued with my secretarial studies all the time, sending off my lessons and beavering away in the evenings when it was cool and the children were asleep. I still had no opportunities to work while the children were small.

I was quite happy to find that I was pregnant for a fourth time, and went on with my life as the child grew in my belly. Then, one terrible day in the seventh month of the pregnancy I lost the child. I had seen it happen so many times to other women that initially I was not too frightened, but I did ask for Doctor Yamani, a friend of mine, to help me. She was a gynaecologist and she gladly came to be with me. As the day wore on I continued to haemorrhage and she grew concerned. By evening I had lost a lot of blood and was feeling weak and dizzy, with no sign that the bleeding was going to stop. Azziz was becoming increasingly anxious on my behalf and kept asking the doctor if she thought things were all right.

'I think you should go into hospital,' she advised eventually.

'I don't want to go into that filthy place,' I insisted.

'I don't think you have any choice,' she said firmly, 'unless you want to bleed to death. Don't worry I will do the job myself.'

'All right.' I agreed reluctantly because I was beginning to feel frightened about what would happen to me if I stayed at home and continued to bleed.

Azziz took me to the hospital and I was led to a small room in the teaching section with just two beds in it. I stood in the doorway, staring in horror.

'I can't stay here,' I protested, 'just look at the place.'

The mattresses were made of sponge, with rubber covers which were torn open to show the bloodstained contents. Brown rivulets of dirt ran down the walls and lumps of phlegm lay in the corners of the room where people had spat. My first instinct was to turn round and go straight back home, but I knew that I was too ill now to do that. However bad it was, it was my best chance. But how could I bring myself to lie in such a place? I was shaking with fear, but I pulled myself together with one last effort.

'Please can I have a bucket and some Dettol,' I asked the matron, 'and a nurse to help me. Azziz, darling, please could you go home and fetch my own mattress and sheets.'

'Yes, of course,' he agreed. The matron looked as if she was going to protest but she saw the expression on Azziz's face and left, tight-lipped, to do as I asked. Once they had both gone I picked up the mattress and threw it out into the corridor, along with the filthy blankets I had been given. A nurse appeared with a bucket and disinfectant and I set her to work on the floor as I did the walls, the windows, the verandah outside and a screen which I used to hide the other bed. I had almost collapsed with exhaustion by the time Azziz returned. I staggered out to the toilet and as I opened the door I saw several rats the size of cats scurrying away through the filth.

'Nurse,' I shouted, 'please can I have a commode in the room.' I expect that by then they would have done anything just to shut me up.

The next morning Doctor Yamani came with Azziz to collect me and take me to the operating theatre. I was too weak to walk without Azziz to support me, but with my arm around his neck and his arm around my waist I was able to stagger downstairs.

'I'm afraid we don't have any X-ray equipment here,' the doctor explained, 'but I'm pretty sure that you have fibroids, so I will open you up to have a look. Don't worry, it's an easy operation.'

'Oh no,' I couldn't stop myself exclaiming as we walked into the room which she was going to use to operate, 'this isn't the theatre, is it?'

'Don't worry,' she reassured me, 'you'll be all right.'

If I had been strong enough I swear I would have run for my life at the sight of that theatre. There was a bench with a brown rubber sheet stretched over it which I had to climb onto. Her instruments were lying on an ordinary tea trolley and there were stained buckets full of equipment on the floor. A Russian woman came forward to meet me as I climbed onto the bench. The doctor introduced her as the anaesthetist. The woman stuck a needle into my arm, but was unable to find a vein. She tried again, still no success. I looked around dazedly for Azziz, but he had left the room to wait outside. The woman tried my arm once more before giving up and starting on my leg. It took two more goes, but eventually she managed to put me out. I was in the theatre for a total of four hours, and after two hours Doctor

Yamani came out to find my husband. She looked worried.

'Your wife is losing a lot of blood,' she told him. 'You must go and find some.'

'Where can I find blood?' Azziz was gripped by panic. If he failed to find the blood, would I die? How long had he got?

'There is a prison across the street,' she explained, 'go over there and get them to take some blood from the prisoners.'

'Certainly not,' Azziz was adamant, 'Susan's not having any bad blood. I have the same group as hers. Take mine and I will find more from somewhere respectable.'

There was no regular method for collecting blood in those days. When someone needed it badly the television company would sometimes make an appeal in their name in the hope that their friends and relations would be watching. Azziz gave as much of his own blood as he could spare and then phoned the station with a plea on my behalf. They put it out over the air and within an hour there was a queue of our friends waiting to make donations. The doctor told me that they managed to take far more than I needed and the hospital was able to store it for other patients.

When I woke up the pain was a hundred times worse than before. I screamed out, bringing Doctor Yamani and Azziz running to the bed. Azziz held my hand, his eyes wide with horror as he watched me helplessly as I writhed in agony. The operation managed to stop the bleeding, and the doctor told me that she had cut out some fibroids, but my abdomen was a mess afterwards and nothing they gave me seemed able to control the pain. I developed a huge blood blister on the wound, which had to be lanced in the hospital room the following day, and cleaned out, and my abdominal muscles and bladder both seemed to have been badly cut during the operation. In the following years I had many more miscarriages, and often ended up back on that terrible operating table with my friend doing her best to patch me up. My childbearing days were now over, even though I was only twenty-nine.

I asked what had happened to the baby. The doctor told me not to worry, that the hospital would take care of all that. I chose to believe her, and only later did I discover that they simply threw the dead babies into the garbage. All dead bodies were treated very casually in those days. There were mounds of earth beside the main roads and when someone from a poor family died relatives would just wrap the corpse in bamboo matting and bury it in the earth, with no documents or official notification. It made it very easy for murderers to dispose of bodies, particularly bodies of women.

I was always left drained and exhausted after these ordeals. Azziz would usually come to pick me up and on one occasion he came his face was streaked with tears. 'My father is dead,' he told me, unable to keep his voice from cracking. 'I have to go to Baghdad for the funeral today.'

'I don't think I'm strong enough to travel, Azziz,' I said.

'You must stay here with the children, I'll only be gone a couple of days.'

'You can't leave me today,' I clutched his arm frantically, suddenly terrified of having to cope without him. 'I've only just come off the operating table, and Mary and Abdul are away in Baghdad.'

'I have asked Bernadette to bring you some food,' he said, but I knew that Bernadette was also recovering from a miscarriage and was unlikely to be able to look after us as well as her own family. He hugged me close and I could feel the tears on his face. 'I have to go, I'm sorry.' I could tell he was adamant, but I kept on pleading when we got home and he packed himself a bag. 'I'll move your mattress down into the sitting room, so that you can lie down and look after the children from there,' he said finally.

The children watched solemnly as their mother crawled miserably onto her mattress in the living room, and their father left for the funeral. No one came to see us until his return two days later. Soon after he had gone I started to vomit, watched by the silent, frightened children. When my stomach seemed to be calming down I lay very still with my eyes closed.

'Would you like a cup of tea, Mama?' I opened my eyes and looked up into four-year-old April's sweet face as she stared down at me, her brow furrowed with concern, 'I can make you one.'

'Yes please, *habibi*' (darling), I could feel tears coming up into my eyes, 'that would be lovely.' A few minutes later she returned with a glass of brown liquid. 'That's lovely,' I said as I sipped it, 'and when Mama is well, she will show you how to boil a kettle so that the water for the tea is hot.'

I think in many ways I envied Azziz the closeness he had felt with his father during his childhood. I remember how I felt when I was twelve years old, waiting in my bedroom for Mum to go out so that I could creep out and find the father I hadn't seen for six years. My aunt was in the kitchen when I finally heard the front door bang and went downstairs.

'Where are you going?' She looked surprised to see me dressed to go out.

'I'm going to find my father.' I probably sounded defiant, but I was just trying to keep my courage up and I wanted to show her that there would be no point in trying to stop me. I was not a rebellious child by nature. I certainly did not want to take any sort of stand against my mother, but I was stubborn.

'How do you know where to find him?' she asked.

'Mum told me last week,' my heart was thumping in my chest, 'she got angry with me and shouted it all out.'

'Oh,' she thought for a moment, 'you'll want better shoes than that for the walk.' She handed me a pair of her shoes. 'Take these, your feet are nearly as big as mine now.' I took them gratefully and she watched me put them on. 'Will you recognise him, do you think?' she asked. 'It's been six years now, he may not be like you remember.'

'Oh, I'll recognise him.' I was quite certain about that. My father's face was as clear to me that day as it had been when I last saw him. I was six years old then and he had hardly been out of my thoughts since.

When I was little we lived in an old farmhouse in the country outside Bournemouth. My father was in the army, so he was away nearly all the time, fighting in the war, even when he was still married to Mum. I used to be able to sense when he was coming back and I would go to the top end of Cuckoo Road, the country lane that led to our house, and sit waiting for him on a grassy knoll by Granny Phillips' pigsties. I would tell Mum that I knew he was coming.

'It doesn't matter to me whether he comes home or not,' she would snap, and continue with whatever she was doing.

My grandmother told me that they never did get on very well. 'Your Dad has an eye for the women,' she would say, with a knowing look. I had no idea what she meant, all I knew was that I didn't get to see Dad as much as I would have liked.

In a fit of temper Mum had told me that he was living at the Wilberforce Hotel, next to Bournemouth Central Station, but she had forbidden me to contact him. I didn't want to hurt her, but I wanted to see him so much. I treasured my memories of him and I wanted to make him part of my life again.

I walked to a small tributary of the River Bourne, and set off along its banks towards the sea, knowing that it would take me into the heart of the town. I went past the backstreets, through the under-gardens and into the Dean. I was so excited, and so sure he would be as pleased to see me as I would be to see him. I was certain I was doing the right thing, but that didn't make it any less frightening. I suppose this was my first really independent action, a small act of defiance against authority, fuelled by a determination not to let other people tell me what I could and couldn't do. It was a small gesture, but I was an obedient child by nature and it took all my courage to make it.

By the time I reached the Wilberforce Hotel my nerves were wound as tight as springs. I was tired from the walk, but my aching feet were nothing compared to the aching nerves inside me. Dad was living in a flat on the ground floor. I think perhaps he had some sort of caretaking job there. I knocked and the door was opened by a woman, pretty and blonde, and I guessed that she must be the one Mum talked about. Her name was Jean. I didn't know what to say, so I pushed the door open rudely.

'Where's my Dad?' I demanded. She was knocked back by the force of the door and I was able to see into the room. It was large, and there were two other women there – they turned out to be Jean's sister and mother. On the table was a yellow bowl of water and Dad was standing, his shirt sleeves rolled up, holding a tiny, wet baby in a towel. They all froze, shocked by my entrance, and I froze too. We all looked at one another for what seemed like ages.

I could feel that the women weren't pleased to see me, but Dad's eyes filled with tears as he looked at me. I must have changed a lot in the years since he last saw me, but he knew who I was immediately. He passed the baby over to Jean and held out his arms to me. I ran over and he swept me off the floor. He sat down with me on his lap, hugging me until I could barely breathe. 'My baby,' was all he could say and we both sat there, crying. They made me a cup of tea and some sandwiches, and I never wanted to go back home again.

'Who's the baby?' I asked.

'That's Paul, my son,' Dad said gently. It felt so strange to think that he might have children other than me and my three brothers. I didn't realise it then but Jean was already pregnant again; she would go on to have eleven children with him in all. She was a wonderful, warm-hearted woman, and once she had got over her fear that I might be a threat, she became a good friend to me.

Eventually I had to think about going home. Dad was anxious that

I shouldn't be out after dark, so he gave me some money for the bus fare back. I took a yellow trolley bus to the square and caught another bus out to Mum's house. As I stared miserably out of the window I concentrated on how soon I would be able to get away from my family and the sadness which I associated with them. Now that I had seen Dad I felt better. I knew that he still loved me, but I also knew that he had another family now, and there was no place for a girl like me who was about to turn into a teenager. It was simply good to know that he was just as perfect as I remembered him, and that he was there should I need him. He is still there for me today, and I know just how devastated I will feel when I lose him, so I can appreciate how Azziz felt that day.

For the next twelve years our lives in Iraq went on much as before, with all our energies going into existing from day to day. The children all went to school and I was highly impressed with the standard of education in Iraq. Whenever we met children who had been educated in Britain or America we were always amazed at how much further ahead ours were. They were doing subjects like physics and chemistry almost from the first day. How I wished that I had been offered such wonderful opportunities to learn when I was their age! But there was always the spectre of politics hanging over the schools. Even before Saddam Hussein came to power children were taught the official version of Iraq's political history, and as the Baathist Party cemented its hold on the country it came to be more propaganda and less history. Officially we were enjoying a socialist government, but that involved practices such as persuading children to inform to the authorities if their parents didn't toe the party line. It smacked of the tactics which the Nazis had used in Germany during the 1930s, and made for an uncomfortable atmosphere.

There were also personal tragedies to contend with. Mary and Abdul had been trying for years to have a child, but Mary continually miscarried. Finally she managed to go the full term and had a lovely little girl. They must have been the proudest parents I have ever seen, they couldn't leave this plump little creature alone for a second. But the baby developed a hole in the heart and Mary went into hospital with her when she was just six months old. Late that night there was a terrible crying and shouting and hammering on our door. We went down and found Mary slumped on our doorstep, with Abdul crouched over her trying to calm her.

'The baby died,' he explained to us, his face streaked with tears. We helped her in and sat her down.

Eventually she was calm enough to talk. 'When they gave up trying to keep her alive, they took the body away from me,' she explained, 'I thought they were going to wrap her up and give her back, but no one returned. I waited for hours but then the nurses I knew had gone off duty. I asked someone where the body would be,' she was having difficulty getting the words out, 'and they said they threw the bodies away out the back. There are all these dustbins behind the hospital, Susan,' she grabbed my hand so tightly I thought she was going to crush it, 'and the dogs were rummaging through them looking for food. They threw my baby to the dogs.' We all wept for what seemed like hours, and Mary never managed to conceive another child.

EIGHT

THE longer I stayed in Iraq, the more idyllic my memories of England became. I used to remember the old farmhouse where I was born and lived as a small child. All around was open countryside, with fruit trees and bluebells, and white dog roses growing up the side of the house. I would tend to forget that inside the house was cold, with flagstoned floors that chilled you through from your feet. Outside, on my own, I was happy, but inside the house I was always cold and lonely.

When the fruit on the trees was ripe my brothers and I would be found scrumping in our neighbours' orchards. Even though we had trees of our own, other people's fruit always seemed to taste better. We used to hold races in the daisies, and creep up on the cows in the fields, drinking the milk fresh from their udders. There used to be snakes in the undergrowth and I remember jumping up and down on sheets of metal which were lying baking in the sun, hoping a snake would be dozing underneath and we would be able to chase it off. Once I went out rabbiting with Dad on one of his rare visits home and we caught an adder with an undigested baby rabbit inside it. It's funny how something as simple as that still sticks in my mind, even after the terrible horrors I have witnessed in the last ten years. My best times were when I was able to go off on my own with a comic or a book and just lie for hours under the trees reading, chewing blackberries or gooseberries, or going out on damp, dewy mornings to hunt for horse mushrooms which we could take home and cook for breakfast.

These were the scenes which I was dreaming of seeing again one hot, airless day, when Azziz came home and announced that he was being sent to England for a training course in a few months.

'Oh darling, that will be wonderful,' I said excitedly, throwing my arms round his neck and covering him in kisses. The children heard the commotion and began to clammer for more information. 'The children will be able to get to know their British relatives,' I babbled on, 'and you can come home to us every weekend . . .' I realised that he had fallen silent.

'They are only sending me,' he said, 'they will not pay for everyone else.'

'Then we must find the money.' I was resolute. 'We will scrimp and save until we have enough for all of us to go.'

'It will be winter by then,' he protested feebly, 'you will get cold.'

Try as he might to discourage me, my mind was made up. I was now set on going back to visit my beloved homeland.

It was the start of winter when we arrived in England and we stayed for a while with Mum, but it was obvious that we couldn't all stay there for the whole six months. Azziz said he would find us somewhere else to live, and eventually came back with the news that the only affordable accommodation he could find was a caravan in a field. There was, he told me, nothing else available within a 50 mile radius.

By the time we reached mid-winter in this caravan, both baby Peter and I had pneumonia. The only water we had access to was a tap in the field for the animals, and that soon froze up. I managed to get John and April into the local school, but I didn't have enough warm clothes for them and was told off by the headmistress. Azziz was finding the course hard work, and when he did manage to get back to see us he was too tired to do anything but sleep. My idyllic English countryside began to seem like a nightmare to me and I looked forward to going back to Iraq again. Azziz did his best to avoid saying 'I told you so', but I could tell that was what he was thinking as he watched me struggling to survive. When we finally got back to the warmth of Iraq I made a vow to myself that next time Azziz gave me the impression he didn't want us to come on a trip with him, I would pay attention.

Under the new regime which had replaced the Hashemites, the people seemed to prosper. There was work for everyone, and girls started to go to university for the first time and were being given hope that things might get better for them. The people loved their leader, Abdul Al Karim Qassem, and credited him with building roads and hospitals for them, putting goods in the shops and increasing salaries. Affluence seemed to be taking root in Iraq.

That affluence, however, was coming at a political price. While our leader was popular with the people whom we knew, many of the things which were done in his name were frightening and threatening and there was some strong opposition building up amongst powerful people. Politics was beginning to seem a dangerous game for everyone, even if they tried hard to keep themselves uninvolved. Political intrigue was everywhere and at the beginning the Baathist Party came close to power. A difference of opinion over whether or not to form a union with Syria and Egypt forced them back into the political wilderness a few years later. Many of the Baathist Party members went to prison and there were some cruel massacres which forced the party underground. This provided an opportunity for the young Saddam Hussein to make a name for himself. He did it by joining a group of men who ambushed the president's car and attempted to assassinate him. Rumours at the time claimed that Saddam was the hero of the day, but later rumours countered that it was because of his bungling that the president was only wounded and not killed. Saddam was a wanted man and had to go into exile. By the time he was able to return things had moved on and he was forced to wait on the sidelines for his next opportunity, building his powerbase and honing his political skills.

During the 1960s the government began to arrest and execute people who had been accused of spying. Often it seemed merely an excuse to eliminate the opposition, or to destroy some wealthy man in order to confiscate his money for themselves. Taking the bus into town one day I was gazing out at the view, lost in my own thoughts, when we turned into the town square and three corpses swung past the window, making me jump back and scream. Everyone in the bus had seen them, but after the initial shock everyone averted their eyes from the gruesome gallows, and no one spoke of what they had seen. That evening, when Azziz came home, I told him about it.

'They were spies,' he said, but I could see in his eyes that he didn't believe his own words. In fact they were all Jewish shopkeepers, accused of having radio equipment on their premises. They had been murdered and their bodies put on display as an example to the rest of us. They hung there for several days and, like everyone else, I averted my eyes and crossed the street, because I had heard that anyone stopping to stare would be photographed and then arrested and asked why they were so interested in the enemies of the government.

One day, when another of my friends, Anne, and I were walking to the wool shop, enjoying a pleasant, warm day, we turned into a street to find an angry crowd gathering. 'I think we should take another route,' Anne said nervously, 'they look ugly.'

'No, don't worry,' I calmed her, 'we'll just walk quietly past. No one will notice us, they are busy with someone else.' Despite my words my heart was pounding in my chest as we approached them, our eyes fixed on the ground.

As we slipped round the back of the crowd Anne couldn't resist taking a look and let out a scream. 'That's a man's arm!'

'No, surely not,' I peered through the crowd to try to make out what was happening. I had often heard the term 'tearing someone apart', but I had never before actually seen it happen, or even dreamt that it might be possible. But that was what the crowd was doing to that man, pulling his limbs off one by one. His eyes had rolled back into his skull and his mouth locked open in a silent scream as they tugged and pulled his corpse one way and then another, like wild dogs with the corpse of an antelope. The crowd was spattered with his blood, some of them covered from head to foot, making them look like savages in war paint. One of his arms was kicked out of the crowd and landed in the dust beside us so that we could see the torn flesh of the shoulder with the bone sticking through, and the fingers which seemed to be reaching out for help when they were frozen in death. We had no idea why they were so angry or what the man had done, but we knew that political and religious rivalries were coming to the boil all over the country. Forgetting myself I let out a shout and several of the men swung round to see what woman had dared to make a sound. Their blood-stained, sweating faces were contorted with fury and hate, and a sort of glee at having a victim. I felt sick with fear and Anne and I both started to run, pushing the babies in front of us at break-neck speed, desperate to get back to the safety of home. But in time even our homes would no longer be safe.

Witnessing this scene was the last straw for Anne, who had been persecuted horribly by a cruel husband for many years. Ever since they had arrived in Iraq he had allowed her nothing but rice to eat, and had been slowly driving her out of her mind. Seeing the man torn apart in the street finally unbalanced her, and her hateful husband sent her back to England to a mental home. He kept their children and later remarried. It still makes me shudder to think of him and what he did to Anne, even today.

It was impossible to protect the children from the realities of what was happening all around us. When John was eight years old he was sitting on the garden wall watching some men digging next door. I saw him put a handkerchief over his mouth and nose as if to protect himself from an unpleasant smell, and then I saw the men lift the head of a corpse on the end of a pole a few feet away from him. He sat there transfixed by the sight for a few moments until I was able to whisk him away.

By 1963 we had a television. We were sitting watching it when it suddenly blacked out. Outside the house I heard shouting and women wailing. I went outside and stopped a passing Arab who was sobbing into his headdress.

'What is happening?'

'They've killed Abdul Al Karim Qassem,' he stammered, before hurrying away.

A few hours later the television screen lit up again. The corpse of Abdul Al Karim Qassem was being filmed, sitting up in his chair, supported by a jubilant member of the opposition. The opposition consisted of the Baath Party, who were making a bid to regain power, and some sympathetic military officers. On either side of him sat two leading members of his government. All three of them had ropes around their necks, their heads rolling to the side, their eyes staring. Abdul Al Karim Qassem was dead and we had a new leader, Colonel Abdul Salam Mohamed Aref, who had at one time been second in command to Abdul Al Karim Qassem and was now supported by the Baathists.

The change-over in power was accompanied by huge battles in the streets of Baghdad, with thousands killed, but we saw little of this in Basrah. Most of the people I came across seemed to be crying over the death of Abdul Al Karim Qassem and the fall of his government, but there was nothing the ordinary people could do about it. As with the previous revolution, there followed a round of political executions, people disappeared in the night and everyone was afraid to speak their mind, even to other family members, for fear of reprisals. We kept our heads down and stayed within our tight social circle and put all our energies into bringing up our family.

All three of our children were good students, bright and popular.

We found that in the beginning the children with foreign mothers tended to gather together in cliques and talk in English to one another, but they soon realised that that did not make them popular with the others, and so they broadened their circle of friends and spoke Arabic all the time. If they were teased about having a Western mother they were kind enough never to tell me about it, and they all seemed to have as many friends as they wanted.

In the summer, when the heat in the buildings became unbearable, people would take their beds up onto the roofs, hanging up sheets to divide the men from the women. We always seemed to have several of the children's friends staying up there with us. The problem with sleeping in the open like this was the early morning dew, which tended to leave us damp and chilled just before dawn, but it was better than suffocating indoors. The modern houses were not built to keep out the heat and it was impossible to be comfortable in the hot season. The children used to soak sheets in cold water, wrap themselves up in them and sit under the fans. I was always terrified they would make themselves ill, but they never seemed to.

April had the same beauty as John, made more striking by her hair which had turned a wonderful copper colour, and her startling green eyes – the same colour as my mother's – with their thick black lashes.

Peter was a blond, but he had his father's soulful brown eyes and permanent smile. I was very proud of them, but fearful that they stood out too much from the crowd. I always took great pride in turning them out in their school uniforms looking clean and smart no matter how short of money we might be, and I think that that may have made them more conspicuous than was comfortable. One night when April came home and I was picking up her clothes to wash she stopped me.

'Please don't wash my blouse tonight, Mama,' she said.

'Why on earth not?'

'I just want to be more like the others.'

When John was eight years old we moved him to an all-boys school for the first time, but after a few months the headmaster asked my husband to go in to talk to him. Azziz returned home with a grave face.

'I think we should look for another school,' he said, and was reluctant to elaborate. I forced him, much to his embarrassment, to explain. 'It seems that John is too pretty for his own good and the headmaster fears that he could be subjected to abuse from some of the older boys.'

This was my first brush with the possibility of homosexuality. The concept had never crossed my mind until then, and Azziz had been careful to shield me from it. In any Arab country, I now discovered, it is not considered unusual for young boys to form strong emotional and sexual relationships with one another because of the unavailability of women. I was appalled to think of this happening with my eight-year-old son. John was moved back to a mixed school immediately, and for years to come I guarded him and Peter fiercely.

The problem of sexual repression became very difficult for all of them as they grew older. Boys and girls, even when they reached university, could not be seen walking together in the streets. If the security police saw members of the opposite sex talking together in public they would swoop on them, push them into cars and take them to interrogation centres. There they would be subjected to brutal questioning, and even if they could prove that they were brothers and sisters or legally married, the women were in danger of being beaten up and raped, and having their legs painted. The boys might suffer similar fates.

This sort of repression makes courtship very difficult, since young people can only meet in private houses under the scrutiny of their families, or in places like universities where the sudden freedom to mix can go straight to their heads. Many of them rush into unsuitable marriages simply in order to have sex, or even just to enjoy the company of the people they love. As someone who had made a hasty marriage, but was lucky enough to have found a good man, I now knew how dangerous this could be, and I feared for my children as they approached maturity. I was beginning to understand why families in that part of the world took such an active role in choosing marriage partners for their children.

Peter was twelve years old before I began to consider getting a job and letting the older children help to look after him. A friend told me about a company which was building a power station locally, and said they needed a secretary.

'Don't worry,' she said, 'they are South Americans – completely crazy. Whatever you do will be better than anything they can do for themselves.'

She was right. They took me on immediately at a salary which was four times as much as Azziz as earning. I was very careful to let him know that he was still the head of the family despite my superior earning power. He had enough trouble trying to justify his Western wife to his family, without having his confidence undermined any further. He is such a strong man in so many ways and the last thing I wanted to do was make him feel inadequate. I would keep enough money to buy the children shoes and a few other things, and the rest I would give to him each month to put in the bank. I bought myself a sewing machine to help with the making of the children's clothes and some little luxuries like new wool for knitting. By the mid-1970s we had been in Iraq for twenty years and we finally had enough money coming in. Our savings grew at a surprising rate and within a few years we were able to buy a car. When the army threatened to take Azziz away we were able to buy him out and finally – the greatest joy of all – we were able to buy a new house and life gradually became more comfortable for us. We grew used to the unsettled political scene and paid it little attention. Perhaps if we had taken more interest in what was happening around us then, we could have somehow protected ourselves and our family before the inevitable explosion took place, destroying all our lives completely.

NINE

IN July 1979 Saddam Hussein became President of Iraq, Chairman of the Revolutionary Command Council and General Secretary of the Regional Command of the Baath Party, which had been running the country since another military coup in 1968. The people of Iraq refer to it as '*thaka yaum aswad*' – a black day.

What this meant was that having been secretly the most powerful man in the country while officially still only the Vice-Chairman of the Revolutionary Command Council, he had now attained everything he had been working for. To the average Iraqi then he seemed little better or little worse than all the other ambitious soldiers and politicians who had been seizing and losing power for the last two decades. Each coup had led to even more executions and fear, and everyone knew of someone who had disappeared mysteriously. But we had grown used to existing in such an atmosphere.

Azziz and I were asked by his employers to move to Baghdad with the children because Azziz was becoming more successful and needed to be where the major government building decisions were made. He was spending more and more time travelling around the world studying the way other people undertook giant civil engineering projects, and attending conferences. At the time we moved to Baghdad he was planning to go to America for six months. I was dreading being without him for so long. I missed him even when he was away for a few days, but I realised that if he was going to get on he had to travel. This time I was feeling very tense and unhappy at the prospect of such a long separation. Before he went he had to make sure that the children and I had a roof over our heads, so he asked one of his half brothers to buy us a house in Baghdad and sell our home in Basrah. Because he was so preoccupied with his impending trip, he did not check up on what was being done in our name, and when we arrived in the capital city we found that his brother had indeed bought us a house, but that it had a sitting tenant in it.

We asked the man to leave, but he refused. We went to court to have him removed, but the court told us that it was the wish of the government that no one should ever be thrown out of their house. If we made too much fuss about it, the court added, they would simply take the house away from us and give it to the tenant. We withdrew from the case. Azziz had to find somewhere else for us quickly if he wasn't going to leave us on the street. Another of his brothers had built a shack at the bottom of his mother's garden, and so we were moved in there. There was no room for all the furniture which I had lovingly collected in Basrah, so it had to be stored on the roof, where it was ruined by the sun and rain. There were only two bedrooms, so the children all had to share, and a man from a neighbouring house would clamber over the roof and look in at them during the night, frightening them half to death. Every day that Azziz was away seemed like an age to me as we struggled to cope in this place.

When Azziz got back I asked him to build us a house, but he did nothing about it. He was busy with his job and I think he was tired too of the struggle to improve our lives. He wanted to relax and pass some time with the other men. But I desperately wanted a nice home. I felt I had worked hard for many years and I believed I deserved a little peace of mind. I had been so happy to have him back, but our relationship seemed to have changed, and I realised that if I didn't make a stand we would go on in the same rut until we died. I was determined that we should make an effort to be more comfortable for the next stage in our lives, but I couldn't persuade him to do anything about it. I needed a break from that terrible little house, so I packed up the children and we all went to England.

'The day you start building us a proper house,' I told Azziz as we left, 'we will come back to you.'

For six months we stayed in England, living with relatives. April, who was fifteen by then, and I worked at Websters, a factory where I had worked before starting my nurse's training. We were hired to test lipstick cases. The boys did what odd jobs they could to make a little extra money. Every week Azziz rang my mother's house to ask me to go back, and every week my answer was the same: 'When you start building us a house we will come back.' I felt terrible being away from him, but I knew that unless I stuck to my guns our lives would never get any better. I knew enough Arab men now to know that if they can get away without doing something for their families they will. I prayed that he was missing us as much as I was missing him.

Although I was miserable at being away from Azziz yet again, I got a lot of pleasure from being with the children in the relaxed English atmosphere. They were growing into such fine young adults and I was so proud of them. April was a real beauty now, with her wonderful hair and eyes, and I could see the way that boys around the factory looked at her. She seemed unaware of the effect she had on other people. John and Peter were changing into handsome young men, both towering over me by now, and both keen to get home to get on with their education.

Finally Azziz gave in. 'Come back please, Susan,' he pleaded, 'and we will draw up plans for a house. I have bought the land.'

I was so relieved I just sat there and wept after hanging up the phone. I couldn't wait to get on the next plane and fly back to him. I never wanted to be parted from him again. All our friends and relatives in England thought I was mad. 'Why go back to that place with all its problems,' they wanted to know, 'when you could stay here in comfort?'

'Because that is where my husband is and I can't live without him,' I explained.

With the wisdom of hindsight I wish with all my heart that I had stayed in England and had persuaded Azziz to join us there. I doubt if I would have succeeded in getting him to leave Iraq then, when everything was going so well for him at work, but I wish I had tried. Taking the children back to Iraq at that time was the worst thing I could have done, but how was I to know that then?

When Azziz met us at the airport I threw my arms round him and just clung on. I didn't care about the stares we got from everyone else, or even the embarrassed protests of the children. I never wanted to let him go.

So we resumed our lives as Iraqi citizens. Azziz was now, finally, earning good money, as was I with a job working as a secretary for an oil company. It was an interesting job and I enjoyed it, but the journey there and back could sometimes be a nightmare. Although it wasn't all that far, the bus drivers would leave when they felt like it, and would travel at whatever speed they wanted, frequently stopping so they could talk to friends or just disappearing for a while, leaving the passengers fuming in their seats. Sometimes I would be travelling for three hours a day.

We built the house to our own design with the help of the children and other relatives. The wonderful thing about building your own house out there is that if a room looks a bit small when you dig out the foundations, you can just make it bigger. You don't have to worry about things like planning permission from the authorities. I loved working with them all, seeing how tall and strong they were becoming. It was a happy time for all of us.

It was a beautiful house, but it took longer than we hoped to finish because the supply of materials like glass and pipes seemed to be drying up in the city. When we first moved in we had to pin nylon sheets over the windows while we waited for the glass to arrive.

I had managed to form an uneasy alliance with my husband's family by this time. I think that now I was becoming an older woman they didn't see me as such a threat, although I'm sure that most of them didn't like me. When my father-in-law died my mother-in-law had moved into a house which she had inherited from her family and which was close to ours. In those years she and I were able to build a good relationship and she gave me a great many insights into just how stoic and strong the Arab women have to be to cope with their lives.

She was a wonderful old woman and I had grown very close to her. She was only a little over four feet tall and she would tell me that I was more of a daughter to her than any of the others. Even when we were living in Basrah she had come to stay with me several times, when the rest of the family was still virtually ignoring me. She was very religious and would never eat any food that I had prepared, since I was a *masihi*, a 'dirty Christian', but I never took offence at anything she said or did, we just understood one another. She would make her own food and would talk to me all the time about religion and about the sayings of Mohammed. I think she was a much better person even than my husband.

Sometimes I would tease her: 'Why couldn't you have made me a better husband than this, Mother?' I would ask when Azziz was doing something to annoy me, and we would laugh together. If she felt ill she would come and consult me and ask me to take her temperature or administer her medicines. I grew to love her very much.

Azziz always claimed that his mother lived to be over a hundred. I'm not sure if this was true, but she was certainly well over ninety. The day she died Azziz was out of the country. I was told about her death by one of Azziz's sisters-in-law whom she had been staying with. I was so upset I insisted that I wanted to be at her graveside during the funeral, representing Azziz who couldn't get back in time. The other men in the family were furious. Women were never allowed near the graves, even of their own husbands or children. I was very upset by the loss of a good friend and I was determined to be there. The men in the family pretended to go along with me and put me in a car with one of the brothers, who then pretended to get lost on the way to the graveyard. I had been prepared for a last-minute trick like this and was armed with a map. I made it just in time, to the fury of the other men. When Azziz returned and heard what I had done he told me off for upsetting the family again, but I could see from the twinkle in his eye that he was pleased I had done it.

Other members of the family would also come to visit us now, many of them young enough not to remember clearly how unwelcome I had once been in Iraq. I had become an 'auntie' to many of them, and the thought that I might once have been labelled a prostitute probably would have struck them as hilarious. It was usually the men, all called 'nephews' by Azziz, who would instigate the visits. I would receive a phone call in the middle of the morning and one of them would announce that they were on their way. 'But you have given me no time to bake anything,' I would protest. I would then rush to the kitchen to make biscuits and a cake, and by mid-afternoon three or four cars would arrive bringing fifteen or more people. I liked to watch the children mixing with all their cousins and aunts and uncles because I could see that they were totally accepted now, despite Peter's almost white-blond hair and April's exotic colouring. I felt that the older family members tolerated me because I was Azziz's wife, but still didn't like me for myself. Everyone likes Azziz.

Soon the time came to think about finding marriage partners for John and April. April was always a strong-willed girl and she chose an Iraqi boy from the university whom I thought was too handsome for his own good. They made the most gorgeous couple to look at, but I felt deeply uneasy. I told her, as gently as I could, that I didn't think it would work out, but she was determined. When we met his family I was horrified by how poorly they lived, knowing that April would be expected to go and live with them. The main bed in the house was propped up on bricks, and there wasn't a square inch of wall which wasn't scribbled on with children's pencils. Azziz told me that I was wrong to make such judgements and that he was a fine boy, but when you have children you worry so much about what will happen to them, and that worry doesn't stop just because they become grown-ups and are supposedly able to look after themselves. You may know that the time has come for you to draw back and let them make their own decisions, but you still ache when you see them taking the wrong ones.

'Okay,' I said, 'let them do it, but I want no part of it.'

Of course I had to relent because someone had to pay for the wedding and provide the things they needed to get started in life. April very soon became pregnant and my first grandson, Majid, was born before things started to go seriously wrong in the marriage. At first April would not tell me what was worrying her, perhaps because she didn't want to worry me, but whenever she came home I could tell she was sad. She always needed material things to help them with their life, but it wasn't just doing without things that was making her unhappy.

Gradually I learnt how badly her in-laws and her husband were treating her. She was barely getting enough to eat and was so thin it made me want to cry. Eventually she admitted that he was hitting her, and even her mother-in-law was physically abusing her. Although I knew by then that this was not unusual in an Arab marriage, particularly with a family of that class, I also knew that April was not used to that sort of treatment. Perhaps she had learnt too many of her mother's independent ways, perhaps she had learnt too much about the outside world at university. Whatever the reason, I knew that she would not be willing to put up with it for very long.

'We have to help April to get a divorce,' I said to Azziz when the truth had finally emerged, 'otherwise those people will kill her.'

'What about Majid?' Azziz asked.

'We must make sure we get him.'

'If an Arab couple divorces,' he explained to me, 'the man's family automatically gets custody of the children.'

'Then we will have to fight hard.'

Fortunately April's mother-in-law was not keen to have another mouth to feed and was willing to give up Majid without too much of a struggle. Normally when an Iraqi woman is divorced she receives an agreed settlement from the husband, but April's husband had no money and Azziz had not insisted on the usual marriage contract before giving his agreement to the match. But the money was not important, as we had enough to support them easily.

April decided that she would like to go back to university, and I was happy to volunteer to have Majid to live with us. I love the fact that grandparents in Iraq are allowed to play such an important role in bringing up their grandchildren. It gave me another chance to enjoy a young family at a time when I was more relaxed and didn't have all the financial pressures which had dogged us when our own children were small. Little Majid stayed with Azziz and me for six years. It was fun having a small child around the house again, and he was able to stay with the neighbours when we were out at work.

I had a potential bride in mind for John, but he said she was too strong-willed. Perhaps he was right. While I was away in England on a visit to my mother Azziz picked a girl for him from his office. She was a pretty little creature who worked as a secretary and I'm afraid it was her looks that convinced Azziz that she was a good choice. Men can be such fools sometimes. When I returned and was told that the match was arranged I felt doubtful; I did not trust either of them to make a sound judgement on such an important issue. Laila was certainly lovely to look at, but when I saw her with her family I could see that she was spoilt and petulant. By then it was too late to do anything and so we set about arranging another wedding.

Azziz built John and Laila a flat on the roof of our house and soon there were two more little children around to play with Majid. Our family was growing, with Azziz and me at the centre of it, and I was very happy in my home. I had a nice piece of garden for the children to play in. There was a lot of wildlife, even in the centre of Baghdad. There were two hedgehogs which would come out at night to be fed, and whenever it rained in the spring the garden would come alive with tadpoles, which would hatch into frogs in the puddles, covering the paths and patios so that you couldn't walk anywhere for fear of crushing them. I used to send the children out to shoo them away so we could move the car on the drive, or walk to the gate, and they would catch them and hold them up by their hind legs to make them spit with anger. I filled the garden with flowers, and in the summer the sunflowers grew everywhere, taller than the people.

A population of cats took to basking in the sun around our walls.

There was a separate feline community outside each of the doors, and at one time I had seventeen cats in all. Some of them were beautiful, well-bred creatures, but eventually all the pedigree ones fell foul of the neighbours who would throw them pieces of poisoned meat, or would simply catch them and wring their necks in the night. The wily Arab street cats were not so easy to dispose of and succeeded in breeding generation after generation around the house.

One tom, of which I was particularly fond, used to sit on the high front wall in the sun, watching the world go by. He was killed like all the others. The children used to like to sit up on that wall too, to see what was happening in the street, but as the political situation became increasingly dangerous we stopped lifting them up and kept them inside the walls.

For the poorer families, of course, there was never even the meagre protection offered by high walls. The streets of Baghdad were full of tiny street urchins whose families were too poor to offer them any sort of security. I used to love these barefooted, scruffy little creatures, none of them more than six years old. Whenever I went out into the street I would be armed with sweets, which I would slip into their pockets. They would call me 'Nana' – Arabic for grandmother, and hug me as tightly as I hugged them. Often these little ones would be killed in the streets by passing cars or lorries, because most people were quite indifferent to them. Their families would just bury them and get on with having the next one.

Because of the numbers of men who were being called up into the armed forces there were rumours that the government was planning to go to war with Iran. Everyone talked about it, but no one knew what to expect. On 22 September 1980 we heard the news on the television: Iraqi forces had invaded Iran at eight different points on land and had bombed Iranian airfields, military installations and economic targets. We were as startled as the rest of the world at the ferocity of this attack. Television programmes were constantly being interrupted by news bulletins. The screens showed jubilant Iraqis chanting and celebrating in the streets, Saddam Hussein appearing amongst them, his face beaming with pride at this great military victory.

Jubilant martial music blared out from the rooftops of nearby schools and high buildings, and everywhere students were to be seen celebrating in the streets. It isn't hard to brainwash students, particularly when they have been brought up on government propaganda. No one I knew felt much like rejoicing. Most of us felt that by challenging Iran Saddam Hussein was taking a tiger by the tail, and that sooner or later the tiger would turn round to bite us. In all the euphoria it was easy to forget just how small Iraq is, and just how big and powerful Iran.

For what seemed like a week we heard nothing more about it, apart from the victory celebrations and endless declarations of loyalty to our great, conquering leader. It was as if we were just waiting to see what Iran would do. The waiting was like torture to me, bringing back all my worst memories of the war in England when I was a child.

Just across the moors from our house the Creekmore ammunition factory nestled amongst the trees. Night after night the Germans sent their planes over to try to find it. We could hear the sirens, even out there, and Mum would herd us downstairs and out to the farmer's sturdy house down the road, where they would push us under the furniture until the danger had passed. How those sirens used to frighten me as they woke me from my deep, childish sleep, far more than the bombs themselves. Once Mum came running into my bedroom and found me literally trying to climb the walls because, in my sleepy, frightened state, I was unable to find the door. Even then I can remember wondering why people in another country should want to kill us, or why we should be trying to kill them. Fifty years later, having witnessed more killing and inhumanity than I could ever have imagined possible, I am still no nearer to finding an answer to that question.

I was playing out in the garden on the day that I heard the German bomber crash in the fields, and felt the ground shake under the impact. I ran towards the column of smoke which rose up into the sky. By the time I got there the two pilots, who had miraculously survived, were sitting in the sun with the farmer and a group of local people, waiting for the police and the army to arrive. I was so curious to see who these terrible people were who kept trying to kill us with their bombs. As I came close one of the pilots smiled at me and beckoned me nearer. He picked up a piece of the shattered fabric from the window of the plane, carved a cross with a knife and handed it to me, smiling. I think it was then that I realised that the people who are made to fight against you aren't your real enemies. Their lives are controlled by others. These two men were not frightening or strange, they were just like my Dad. It was very puzzling to me as a child, and even now I can't believe how easily good people have been persuaded by their leaders and politicians to do some of the terrible things I have witnessed.

My terror at the sound of sirens became even more acute when we had to move to a new house nearer to Bournemouth, since there was a siren right at the bottom of our garden. Over the next few years that sound was to become so deeply imprinted on my brain that decades later it would come back to haunt me, setting my nerves jangling and my heart pumping with fear.

Many other planes were shot down above us in the last years of the war. With a group of neighbours I remember staring open mouthed at the body of a German pilot tangled in the telephone wires. And now I was sitting in Baghdad waiting for the whole thing to happen to me again.

TEN

THE first bomb fell at one in the morning, the explosion bringing dozens of families out onto their roofs in their nightwear, shouting questions to one another across the narrow streets. It was a one-off explosion, all over before we had time to feel in danger. It brought back all the childhood terrors which I had been repressing, but I felt able to control them at that stage. We were all more interested to find out what had happened than frightened. As the sun came up we could see a column of smoke rising from the centre of the city. We tuned into our radio, desperate to know what was happening, but no announcements were made, so we started to telephone everyone we knew in the city to try to piece together a picture of what was going on. The worst thing in a situation like that is not knowing exactly what has happened. The truth is often less fearful than one's imaginings, although in the years to come the reality of our lives became worse than any nightmare or black fantasy.

At first we could find out nothing, so Azziz left for work as usual. I didn't like him going, but I knew that I had to face up to the fact that if we were entering a war I would have to cope with it. I wanted to beg him to stay with me, but I bit my tongue. As he drove through the centre he noticed that Rashid Street was closed. I kept phoning, like most other women. As the telephone lines continued to hum, rumours grew that the explosion had been caused by a bomb placed in the Central Bank, the tallest building in Baghdad, by the opposition to the government:

'They have blown up the tenth floor, totally demolishing it ...'

'There is damage for 200 metres in every direction ...'

'The poor residential area has been the worst hit ...'

'Six Egyptians were killed in a lodging house just behind the bank ...'

As the day progressed the rumours became more grounded in fact.

'It wasn't a bomb inside the building, it was a land-to-land missile from Iran ...'

So the tiger had turned on us and bitten back, but what would happen next? In the absence of official information anxieties grew. Soon more explosions erupted and all our questions were to be answered. A rocket hit part of the *Al Iraq* newspaper office and demolished ten houses in the vicinity, killing many families, and the government had to admit that the damage was being inflicted by Iran. 'But,' the officials assured us over the television, 'they are failing to hit their targets, only managing to strike empty areas of the city.' Nobody believed that for long as eye-witness accounts of the mass destruction began to circulate. Everyone knew someone who now had first-hand experience of how much damage and destruction were being inflicted on us, and my childhood nightmares rose up by the legion to torture me.

For the next six months the Iranians sent over a steady stream of planes, and rained bombs and rockets down on Baghdad. The attacks went on throughout the eight years of the war, but for us the first six months were the worst. The noise never stopped for more than a few hours at a time, day or night, wearing at my nerves, making me jump and scream whether I was awake or asleep, as I fought to control my fears in front of the children. Sometimes the planes would by-pass us and we would feel and hear the explosions hitting buildings a few miles away. We would all run up to the roofs to try to work out where the damage was and whether we knew anyone in the area which had been hit who might need help. At other times they would land in our district, shaking the house and breaking the windows. For me the worst part was the sirens. All the terrors of my childhood returned, leaving me shaking with dread at that wailing announcement of approaching doom; and after the bombers had gone there would be the equally plaintive sounds of police vehicles, ambulances and fire engines.

How I regretted building a home with such huge picture windows. I was frightened to stand at the sink for more than a few minutes in case the kitchen window exploded in my face, or to pass the glass front door in case it blew in. The safest room in the house was the bathroom, and Majid and the other children would cower in there, wide-eyed and shaking, as soon as they heard the sirens. As the war continued the local urchins seemed to become so used to the noise they didn't notice it, playing happily in the streets and cheering as the bullets sprayed around them and the rockets plunged out of the skies.

'We need a bomb shelter,' my neighbour, Nancy, told me one day as we drank coffee, watching the planes go by and listening to the pounding of the powerful anti-aircraft guns.

'Let's dig one,' I said. 'We can use my garden because it's sheltered by the high walls.'

We spent a week digging out the hole, then we lined it with bricks, put timbers across the top and sandbags on top of that. As we stood back to admire our handywork I felt a twinge of doubt.

'Do you think it will work?' I asked. 'I don't fancy being buried alive.'

'Yes, I think it will.' Nancy didn't sound any more sure than me.

For the next few raids the two of us sat in our new shelter with the children, but I didn't feel any safer and within a few days I stopped using it. One morning a bomb landed just the other side of the house. The explosion funnelled inside our garden walls in a way I had never anticipated, lifted everything into the air, including our bomb shelter, and dropped it like the pile of rubbish it was. When the dust cleared and the drone of the planes faded I stood at the window and looked out at the shambles which could easily have had us underneath it. I decided from then on to put my trust in the strength of our bathroom walls.

The Iranians were trying to wipe out our light industries, but they were very bad shots, and many of their planes were brought down by anti-aircraft fire before they could get away. No doubt some of the bombs hit their targets, but the majority landed on the houses of the people, and usually in the poorer areas of the city. As in any war the leaders were safe in their well-prepared shelters while the ordinary people were left to take the brunt of the onslaught. We saw many civilian districts reduced to rubble, their dead piled high.

The endless noise was having a terrible effect on the children, who were often subject to air raid warnings while they were at school and had to dive under their desks for shelter. Majid was very frightened at the thought of leaving the house or me, but the bombings could go on for years and he had to go to school.

One of my biggest worries during this period was that the Iranians would invade Iraq and take over the running of the country. This often seemed a real possibility as the war swung this way and that, and the thought of being under the rule of the Iranians was very frightening for me as a woman. By that time Muslim fundamentalism had taken a firm hold on that country, and all Western influences were being brutally expunged. The fact that I was British and Christian would cause the family great suffering if such people had control of our lives. Under Iranian rules women now had to wear the traditional robes, covering their faces in public and behaving as they had in the Middle Ages, rigidly obeying the laws of the Koran.

In Iraq the rules of the Koran are more liberally interpreted, and I was sure that I would have great difficulty conforming to that sort of oppression. I had, after all, found it hard enough to toe the line in the relatively liberal atmosphere of Iraq. Although many of the young women in Iraq were choosing to adopt the aging style of dress which was compulsory in stricter Arab countries, including headscarves, long dresses and thick black stockings even in the heat of summer, we were still more or less free to wear whatever we liked, apart from very short skirts or shorts and the sort of brightly dyed hair which was becoming fashionable amongst young people in the West. If the Iranians took over all that would change.

John was called up into the army, which meant that we were in constant fear for his life, never knowing where he was being sent or what he was being asked to do. Laila and the children went on living with us. I preferred having my family around me so that I could look after them, especially the babies. I loved all the babies so much, they were all so beautiful, but their nerves were being battered by the constant noise and danger and destruction which they witnessed. Then Peter was taken off the street by army officials and pressed into service and we had something else to worry about.

It is surprising how you become used to war. As the months turned into years we grew accustomed to the situation and channelled all our energies into simply surviving, moving around the streets as if nothing was happening. If the sirens went off during the day we would be waved into the shelter of shops or doorways, and once we had heard the explosions we would come back out and continue with our business, hoping that no one had been killed this time. We became strangely hardened to the sounds of the explosions, even though each one could wipe out a whole family or a whole street. My fears never wholly subsided, but I learnt to live with them.

Initially there appeared to be no problems with food as the government seemed intent on filling the markets to keep the people happy, although rationing began to be introduced towards the end of hostilities. It was always hard to get cigarettes because they had been given to the forces, and eggs became very expensive.

As the years passed, however, the prices of all foodstuffs started to rise and life became an increasingly hard struggle. Every time Azziz went out searching the *suq* for vegetables he would find that the costs had multiplied overnight and the quality was constantly deteriorating. Tomatoes, which were usually so wonderful there, were now sold as a squashy, over-ripe mess, onions became non-existent and I would have to chop up chives, if I could get them, in order to combine them with my store of dried herbs to give the cooking any flavour at all. Milk had risen so much in price that we could only afford to buy two cans a month for the children. I would have to try to make meals from meat which normally I wouldn't have given to the dogs. By the time I had cut away all the fat, which it was compulsory to buy with the lean, cleaned away all the broken bits of bone and washed it thoroughly to ensure none of the flies which always swarmed around the butchers' stalls had left any eggs, I would be left with barely enough for one person, let alone a family.

Even two years after the war finished basic foodstuffs continued to be rationed, and we would not have been able to survive without the black market. Life was a constant worry. There were no streetlights in the city through the war years and we had to save water and electricity whenever possible and observe the blackout at night, but those sorts of things are not so hard to live with. What was hard was the constant news of death as the troops continued to be slaughtered. The bereaved families would drape their houses in black banners which carried the dates that their boys had been killed; there wasn't a house in our street which did not have banners out.

Every month I would join a family somewhere in the street for a *fatha* (wake). If the people were rich they would erect huge tents for the traditional three-day wakes, but the poorer families just held them in their sitting rooms with all the furniture removed and mattresses forming a square around the room. I would arrive amongst the black-swathed, wailing women and the crying children and sit with them on the floor, drinking tiny cups of bitter black coffee, smoking cigarettes, eating from saucers of nuts and offering my sincere condolences, wishing them in turn a long life – '*Baqi fihi atiqum.*'

I would give the mother or wife of the dead youth a traditional envelope of money to help with the funeral expenses. We always had to stay at least half an hour at these events, anything less would have been disrespectful. The chief female mourners would stay indoors for forty days before emerging and coming round to thank us all for attending and showing our respect. In Iraq a bereaved wife must not enter society for forty days just in case she is pregnant. If she were not pregnant when her husband died, but became so during that forty-day period, she would be disinherited by the family.

The men would join the bereaved fathers in the streets if they could not afford a tent, and would bring sacks of rice and sugar, or tins of fat or even whole sheep to the family. The chief male mourner would keep an exact tally of how much money or what gifts were given by each visiting family, and should that family suffer a bereavement they would receive exactly the same value of gift in return. How long before it would be our turn for such a terrible ritual in our house?

I also attended a number of hastily prepared weddings, young soldiers marrying in order to produce heirs just in case they were killed. So many of them were killed, leaving these young women and babies behind. Few of these young widows were ever able to marry again, unless it was to some other male relative, and they had to bring up their families on their own with all the extra pressures of politics and war to contend with.

The most ferocious fighting during the Iran–Iraq conflict did not happen in Baghdad, much of it was going on in Basrah, and I was glad that at least we had moved away from that area. But we knew that many of the boys from our area were down there fighting.

One day Azziz was due home for lunch. He left work at the usual time, and drove his usual route across the city towards home. There was a long queue at the first checkpoint which he had to cross, slowing him to a crawl. Eventually he reached the front and a soldier came up to his car window.

'Is this your car?' the young man asked.

'Yes.'

'Draw in over there,' he pointed with his gun to a lay-by where other vehicles were already congregating. Azziz noticed that they were all commercial vehicles or cars like ours with roofracks. He parked and climbed out, waiting beside his vehicle like the other drivers. The ones in front were talking in hushed voices, all of them frightened and unsure why they had been picked out for special treatment.

'You!' another soldier came over to him and thrust an official looking piece of paper into his hand, 'You are to go to collect the body of a martyr to bring back to his family. This is the name and this is where you must go for the collection, and where the body must be delivered to.' A martyr was anyone who had died for his country in the battles with Iran.

Azziz nodded. There was no point arguing, and he wouldn't have wanted to get out of the job anyway. One day, as he told me later, it might be one of our boys who needed to be collected, and he hoped someone would be kind enough to do it, otherwise the body would be thrown into some communal grave or lime pit. His licence was taken and he was told to go immediately. If he got the police to sign for the body at the other end he could reclaim his licence when he got back to Baghdad. Following the instructions he drove to the collection point out in the desert outside the city. There, in a wire compound with guards on the gate, were twenty or thirty containers from the backs of articulated lorries, still advertising fruit and vegetables on their sides. Azziz was told to wait with fifty or more other drivers until his turn came. By the time he was taken to one of the lorries it was already dark, and he hadn't been given anything to eat or drink all day. Inside the container were piles of makeshift coffins. The guard looked through to find his designated one.

'These aren't freshly killed,' he explained as he searched, 'these were buried in the desert by the Iranians. When we retook the land we dug them up and brought them here.' The smell of rotting flesh made Azziz gag as the guard pulled down one of the boxes. He opened the lid and inside was a body, its head blown clean off its shoulders, but the dog-tag and papers were still there.

Other bodies were being given to other drivers; many were missing limbs, or had holes blown in their stomachs or rib-cages. Many of the faces were too disfigured or blackened to be recognisable. The only means of identification were the name tags tied to their toes. The guards nailed the boxes shut before they left the compound.

Once these boxes were sealed no one was allowed to open them.

The government said that it was to save the families from the distress of seeing their sons and brothers badly mutilated – in fact it was because more often than not the wrong body was in the box. There would be people watching at the funerals to check that the boxes had not been tampered with, but many families took the risk to try to get one last look at their boys, and that was how so many discovered that they had been sent the wrong bodies, leaving them in an emotional limbo, never knowing whether to grieve for their boys or pray for their safe return.

Azziz loaded the box onto the roofrack and started the long trip out to find the family. It was now pitch black and he wasn't allowed to use headlights. He didn't know the road he was travelling on, and could easily have driven over a cliff, but he made it to the area. He found the police station on the outskirts to get a signature and then continued. As he approached the destination he saw that there was a crowd waiting for him. The whole village was standing silently beside the road. All the men were armed. As he drove up they began to shout and scream, terrible blood-curdling sounds, and they were shooting into the air, charging at the car. They tore at the ropes which held the coffin, rocking the car with their weight, drumming on the roof and windscreen, wailing and shrieking and firing off their guns. Azziz was terrified, but managed to escape alive.

By the time he got home it was light and I had been up all night, convinced that he had been killed by a bomb. I was so relieved to see him I just threw my arms around his neck. The moment he walked into the room I could smell death on his clothes. It was a smell I had grown used to over the years, not only from the bodies of people which I had come across, but from the carcasses of animals which often lay rotting in the streets for several days before being cleared away. It was a sweet, sickly smell, like raw sewage.

He made many more such trips over the next few months as the young men from the north of the country were brought back to their grieving families. He would often come home in tears with stories of the distress which his missions had caused to the innocent people he had had to visit. Everyone with a suitable vehicle was forced into this service.

One New Year's Eve during the war years Mary and Abdul invited us back down to Basrah. We knew that it had been an exceptionally bad year for rocket attacks down there.

'Should we risk it?' Azziz asked, voicing my own fears.

'I think if Mary and Abdul and the others have been able to put up with it all this time, then the least we can do is go down for a few days to cheer them up,' I said. 'New Year was always good fun down there.'

Azziz thought for a moment before answering: 'Okay,' he nodded, 'let's do it and hope for the best.'

It is nearly 500 kilometres from Baghdad to Basrah and we knew we would not be able to get petrol on the road so we filled extra tanks and put them in the back of the car. It was our first trip back for many years and we weren't prepared for the damage we would see. Mary and Abdul were spending a great deal of their daily lives hiding out by the telephone in a dark hallway in their sand-bagged house, with rockets showering down on them. As we walked into the house we saw the broken windows and gaping cracks in the walls. There was no electricity or water. But their obvious delight at seeing us made all the risks worthwhile. Mary had lost a lot of weight and I was surprised by how lined she had become. I guess we must have aged since we had seen them last as well. Abdul had become very elegant and distinguished looking.

'We are going to celebrate New Year at the Port Club,' they said. 'There will be so many people there that you know, you must come.'

We arrived at the club at ten at night. The atmosphere was as heavy as lead. No one was dancing, they were just sitting at the tables in gloomy silence. As we walked in everyone seemed to recognise us, it was like receiving a standing ovation. Dumping our coats and bags down at the table which had been prepared for us I turned to Azziz, '*Yalla!*' (Come on) I said, 'let's have some fun.' Once out on the dance floor, gyrating to Tom Jones's 'Delilah', I called other friends out to join us, 'Come on, up you get, let's dance. The rockets aren't coming tonight, it's New Year, let's celebrate!' Within minutes the floor was crowded and we were surrounded by old friends hugging and kissing us and welcoming us back. Nizar was so pleased to see us he practically crushed us both in an enormous bear hug. I was so proud of them in their terrible ordeal. So many of them were to lose their homes and families in the horror that was to come.

The next day we went round the city visiting Nizar and Bernadette and other friends in their homes. As I looked around at all the destruction in the familiar streets I couldn't stop the tears from flowing. Not one rocket fell in the two days we were there, but within an hour of us leaving for Baghdad the attacks restarted. For once we seemed to have been leading charmed lives, and I was so glad that we had decided to go.

ELEVEN

ALL the young men in our family were gradually taken into the army, and then the government began to spread its nets further and look for older men who were fit enough to be sent out to fill the gaps left by the early casualties. Azziz was determined not to fight, and I was determined not to let him. We had been adamant that we would not join any political party; we wanted to stay right out of it because every allegiance was fraught with potential dangers.

The Baath Party organised groups which worked like the press gangs which the British navy had used in the eighteenth century. They would be given lorries and told to fill them with recruits for the army. If they failed to fill their quota then they themselves would be sent to the front. These men, who all looked like backstreet murderers, became desperate to find enough people. They would stop buses in the street and drag the men out, or they would swoop on young boys playing outside their houses, or knock on doors to find the men inside. Our doorbell was always going – either they were looking for my husband to find out why he wasn't fighting, or my sons if they were home visiting, or they wanted to know why we hadn't joined the Baath Party. The moment you opened the door they would begin to shout their questions at you.

'Where is your husband?'

'Where are your sons?'

'Who is your daughter married to?'

'How old are your grandchildren?'

'Why do you not join the party?'

I always replied that I had no idea where the men were, that they had gone to a meeting somewhere that I knew nothing about. I told them we knew nothing about politics. If you were not careful what you said they would start screaming that we did not love Saddam Hussein and that we were traitors. Men who refused to get into the lorries were shot on the spot for treachery, so they would all go.

There were always so many pieces of paper to be filled in. They would push a form into your hand at the gate one day, ordering you to have it filled in by the following day, when they would be back to pick it up. The questions were always the same: trying to ascertain exactly who we were, how many of us there were, what our politics were and whether there was anyone eligible to fight. When you live in a police state you grow used to this sort of behaviour. You have no privacy, they know everything about you and if you try to withhold anything they have the power to take you anywhere they choose and do with you whatever they like. They can torture you, rape you, lock you up or simply shoot you on the spot. So many people we knew had first-hand experience of all these things. If you have a family it is impossible to take a brave stand, because they will not just come for you, they will come for all your friends and relatives, and anyone who is thought to have had dealings with you.

'These people are driving me mad,' I told Azziz one evening when we were sitting alone together in the bedroom, 'they frighten me.'

'We'll make the house more secure,' he promised, holding me tightly to him and stroking my hair soothingly.

We already had a high wall around the front of the house, encircling the drive which was big enough to take four cars. That meant that we could close the gates with the whole family inside. The gates, however, were just wrought iron, so anyone could look through and see that we were there. Azziz brought home some steel plates and welded them to the gates so that no one could see through, and put large bolts on the inside. We then devised a coded ring on the doorbell which only the family knew. If the bell rang in any other way we didn't answer it. The only way they could see in was if they stood on top of their lorries and looked over the walls. It made me feel more secure, but I still knew that they were watching us all the time.

We lived in a police state, and we had a family to protect; there was nothing we could do but comply with all the regulations, however ridiculous they might seem. At one time the government ordered that every typewriter in the country must be registered to one person only and that no one else should be allowed to use it. As a secretary I needed to be registered to the typewriter I used at work. I had to take the machine all the way to a government building, sit down with an official and produce a sample document, and have that sample registered in my name. That meant that if any subversive propaganda appeared, they would know who had typed it. I was always terrified that someone else would use my machine when I wasn't in the office and get me into trouble. The same rule applied to photocopiers. I also had a typewriter at home which I had learnt on, and which I was very fond of, but Azziz insisted on destroying it. When you had as many children and grandchildren as we did, you didn't want to take unnecessary risks with their safety.

Most of the Iranian bombs missed the targets they were aimed at and fell on people's houses or shops, but occasionally they seemed to be getting help from other places. One hot, bright afternoon in June 1981, my neighbour Nancy and I were sitting on the roof of my house chatting and having a cup of tea. We heard some planes coming in along the route used by the Iraqi fighters to a nearby airbase.

'I can hear planes,' I said. 'Let's just check they are ours and not theirs.' As we looked up into the sky I saw five huge, black bombers heading towards us. They were not like any of the planes we were used to seeing. 'Those aren't our planes,' I said, 'but they're not Iranian either.'

'Are they going to land?' Nancy wondered. We watched to see what would happen next. The planes went past us and dropped down much lower.

'They're heading for the nuclear plant,' I said, horrified. A few minutes later, when they were out of our sight a spiral of heavy black smoke rose up in the distance. We ducked down, expecting an enormous explosion, but when it came it was muted, as if it had happened somewhere underground. We stayed crouched down as the planes flew back the way they had come, but there was no anti-aircraft fire. As the sound of their engines died away we started to hear the bells of the ambulances and fire engines as they rushed to the scene. The roads outside were full of people asking one another what was going on. We all knew the dangers of a nuclear explosion, but no official announcements were made to calm our fears. Later we heard rumours that the Israelis had managed to locate and destroy a chemical weapons factory. For many months after that every time we took a trip to a doctor, either for ourselves of for one of the children, they would give us a blood test. I was even given one when I went complaining of a sore throat. I don't suppose we will ever know exactly what happened that day, or what long-term effects it has had on our health.

Azziz and I had grown very contented with one another through the war years. Age and experience had mellowed us, and having enough money to get by and to look after our children made everything easier. Marriage is always smoother if you have a house big enough to get away from one another when you feel like it, and when you aren't having to scrimp and save all the time. When I wanted to be alone I would go along to our bedroom and paint or write poetry, but most of the time I was busy working and running our home. Azziz had his work which was going well, but he also had our constantly growing family, all of whom loved and respected him, and he seemed to want to spend more and more of his time with them.

If you are lucky in your choice of partner the passion which first brings you together will develop into a friendship, rich in mutual trust, reliance and companionship. That is how it has become for us. We have been through so much together it is easy for us to forget where we started all those years ago; we are almost like one person.

In 1980 any foreign wives in Iraq who had been there more than three years were ordered to take Iraqi nationality or get out. I was horrified by the prospect. Somehow the fact that I had a British passport had been a comfort to me through the years, allowing me to feel that should the worst happen I did have an escape route. It had helped me to face up to many of the tribulations of living in the Middle East with more courage than I might otherwise have been able to muster. For days I haunted the British Embassy, trying to find out if the Iraqis were within their rights to demand this of us. My panic began to turn into a boiling anger, and there were many others who felt the same. Our main fear was that the new rule would curtail our freedom to travel outside Iraq, particularly back to the UK.

One morning, at a coffee party, I was able to get the ear of the ambassador's wife. I begged her to speak to her husband on our behalf, admitting that many of us were coming to believe that he was indifferent to our plight. Two weeks later I heard through the grapevine that the ambassador had been to see the president and had been assured that should we take up Iraqi nationality we would not have to surrender our British passports, that we could hold dual nationality. I wanted to have this in writing and went down to the embassy. There was only two days left before the deadline.

I wasn't alone in my concern. There were dozens of other girls milling around at the embassy when I arrived, all clutching official-looking forms and moving from one queue to another. Many of them were there to get exit visas, having no intention of agreeing to the government's demands. If my children had been younger and I could have been sure Azziz would have come with me, I would gladly have joined them on the plane back to England.

Instead I became the possessor of an identity card (*huwiyah shakhsiyah*) and a national certificate (*shahadat al-jinsiyah*), both documents which many people whose parents and grandparents had failed to claim Iraqi nationality in the past were unable to obtain. Unless they could prove their ancestors were born in a particular stretch of country previously included in Mesopotamia, these people could not be classed as full Iraqis – a claim I was now able to make. Most had entered the country generations before and had never bothered to claim full nationality. Known as *Tabiyah*, these poor people were now floating, without the right to claim university schooling or travel. Many of them later had to escape over the borders into Turkey and Iran in the hope that they would be accepted as refugees by other countries.

Receiving those papers and becoming an Iraqi citizen seemed to break down some of the barriers which still existed between me and Azziz's family. Suddenly they accepted me completely. Azziz was so proud when he told them I had become an Iraqi citizen and they all rejoiced as if it were a great victory for them. I was given presents, something which had never happened before, and was greeted with smiles, kisses and congratulations at family gatherings. Like the other foreign wives, however, I felt very uncomfortable about this new development, even though it made some things easier, like finding jobs.

Now I was governed by new rules regarding my rights to travel. When I next decided I wanted to visit my family in England I had to put in a written request for permission from the president and the Revolutionary Council, permission which had been known to take up to four months to come. This time a ring at the gate signalled the arrival of a Baath Party official bearing a letter with the seal of the palace on the envelope within a couple of months. This letter opened doors for me at the exit visa office, but also caused considerable jealousy amongst those who, for various reasons, were unable to get visas. The visa was not unconditional: while I was away Azziz was not allowed to leave Iraq, even on government business, none of my children was allowed to travel with me, and I was not allowed to stay away for more than two months. Every day it seemed that our freedoms became a little more restricted.

I soon grew tired of commuting by bus to my job, and when I was offered a post by one of the international airlines, with the offer of a car to pick me up and take me home each day, I jumped at it. One of the perks of the job was free air tickets home from Jordan. In 1982 I decided to go home to England for Christmas.

Christmas has always been my favourite time, even in a Muslim country. I would start preparing for it in about August each year, collecting presents for my whole family. I would knit clothes and sew for all the children, making toys out of scraps or knitting them from odd bits of wool I had scrounged over the years. I had secret hiding places which by December would be overflowing with packages I had wrapped months ahead. I would also give my beloved street urchins balloons, sweets, homemade cakes, biscuits and other small gifts. They must have been very puzzled by the whole thing. One year, just when things were hardest, I managed to buy a small truck load of toys from a departing expatriate. The children couldn't believe their eyes. Because they were all Muslims it was 'Nana and Gidu's (Grandmother and Grandfather's) Day', and Azziz would dress up as Father Christmas in a suit I had made for him out of a piece of red satin, coated with cotton wool and Christmas tree decorations.

This year, I decided to treat myself to a real English Christmas. The trip involved a cold, sixteen-hour coach journey to Jordan, with numerous checkpoints along the way. At Safwan, a windswept desert outpost on the Iraqi side of the border, we had to queue for more than two hours in the bitter cold. I was travelling with a girlfriend and her two-year-old daughter, and my heart sank when it came to our turn and we were asked to come into the office.

'Where are your visas?' the official barked at us as soon as we entered. 'Why didn't you have your passports stamped with exit visas while you were in Baghdad?'

He seemed an inexperienced young man, even more nervous than us, so I started to gabble away at him. 'We went to the office, but because we are married to Iraqis they said we didn't need exit visas.' He shook his head, and I could see he didn't believe me. Taking a deep breath I tried one last bluff. 'Look, ring Mr Khada (a senior official at the passport office). He will know my name.' He stared at me for at least a minute, and I held his gaze calmly, although I was trembling inside. Then he stamped the passports and handed them back to us. One other British woman wasn't as lucky; because she didn't have a letter from her husband, giving her permission to leave the country, she was sent back to Baghdad.

At one of the checkpoints on the Jordanian side we were told that we were all going to be subjected to body searches. Since the temperatures outside were now below freezing and icy rains were falling, I did not relish the prospect, so when my turn came I decided to try something which I had never been able to bring myself to do before: I slipped the woman some money and she allowed me to climb back into the warmth of the bus. I always knew that bribes would get you almost anywhere with officials, but I had never had the nerve to try it before. I was amazed by how naturally and easily she accepted the arrangement.

After a night in a painfully cold hotel in Jordan I caught my flight and finally I was on a British bus to Bournemouth, eating sandwiches, drinking hot tea and watching the peaceful English countryside slip by. It was a wonderful Christmas, but I missed my family terribly, phoning them every day, pestering them with questions about whether they were eating properly and looking after themselves. To compensate myself for missing them, I headed for the January sales and bought a mountain of presents for them all, particularly Azziz. I bought him suits and shirts and shoes, many of which I knew he would never get round to wearing, but I just wanted to spoil him. I also stocked up on essentials which were hard to get at home in Iraq like candles and torches and an Alladin heater which Azziz had asked for. I bought a huge cheddar cheese, packs of bacon and bottles of HP Sauce for Majid, a big Christmas cake and packets of jellies and trifles for a children's party. I also bought loads of brightly coloured wrapping paper, but there was no point in wrapping anything until I got home because the Customs people would only rip it all open again.

So many people came to see me during that holiday, and I was able to spend time with my Gran, and to go on quiet walks in the country. Being back in a land of plenty made me all the more aware of how hard life was becoming in Baghdad with all the shortages. If I heard anyone grumbling that Christmas I would beg them to count their blessings at being able to live in a country which had so much.

Loaded down with all my boxes and cases, I flew back to Jordan, sad to leave my English family, but desperate to see Azziz and all the children. In Amman the cold was far more intense than anything in Britain, and the bus back to Baghdad had no heating or proper luggage facilities. Clutching my cake under my arm, and with bags bulging on every side, I stumbled down the aisle, hitting the other passengers over the head and tripping over their feet, until I fell into one of the uncomfortable little bucket seats, forcing the paraffin heater down behind me and stuffing the bags under my legs. I had managed to persuade one of the air stewardesses to make me a thermos of tea on the plane, and this was the only source of warmth I had for the rest of the day.

We set off in the early hours of the morning and delays along the way meant that we were still crammed into this cattle truck as evening approached. There was a curfew operating in Baghdad from seven in the evening and I was very afraid that we wouldn't get back in time. Sure enough it grew dark outside and the bare desert road disappeared from view. At midnight we reached the outskirts of Baghdad and saw a few dim lights showing from the bare bulbs which hung in the army tents surrounding the city where the Iraqis waited for the Iranians to invade. When we finally arrived at the depot the other passengers, all nervous of being out so late in a city at war, faded away into the night, leaving me, with all my packages and parcels round my feet, sitting on the steps of the bus. I didn't know what to do. The only other person around was the driver who was looking at me despondently, as if wondering what he was going to do with me. I went over to him.

'Would you drive me to my home?' I asked, hopefully, holding out a handful of banknotes. He looked at the money for a moment and then shook his head, brushing the bribe away dismissively. He walked off, shaking his head, reached the door and turned back. Striding over to me, he picked up my cases and threw them back into the bus. Just when I had been about to despair of ever again finding someone who would do me a favour for its own sake, he restored my faith.

'Okay,' he grinned, 'let's try. It's against the law and we might get stopped by the police, but if we tell them you have been travelling all day from Amman, perhaps they will take pity. We will say your husband is sick and needs you.' We set out into the blacked out city again, crashing over potholes and cutting through narrow backstreets in the hope of avoiding the police. By some miracle we weren't stopped. At the only army checkpoint we passed I showed them my passport and explained what was happening and they waved us on wearily. When we finally reached the gates of the house, nearly twenty-four hours after leaving Amman, I stepped straight into a mud puddle in the dark. By the time Azziz answered my frantic rings on the door the bus had disappeared, leaving me and my sorrowful pile of luggage on our own.

'Susan, thank God you are safe,' he swept me off my feet into a bear hug. 'We waited for hours for the bus, and then the curfew came and we had to come home. We thought something terrible must have happened.'

'That is the last bit of travelling I want to do,' I said firmly. 'I never want to be away from you and the kids again.' Little did I know just how much travelling lay ahead of us, and how all the discomforts I had suffered on this trip would one day pale into insignificance beside the suffering we would then have to endure.

TWELVE

THE bombs which the Iranians were throwing at us were only one of the dangers which we had to face during that time. Political groups opposed to the government were frequently letting off bombs and causing disruption to the roads and railways and to public buildings.

The government accused Syria of being behind a series of explosions in cars in the streets of Baghdad. The problem became so acute that they built giant concrete blocks shaped like flowerpot holders to act as shields for important buildings all over the city, blocking in narrow lanes and stopping traffic from getting close. Even the car parks became unsafe after several massive explosions, although the diligence of the traffic control police saved many lives. I found that these internal troubles disturbed me even more than the rockets from Iran. It is somehow easier to cope with an enemy when you know who they are and why they are attacking you. The internal politics of the country were so complex that it was difficult for me to understand who were our enemies and who our friends.

April had to travel by train to her university course in Basrah, and on one of the trips she found herself sharing the carriage with a dozen or so soldiers. They were taking up half the compartment and she was in the first set of seats that they weren't occupying. They were a cheerful bunch of young men, probably new recruits who had not yet been hardened by any serious fighting. They were good-naturedly teasing April and the other girls she was with. The atmosphere in the carriage was relaxed and pleasant. Then, half way to Basrah, everything ended in an enormous flash and a mess of flying debris and bodies. An explosive device had detonated under their carriage and the explosion had come up through the floor, virtually cutting it in half. All the young soldiers were killed, their bodies ripped to pieces, and April was thrown forward in the blast, entangled in the dead bodies and twisted pieces of metal but alive and only superficially hurt. If she had been one seat further down the train she would have been killed too.

From then on she shared taxis back and forth to Baghdad with fellow students. Not long after that the Iranians started to target Basrah University itself. Several times April had narrow escapes, having to throw herself to the ground as planes overhead sent bullets spitting into the dust around her. The government said that any students who wanted to move to safer universities were free to do so, so she came back to Baghdad.

Despite these dramatic incidents, our day-to-day life in Baghdad was fairly quiet. The Iranian bombing attacks would die away for several weeks sometimes, and would then return with renewed ferocity, but we learnt to live with them. Our main preoccupation was trying to find enough food to keep the family healthy. Azziz and I used to go to the British Club quite a bit. Times had changed a great deal since the days when the colonial British had filled places like this. Now most of the expatriates were ordinary working people who had come out to do specific jobs like build sewers or power stations, hospitals or roads. They were nice people who had none of the snobbery of their predecessors. The club was a beautiful old building with swimming pools, indoor and outdoor cinemas, a restaurant and a bar. There was a new hall for social gatherings, with a stage for special events and performances.

We used to go there for parties, or just to swim or watch films. It was like a social centre for us. I became involved with fund-raising activities, spending hours making items for raffles and other charitable ventures. We also gossiped a great deal about the war, the government and the future of the country. Nobody was optimistic. We would talk endlessly about the news and the propaganda which the media was pumping out.

'Did you see that man they tore apart?'

'What was that?'

'They tied him to two jeeps and then drove them in different directions – he was just torn in two. It was on the news last night.'

'My God, but who did it?'

'The government said the Iranians did it, but people say it was propaganda to make the Iranians look like butchers.'

We all had opinions, but none of us ever knew the truth of what was going on. There was so much rumour and speculation, and so much propaganda and false information fed to the people that it was impossible to know who was behind what.

A lot of people used to ask me why we didn't give up and go back to England. 'Iraq is my home,' I would answer. 'My house is here, my job, my children, my grandchildren and all the friends I have made in the last thirty years.' There were some attractions to the idea of leaving Iraq, but we didn't seriously consider it at that stage, particularly after my awful journey that Christmas and all the problems with getting visas. It seemed better to stay put and make the best of things. With hindsight that was one of our most terrible mistakes: we should have done everything we could to get ourselves and as many of our children and grandchildren as possible back to England. When you are living somewhere for many years you get into the habit of thinking that that is your destiny and of believing that there is nothing you can do to avoid it.

With the departure of so many of my friends I found my leisure time passing more and more slowly. I was finding it difficult to sit down and read a book, always waiting nervously for the next explosion. I hated cooking because the kitchen had so many windows and I was frightened they might be blown in on me; most of them now had cracks in the glass. I used to spend hours chatting on the phone or meeting up in other people's houses, but now there were fewer and fewer people to talk to as our friends took opportunities to move to other countries. Mary and Abdul had left for Jordan, Nizar and Bernadette were back in England with her family. By the end of the war even the phones were cut off. Every day the sirens haunted me, sending me scurrying for the bathroom with the grandchildren under my arms. Sometimes the 'all clear' would be sounded and we wouldn't even know if any bombs had been dropped, but the terror was the same.

I was so proud of the way our children had grown up. John was doing well in his job and was discharged from the army in order to work for the government. He and I were very close. I could talk to him about anything and he would tease me a great deal. He and Laila had four wonderful children. April was excelling at university and soon came home with a new man and announced that she wanted to marry him. He was a professor of Kurdish studies, a jovial, round and intelligent chap called Hilall. He was certainly very different from the tall, good-looking young man she had married the first time, and he seemed very nice, but this time Azziz was taking no risks.

'This time,' he told April, 'we are going to do everything the traditional way. Your mother and I want to meet his parents before we give our permission, and he must put down some money to guarantee that you will be looked after if he leaves you.' April was indignant at these restrictions but Azziz was adamant, and I think he was right. Hilall wasn't at all concerned.

'I will give her all the money and property I possess if you like,' he said cheerfully, 'I don't mind what she has.'

Once we were satisfied that he was as good a man as he seemed, we agreed to the marriage and we have never had cause to regret it, although it was Hilall's fluency in the Kurdish language which was later to lead us into making the worst mistake of our lives. They bought a house on the outskirts of Baghdad and April eventually had three more children.

During those years the press gangs were continually working in the streets, taking off young men for a day's training in how to use a gun and then shipping them out to fight the Iranians or the Kurds or to guard some mountain or other. Most of the boys went and did their time and got out as quickly as they could, but Hilall fought them all the way. The first time he was picked up he turned up on the doorstep the following day, looking very dishevelled.

'How did you get out of the training camp?' I asked.

'I climbed into an empty soup tureen and came out with the catering staff,' he explained with a wicked grin.

Another time he simply stole an officer's cap and marched out of the gates, cheekily returning the guards' salutes. In all he escaped six times, but eventually they managed to keep hold of him and sent him up into the Kurdish mountains. It was there that he first learnt about the ruthlessness with which the Kurds were fighting their enemies.

'I was on duty one day,' he told us on his return, 'and my group was relieved in the evening by some new recruits. The oldest was fourteen, and there was one twelve-year-old boy who was crying for his mother.

We were worried about leaving them alone, but we had orders and we needed sleep. During the night the Kurds slit their throats and threw them over the edge of the mountain. Those mountains are dangerous places.'

Azziz and I were both very happy that April had managed to find such a good man. That just left Peter, who also managed to finish university in between bouts of military service and met a girl in Basrah. Hala was the daughter of a wealthy family of traders and a lovely girl, so we had no hesitation in giving our blessing to the union, and soon they too started to produce children. How I loved all those babies. I would have been happy to have had all of them with me all the time. I adored being the centre of such a growing and happy family. We all had our differences of opinion, of course, and occasionally there were bad feelings between some members of the family, but somehow we always managed to smooth everything over and bring them all together in our house for special events and holidays. Compared to most of the families we knew we were very lucky.

The war was costing the government a lot of money, and they passed a law called War Support. This meant that part of your monthly salary was taken, and money was collected from anyone working in the streets and shops, to help with the war effort. No one minded this law, as long as we felt it was helping our forces in some way. When the gold reserves started to drop a message came out over the television and radio asking that everyone should hand over their gold, right down to their wedding rings. People who gave a lot, such as goldsmiths, were thanked personally on television by the president. No one was given a receipt and none of the gifts was registered, so no one expected to receive remuneration once the war was over. Anyone who said they didn't have any gold had their reluctance to support their country recorded against them.

On the president's birthday and on Revolution Day, we were all expected to put decorations up and candles on the houses and front gateposts. Once again it was recorded against you if you didn't. As the years passed, however, and the government became more unpopular, people stopped doing this and the decorating of government buildings and shop fronts had to be done by members of the party.

One spring day the pressures of life in Baghdad finally got Azziz and me down. 'Let's take the family up into the mountains for a week,' I suggested, 'just to get away from it all.'

'Okay,' Azziz agreed, 'we'll go to Sirrarush. It's a holiday resort at the top of a mountain in the province of Salahuddin. Hilall and I will go down to the town and hire a chalet up high somewhere.'

'That would be wonderful,' I clapped my hands with delight, knowing how beautiful that area was at this time of year. 'Perhaps there will be some snow for the little ones to play in.'

The arrangements were made and we set off early one morning, intending to reach our destination by the evening. We took our car and Hilall's so that there was room for us all to travel in comfort and bring enough luggage. We had Majid and his new baby half-brother Ali. We sped across the plains towards Kirkuk from where we intended to take the road to the summer city of Arbil. We reached Kirkuk all right, but at the beginning of the road to Arbil we were stopped at a checkpoint behind a long line of other cars.

'You have to have an armed escort,' we were told by the soldiers manning the checkpoint. 'The Kurds are attacking the army outposts along the highway.' An armed escort? We were travelling to try to get away from this sort of thing. 'You won't get to Sirrarush today,' we were told, 'it's too dangerous.'

We didn't feel like heading back now, having come so far, so we decided to get as far as Arbil and see what happened. The line moved out.

'Do not slow down or leave the safety of your cars,' our escorts ordered. 'If the children need to relieve themselves they must do it in the cars. Stay with the other vehicles.' We set off at a good speed, but I was sorry not to be able to stop and take in the beautiful scenery along the way. I would have loved to let the children loose on the green slopes and fields either side of the road.

In Arbil we found a hotel we had been to before and enjoyed a meal in the gardens with freezing cold beer, waiting for daylight to return so that we could try again to reach the mountains. Up here was a land of plenty compared to Baghdad. We saw crates of cold drinks stacked up at the next checkpoint and cigarettes on sale everywhere.

We were now allowed to go on our way and our spirits were lifting. We sang out loud with the children all the little songs that they had learnt back home, while they clapped their hands and stamped their feet. The sunny weather was turning to rain squalls, but we didn't care, we were on holiday and there were no rockets. From Arbil it took us less than two hours to get to the base of the mountains. The rain was beginning to turn to snow and the roads ahead would be more difficult to negotiate than the flat plains, but we weren't bothered, inside the cars we were warm and cosy.

As we zig-zagged up the mountains the snow was thickening. 'Tomorrow we will be building a snowman and having snowball fights,' I told the kids, and they squealed with joy.

The road began to become more slippery and dangerous. High on a narrow road, with only a half-metre wall stopping us from sliding back down to the bottom, we came to a halt behind a queue of traffic. Dozens of cars had stopped ahead of us and we had to creep forward in first gear. By the time we reached the top of this particular stretch of road the snow was coming down like a blanket, the gullies beside the road pouring water and ice, and the temperature was dropping. Even inside the car it became cold. We finally reached Salahadin roundabout where we were forced to get out to ask directions in the sleety snow. We hoped it would only be another hour. The snow was now a foot deep and the cars were getting into trouble; it didn't look as if Hilall's would get any further.

'Everyone will have to get in with us,' Azziz said, 'we'll come back for the other car tomorrow.'

'We can't leave the car out all night,' Hilall argued. 'I'll stay with it.'

'All right,' Azziz agreed, 'I will drop the others and come back to help you.' Had we known that there were wolves in the area as well as Kurdish separatists, we might not have been so willing to leave Hilall on his own.

Azziz managed to get us to the chalet and then disappeared back into the storm. There was no electricity and no water. We did, however, have gas, so I dug up the virgin snow outside with a cup, filled a nylon bag with it and took it inside to melt for tea, for the baby's bottle and to flush the toilet.

There was no food in the house, and no restaurant, and even the children didn't want to go outside because of the intense cold. It was midnight before Azziz and Hilall returned. The following day we discovered why things were in such a bad state. Apparently the Kurds, who wanted to discourage tourists from coming to the area, had cut the electric cables and broken the water pipes leading to the resort. The restaurant was closed as no provisions had been able to get through due to the attacks on the roads. I couldn't help thinking of those young boys having their throats cut in the dead of night, and their bodies tossed away. Every sound outside the house made me jump.

'There could be a full-scale attack on the town any time,' a local told us, 'and these chalets are not built to withstand bullets, they are only made of wood. The best thing you can do is get back down the mountain as quickly as possible.'

By now the roads were impassable, so we had to stay there for two days with no food, help or heating, no water other than melted snow, and two small children. We kept the baby wrapped up in blankets inside the chalet and wore every item of clothing we could find, but still we were all freezing. On the third day we slid back down the mountain to Salahadin, where we managed to find a restaurant which sold the most delicious kebab and *tikka* with hot *khubiz* (a flat, unleavened bread). We stuffed everyone full of hot food, buying extra for the journey back into Arbil and joined a line of other cars zig-zagging round the treacherous mountain bends. Eventually we reached the plains and headed home as fast as we could.

Despite this disastrous attempt at a holiday, the following year we set off once more for the mountains to escape the rockets, having been told that the government was now fully in control of the area again. By this time April had another newborn baby, a little boy called Hosni. We stopped off for lunch at a village nestling at the foot of high, red, sandy cliffs, called Shuklowa. Here the icy mountains were just a distant, if fearsome, backdrop. Armed soldiers patrolled the streets, making us feel safer. Our destination was a place which the Arabs called Al-Ain al-Sahariyah (the Magic Eye), a place where the waters from the high ice fields thunder down the mountainsides and end in a deep gorge used by the Iraqis as a holiday resort. Holiday-makers from Baghdad would pitch their tents by the water and eat in a local eatery. I loved this place, its beauty, the towering mountains enclosing a well of peace, quiet except for the noise and spray of the waterfall. I could have stayed there forever.

On the way home we stopped off in a field of sunflowers, their nodding heads heavy with seeds. I buried my face in the earth, feeling the warmth of the sun and never wanting to return to the explosions of Baghdad. We picked sunflower seeds to plant in the garden, to bring a little of that peace and beauty into our lives.

On another outing we visited a place called Rawandiz, one of the highest points in Kurdistan. There is a cave carved out by the waters which form a pool on the floor so pure that you could drink straight from it. Makeshift coffee houses set up under canvas were selling hot, spicy food, rice and meats cooked over charcoal burners and *hubbas*.

After lunch we decided to take a walk around the area and found what looked to be a well laid out garden with pathways circled by narrow channels running with mountain water.

'I feel we are being watched,' I muttered to Azziz.

Azziz looked up with a start and suddenly, as we rounded a corner, we found ourselves face to face with a battalion of Kurdish warriors. There must have been several hundred of them, all dressed in the same filthy brown clothes and headdresses, their chests crossed with ammunition, guns and knives in their belts. The stink of them filled the garden. All their eyes bored into April and me, looking hungry, angry and suspicious; God knows when they had last seen women. Some of them stirred and moved towards us. We were too late to stop Majid running towards these dirty, unsmiling soldiers as they lolled in the sun, dragging little Ali along behind him by the hand. Ali's plump little legs were going as fast as they could to keep up with his big brother, and his eyes were wide with wonder at the sight of these awesome men. With no sign of fear Majid ran up to them and asked to see their guns. There was not a flicker of response to his childish request. It was as if the whole valley had fallen silent, and even the mountains were staring in horror at the foolhardiness of the two small boys. A voice shouted something from behind us in Kurdish which sounded like a warning. Someone in a café had seen where we had got to. Hilall went up and talked to the man for a moment, as the rest of us stood frozen to the spot under the malevolent stares of the soldiers, then he returned to us, walking deliberately slowly as if trying not to alarm some particularly dangerous wild animals. When he reached us he spoke in English.

'Get back to the cars, quickly,' he pushed us up the slope. He seemed to be panicking and trying not to show it. 'Come on, Baba,' he said to Azziz, 'let's get them out of here.' We could tell that something was seriously wrong and obeyed him without question, hurriedly lifting the boys and carrying them with us. They must have sensed our fear because they didn't protest at such manhandling. We climbed into the cars and once we had driven several miles down the road Hilall pulled over and came back to explain.

'They were Kurdish warriors just back from fighting in Iran, mercenaries hired by the Iraqi government to plunder and kill. This is their mountain base. The man told me that they don't like tourists gaping at them and they don't hesitate to kill people who annoy them and just walk away from the bodies. These people are untouchable because they have nothing to lose.' Remembering their faces I had no doubt that those men would have been capable of anything.

That was our last attempt to go to the mountains until we were finally driven up there against our will. I had grown to fear the whole area. I did not understand what was going on up there, but I knew that danger was everywhere and that when we were there we had no one to protect us.

THIRTEEN

IN 1988 the war with Iran ended, but the people were not convinced that that was the end of the troubles. We knew that no agreement had been signed, and we imagined that now that Iraq had annoyed Iran, sooner or later our giant neighbour would hit back in some unexpected way. We knew that they were building up their arms supplies; it seemed that it could only be a matter of time. Everyone was still excited by the news of peace, because it meant that our men would be coming home, but of course many of them didn't. Every day lines of taxis and other vehicles would bring the bodies of loved ones home for burial. Up to two years later bodies were still being released to their families. Even now I know of families who pray that their sons are prisoners in Iran and will one day come home – but of course they never will.

While some of the soldiers left alive were discharged, that didn't include the men in the most important age groups; they were being kept on and no one would say when they would be allowed to go.

'They haven't finished with the fighting yet,' I said to Azziz, 'otherwise why are they keeping our boys?' He had no answer either.

Peter never was discharged and within a few months of the end of the war John was called up again. Because of his job at the university Hilall was spared, for the moment. On the television each evening they showed army recruitment and training films, telling the university students to expect to do military service during their holidays. Why would they show those films if the war was truly over and peace had come as they said?

They made some attempts to rebuild the bomb-damaged buildings around the city, but no one's heart was in it. 'Why rebuild the city if the Iranians are going to return to destroy it?' people said. There was a feeling of hopelessness, as if the war had never ended and we were just waiting for the worst part to come. No one trusted the government, or believed that they had the interests of the people at heart. There were terrible food shortages and most of our time was spent searching for the essentials of life.

'They will do anything to maintain power,' Azziz said one evening. 'That will probably mean another war, anything to allow them to keep a state of emergency going.'

All the foreign business people kept being called into their embassies for 'trade meetings'. They all looked very worried when they came out, but no one would tell us exactly what had been said.

One evening I was at the British Club with a group of people including my neighbour Nancy. Everyone was talking about the situation. Suddenly one of the men motioned the others to be quiet and I heard him whisper, 'Careful what you say, remember Susan and Nancy are married to Iraqis.' These people were our friends and yet they didn't trust us, in case we were spies working for the enemy. From then on whenever they were gathered in groups around the bar or swimming pool, the expatriates would break off their conversations when we came near, looking sheepishly away into the distance.

'Why are they behaving like this to us?' I asked Azziz.

'They know something,' he shook his head and held my hand which was trembling, 'something which the government is planning, but I don't know what.'

It seemed we were going to be the last to know. Our relationships with all our remaining foreign friends became strained. My Scandinavian boss, Ole, threw a party at his house on New Year's Eve to which we were invited. I was grateful to him for inviting us. It was a wonderful event and took our minds off the worries which we all had. Towards the end of the evening I was standing on my own looking out of the window at the lights of the city.

'Hello, Susan,' I turned to find Ole standing beside me. He looked very tired. 'Are you enjoying yourself?'

'Yes, thank you. It's lovely to be with friends at a time like this.'

He chatted on for a few minutes before getting to the point. 'May I give you some advice, Susan?'

'Yes, of course.'

'Pack up and get out of Iraq for a while.'

'Why?'

'They expect things to get very bad. The embassies are telling the foreign businesses to sell whatever they can, collect their assets together and leave, otherwise they think we will lose everything.'

'What do they think is going to happen?'

'There is going to be a war against Kuwait, and the international repercussions will be enormous. They think it might even lead to a nuclear strike against Baghdad.' This was the first time that anyone with any inside knowledge had actually put my fears into words for me. I felt my blood run cold. 'Get your family out.'

'How can I? My sons are in the army and I have to look after their wives and children, and my daughter is also an Iraqi.'

'Then take as many precautions as you can. This isn't going to be like the last war. This could be the end of Baghdad.'

I thought deeply about what he had said and talked to Azziz. He agreed that we were in danger on a number of fronts. Firstly, there was the risk of the boys being killed in the army. Secondly, it was likely that Baghdad would be wiped off the map, killing everyone. Thirdly, it was likely that I, as a foreigner, would be seen as an enemy by the Iraqi people once the war was under way; that could mean anything from being spat at to having my assets seized and being imprisoned or shot.

I didn't think that it was likely we would be able to leave the country, although we talked about the possibility a great deal. It would have been impossible to get all of us out, and Azziz and I had no intention of running for safety at a time like this, leaving our beloved babies behind.

If we were going to be trapped in another war we had to prepare ourselves. First we would need supplies and money. Whatever happened there were bound to be shortages and anyone who had the money to pay for things would be in an advantageous position. If we were going to have to leave Baghdad we would need to have enough money to buy food and shelter wherever we ran to. I didn't like the idea of trusting the banks with our earnings. It was more than likely that they would be closed down if there was an emergency, or their funds would be confiscated. I wanted to have our money liquid. Over the next few weeks I drew out several thousand pounds and put it in a bag at the back of the wardrobe. From then on we put no more money in the bank, we just hid it. I began to stock up on dried foodstuffs and anything else which I felt would last us through the coming shortages, and I distributed my more valuable possessions around the homes of Iraqi friends and relatives. This time I was going to be ready for war.

As the months went on we received many more warnings from people who had reason to know what was being planned. We knew now that Saddam Hussein intended to attack Kuwait, we just prayed he would change his mind. Everyone told us to leave Baghdad and most of them urged us to leave the country. As a precaution Azziz and I booked two air tickets for August. If we had managed to find safe places for all the children and grandchildren by then, and we could find a way to get visas, perhaps we could afford to take a few weeks holiday to see what happened. Still, neither of us felt comfortable with the idea, or believed that the authorities would ever let both of us go at once.

The telephone was always ringing, everyone was desperate for any scrap of news they could lay their hands on. Everyone was fearful of what was coming. Many people, like Mary and Abdul and Nizar and Bernadette, were now safely out of the country. They all tried to contact us regularly to check that we were all right, and encouraged us to look for ways to escape before it was too late. I was becoming frantic with worry and often cried myself to sleep as I thought of what might be going to happen to my family and my country.

FOURTEEN

ON 3 August we were awakened by the jubilant blare of loudspeakers all over the city, joyfully telling us that once again Iraq had succeeded in invading a neighbouring country. From now on we were continuously bombarded with news about what was being carried out in the name of the Iraqi people. The television told us about the glorious invasion of Kuwait and the international outcry which it was causing. Suddenly Iraq was the bad boy of the world, and the government closed all the entrances and exits to the country. Our airline tickets were as much use to us as confetti. In a way I was relieved not to be going anywhere; I would have worried so much about my family if I hadn't been with them. Now it was too late, the doors had been slammed shut, and it seemed likely that our city would be razed to the ground.

We waited, with the rest of the world, to see how the Allies would react, only for us there was more at stake. We followed every diplomatic move, and we prayed that someone would find a way out for us. The whole world seemed to be united against our government, and they kept setting deadlines for withdrawal and then waiting for Saddam Hussein to comply. We knew in our hearts that he would never withdraw from Kuwait voluntarily, it just wasn't his way. Unless there was some miracle we were bound to be attacked.

There were many political opinions voiced privately in street conversations, but no one dared to stand up and say what we all felt. Everyone talked politics day and night, in the cafés, outside and inside the houses, in front of televisions and over the telephones. The Americans had never been popular in Iraq, always giving the impression of being rather arrogant, big and brash, looking down on the locals. Their approach to everything, from work to socialising, was so different to the Arab way. But now most people prayed that the Allies would find a way to assassinate Saddam Hussein so that the troops could be brought home and the destruction of Baghdad could be avoided. We didn't want to go to war with anyone, and we knew that if the Israelis did the job that might lead to terrible hostilities all over the area. But if the Allies were able to find a way of eliminating him we stood a chance of escaping from the situation and cleansing our government of evil.

Many people believed that there was some sound historical reasoning behind Iraq's claims to ownership of Kuwait, but no one I knew believed that it was right for us to take it back by force in this way. Many people believed that our leaders really only wanted to secure a route to the sea so that they could later attack Israel from the water, and become the heroes of the Arab world. Not everyone was against such a scheme in principle, but no one believed that it could be achieved now that the forces of the Western world were mustering on our borders.

The whole world was waiting with bated breath as the inevitable war drew nearer, but no one had as much at stake as the people of Baghdad.

'*Musta'jil*,' the people were saying as the tense days dragged by, 'hurry up and get rid of him, so that we can live our lives in peace.'

At the same time as we feared what was going to happen to Baghdad, we also feared for our soldiers, and prayed that the Allies would realise what a weak force they were and would spare them, putting all their energy into finding and killing Saddam Hussein. We knew just how impossible it was for our leadership to climb down and be seen to lose face. Much of the outside world had only been hazily aware of Saddam Hussein until now. Suddenly he was the greatest international criminal since Hitler, but we were the ones standing in the path of their bullets and bombs. We had no idea when we would be hit, but we felt it was inevitable.

'He will attack the Jews,' people said, 'and then there will be a nuclear holocaust and Baghdad will be gone. Why can't anyone stop him?'

Azziz, Hilall and the other men in the family argued and discussed the situation constantly, one minute suggesting one solution, one minute another, and often despairing that we would ever find a way out. I listened to them all until my head spun. The Allies weren't the only enemies Saddam had; within his own borders there were the Kurds and the Shi'ites, both of whom had reason to hate him and either of whom could have taken advantage of his problems in Kuwait to attack him. Then there were his political opponents, the ones who might one day succeed him, but none of them seemed to stand a chance against such a ruthless power. It would only take one bullet, but who could get close enough to fire the gun? Day after day he was still there, broadcasting to the nation with his beaming smiles, boasting of how he would defeat all the enemies of Iraq. It seemed as if he was untouchable, and we were doomed.

The people in Iraq listened to radio news programmes transmitted from Cairo and Monaco, ignoring the ridiculous propaganda being put out by our own media. Hired thugs were forcing people to cheer in the streets and shout the praises of Saddam Hussein for the cameras. We knew exactly what was going on, even the kids on the streets were talking politics. International reporters and television crews were still inside the city, telling the world how calm we were considering the might of the armaments which were being amassed in Saudi Arabia to attack us. We didn't feel calm, we were terrified, but what could we do about it? If anyone had shown disloyalty to the government by talking to the foreign media they would have been killed instantly for their treachery. We just went on preparing for the worst and saying nothing – in public at least.

When Saddam Hussein announced that the foreigners who had not yet left the country would remain as a human shield to deter the Allies from attacking key installations, the people of Iraq were disgusted.

'How can he do such a thing,' they wanted to know, 'it is inhuman.'

'How can he believe that anything will stop them once they are ready to attack?'

We were relieved when the hostages were finally freed, but it did nothing to help Saddam Hussein's popularity within the country. Now he was accused of being America's 'yes man', agreeing to everything they demanded.

Azziz continued with his job, but it became harder and harder to travel around the city. Everywhere there were checkpoints springing up. The city itself was emptying out as more men were called back into the armed forces and more and more families fled to the countryside.

We were all issued with ration cards and we travelled all round the country to find things like soap powder and dried food, storing everything in our bedroom. It was all so worrying. We needed a supply of petrol in case we had to make a run for safety. Every day the men went out and queued at the petrol station. Only car tanks could be filled, no containers, so the men would go down to fill up the cars, come home and syphon it off, then return to the petrol stations to refill, standing in line with all the others who had the same idea. We knew that soon it would be rationed even more severely and only given to army vehicles, ambulances and taxis. That petrol was later to give us some freedom of movement, but we might have been better off without it. If we hadn't been able to use the cars we would not have been able to travel so easily into the mountains, and would have been spared so many of the horrors which were to come.

The government told us all about the 'Mother of all Battles' which was going to be fought in the desert, and how the Allies were going to be defeated by the powerful Iraqi army, but we knew that a lot of the poor men down there didn't even have uniforms, food or water, let alone ammunition. 'Please God,' we all prayed, 'spare those poor boys and attack the ones who matter.'

The Allies were claiming that they were only going to attack military targets. Is a boy who has been forced into the army and sent to the front lines without a gun a legitimate military target? On the media they talked about Saddam's 'crack troops', but how would they differentiate them from the poor hopeless cannon fodder that made up the majority of the army – our sons and husbands and brothers?

We could all see how the real military targets were being moved and hidden. You would be walking down a suburban street and you would see a gleaming new jet fighter concealed under a grove of trees. The government had been moving and hiding things for months, or even years. We knew there was little hope that the Allies would be able to find the targets they wanted. It wouldn't matter how accurate their technology was, they would be aiming at the wrong things.

The official sources told us that to be safe from nuclear attack we should all be ready to move 40 kilometres from the centre of Baghdad at a moment's notice. They held practice evacuations, when buses would arrive to take the people and all their possessions from certain areas out to their designated safe havens. There they would find villages of tents which they would spend the day in before returning to their homes. It was all a farce. If there had been a nuclear strike we would still have been well within reach of the effects, and they would never have been able to move so many people out in time. During the war with Iran the Iranians blew up the Al-Qa-Qa weapons factory in Hillah. It was 100 kilometres away from where I was in my kitchen with a cup of tea in one hand and the backdoor handle in the other, on my way out into the garden to sit in the sunshine under the sunflowers. The door came in like a giant hand slamming across my arm, and seven giant vibrations sent the windows shaking and nearly pulled the internal glass door off its hinges. The explosion had travelled easily across the flat terrain – so what hope would we have in a nuclear strike?

Few people bothered to go on the practice runs, they preferred to shut themselves in their houses and close the curtains. When it was our turn we would drive out to visit members of the family who lived outside the city.

April and Hilall now had a little house in one of the suburbs which was designated as a safe area, where they lived with Majid, Ali, Hosni and a new baby girl called Sabha. We decided that that was where Azziz and I would go when the time came. We knew that there were some good shelters in the area because Hilall had some political influence and had been shown them.

'Why don't we get right away from Baghdad,' I suggested one day when we visited them, 'and rent a house or some hotel rooms in the country for a few months. Then if things get bad we will at least have somewhere to go.'

The others agreed and on 13 December we set off in two cars, with all the children, to go to Khanaqin on the Iranian border, having telephoned a family we knew to ask if we could stay the night.

The drive there was beautiful. Although it was winter the sun was shining and we bowled along, singing songs and making the children laugh, telling them we were off on a picnic. We reached the small town at around midday and we all fell silent as we looked at the damage which the Iranian bombs had inflicted during the last war. Everywhere there were houses which were little more than blackened shells.

'There are a lot of underground shelters,' I pointed out, 'there seems to be one in every street. They must have needed them during the war. It would be good to have access to them when the attack comes.'

The others didn't answer, they just stared glumly around.

Reaching our friends' house we had lunch with them and their many children, and then set off in search of accommodation to rent. It was impossible. Everywhere there were Baghdad families trying to do exactly the same thing, their cars lining the roads like ants. The only house we found had no windows, doors, power or water and had been used as an animal shelter. In the months to come we would have been grateful for such a place, but then we were horrified by it. Our friends kindly offered us nylon sheets to pin over the windows and sacking for the doorways.

'We would help you clean up the mess,' they promised, 'and make it as comfortable as possible.'

'We can't do this,' I said to Azziz under my breath, 'the babies would die of cold, and how would we manage without water?'

By the end of the day we had exhausted every possibility, and knew there was nothing in the area big enough to take the whole family. We spent the night with our friends and then returned to Baghdad with our hopes dashed. It was as if the steel jaws of a trap were closing around us.

We learnt during those months that it was unwise to tell anyone anything. If we were going on a visit we would be stopped at innumerable checkpoints and we would tell the soldiers that we were just going for a drive for a change of scenery. If you told them where you were going they would want to know everything about the people you were visiting and then those people were likely to get into trouble as well.

Everyone was suspected of being a spy, everyone was thought to be trying to keep their men out of the army. There was no trust anywhere. We learnt to lie all the time and I found that my age was useful in making them believe us. The jumpy young men on the checkpoints referred to me as '*hajjiyah*', which means respected old woman, and they could see from my husband's grey hairs that he was past military age.

I spent much of my time scurrying around looking for any foodstuffs which I could store. They were issuing warnings against hoarding goods on television, but I didn't care. Anything I could find I bought, because I was determined that my family would be able to survive as well as possible. Cigarettes and tins of milk had already disappeared from the shops and roadsides again, probably redirected to the boys in the army.

When they introduced stricter rationing you had to be on the ball the whole time to ensure that you were the first one to the shops. To start with every month we were allowed a kilo of rice per person and about one and a half kilos of sugar per couple. We were allowed a cup of dry tea each month. We were able to get reasonable amounts of flour, although it was a different colour each month and gradually became less and less usable. As the months passed these allowances were cut still further. Families with children were reduced to begging from neighbours and from shopkeepers to give them more flour so that they could at least make the daily *khubiz* for the children. The professional classes and shopkeepers didn't do too badly, but as usual there was nothing left for the poor. Many of them were reduced to stealing, and we would see the ones who had been caught publicly displayed by the police on television. I was so pleased that I had been squirrelling food away since the end of the last war. I also had boxes and boxes of soap powder stored away, so I was often in a position to be able to help other families who had worse problems than us.

Driving around Baghdad was like travelling through a ghost city. The streets were empty of people and vehicles, especially in the evenings. Normally the wide boulevards were crowded with teenage boys in their cars, tearing along, bumper to bumper, or swerving in and out at dangerously high speeds, their horns blaring. But all those boys had been taken. Lots of the shops were boarded up and the streetlights had been dimmed to save power.

Outside the city were massive army camps stretching as far as the eye could see, and batteries of anti-aircraft guns. The feeling of fear was gripping me tighter and tighter every day. It felt as if we were witnessing the approach of the end of the world.

'They have encircled Baghdad,' Azziz explained as we drove past them one day. 'They are afraid that when the Allies attack the Kurds will take advantage of the situation and sweep down into the empty city. They intend to protect Baghdad from that, even if they can't protect it from the bombs.' I could see there were tears in his eyes and I squeezed his hand on the steering wheel.

The embassies had all closed now, and the expatriates had gone home, leaving everything behind. The British Club was still open. Nancy and I went down there for lunch one day during the final preparations for war. The kitchen staff were still there and delighted to make a meal for us, but there was no one else around. We ate in solitary splendour and helped ourselves to drinks from behind the bar. There was no one in the video library so I took half a dozen in the hope that they might help to entertain the children in the coming troubles. I don't know what made me think there would be any power once we were under attack.

After lunch I wandered around the place on my own, past the huge swimming pool which was usually so crowded and alive with shouting and splashing, but which was now as calm as a millpond, waiting for the algae to grow. I mooched into the beautiful hall which I had seen built from scratch and climbed up onto the stage. The room was built on stilts and I could feel an icy cold draught coming up through the floorboards. There was an upright piano at the back and I played myself some hymns and tunes which I had taught myself over the years, some of them the same ones I used to play on my organ upstairs in Bournemouth. What a long way away that life seemed now. The music did little to lift my spirits, the echoes merely underlining the emptiness of the city and my own loneliness.

By the time I left the club even the kitchen staff had gone home, and there was no one left to lock up. There wasn't even a guard on the gate as I made my dejected way home.

Christmas was coming and I was determined to make the best of it, after all it might be our last as a family. As always I set about making soft toys, and knitted warm trousers and tops for all the children. Keeping busy helped me to forget the craziness which was going on all around. Although the price of food was sky-rocketing, things like toys could still be bought cheaply in the markets; I guess no one had the money for such things any more. Azziz dressed up as Father Christmas as usual and I managed to bake a cake with dried fruits saved from years before and with ordinary sugar which I ground down to make my own icing sugar. I managed home-made buns and biscuits and laid them out before the children. We played games and sang songs, trying to lose ourselves in the festivities and to forget the reality for as long as we could. None of the adults was able to keep their spirits up for long. The men kept going off into huddles to talk in whispers and all of us had moments when we could hardly hold back the tears as we watched the children laughing and playing so innocently.

Everyone felt in need of human contact in those last days, and we would all meet in one another's houses to talk and try to cheer ourselves up. No one wanted to be alone with their thoughts and their imaginings. There was enough time for that in the middle of the nights, as

The Shatt-el-Arab River, a café where we would sit and share a Coke and watch the passing scenery.

Basrah – some of the beautiful houses and waterways in the old city.

Life on the rooftops of Baghdad – a mixture of the modern and traditional.

One of the shopping streets in Baghdad.

A bridge destroyed by the Allied bombings on the Euphrates River in Baghdad.

Allied bomb damage in the centre of Baghdad.

A cloud of smoke to mark the damage of an Allied air raid in Baghdad.

A bombed telecommunications centre in Baghdad.

Iranian bomb damage in Basrah – a family home in ruins.

Kurdish rebels in the North, using Saddam's picture for target practice.

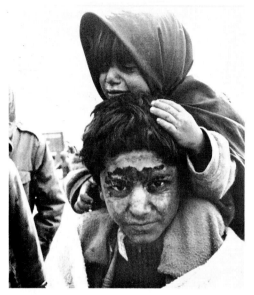

Kurdish refugee children injured by Iraqi phosphorus bombs.

Refugees head into the mountains, carrying their families and their possessions.

Refugees use whatever transport is available for those too weak to walk.

Refugees scrambling to gain
footholds in the mud.

A despairing child in the mud.

Families would huddle together in the snow for warmth and safety.

An endless line of people escaping over poisoned waters.

The snake of traffic moving forward inches at a time under the gaze of the Peshmerga.

we all tossed and turned in our beds, picturing our future once the attack came.

Two days before the final deadline set by the Allies, we called a meeting of the whole family. John and Peter were both in Baghdad, and they were both taking their wives to their families before joining their regiments – I could not bear to think of them as soldiers in the line of fire, and concentrated my mind on how to look after the people who would be staying behind. I found it impossible to believe that I was actually going to have to watch my sons walking off towards a battle which everyone knew they couldn't possibly win, and probably wouldn't survive. How could I think about such a thing and stay sane? Azziz and I were going to go to Hilall and April's house. That was decided.

'We must make this house safe before we leave,' I said, 'it mustn't be easy for people to break in. God knows what will happen in Baghdad before we return. There is bound to be looting.' The men started work. They nailed mighty wooden beams across the side doors and reinforced the metal grills which covered all the windows. There was a metal back door which they welded shut. That just left the front door for us to secure when the last ones left. We prepared chains and locks for that.

On 16 January 1991 a last phone call came from a friend down in Basrah. 'Go now,' she said, 'they are going to attack.'

FIFTEEN

IT felt to us as if Baghdad had become a target in the sights of the whole world. Everyone wanted to see us wiped off the face of the earth, yet we had done nothing but go about our normal lives, like all the other families who were watching their boys go off to be slaughtered and were waiting for their homes to be destroyed. It is hard to understand why you should have to die for a political cause which isn't yours.

That evening, with our house firmly bolted and shuttered behind us and our family dispersing around the country, Azziz and I loaded the car with as many provisions as we could fit in, including a small stove, paraffin, spare petrol, blankets and a case full of money, and then climbed in on top of everything ourselves. It felt so sad to be leaving behind everything which we had built up, our family scattered far and wide. We had no idea if we would ever see our home or our city again. We had no idea how many of us would die in the coming holocaust – possibly all of us.

There were so many 'if only's' in our lives: if only we had stayed in England when we were first married and made lives for ourselves there; if only we had returned to England earlier; if only I had gone home to England to have each of my children, so that they would have British passports; if only we had made some arrangements earlier for a safe house somewhere in the country. But now it was too late to worry about the mistakes of the past, we had to think how we would survive the next few days. To be honest, we hadn't the slightest idea if what we were doing was wise or foolish.

Hilall and April were waiting for us to arrive. They greeted us with open arms and the boys excitedly jumped all over us. I think for them it was something of an adventure, although the two older boys could still remember the bombs in Baghdad and were frightened at the prospect of the terrible noise and destruction starting all over again. Little Sabha was too tiny to take in any of what was happening. She was only just starting to sit up, looking around her with wide, surprised eyes at everything that was going on, her shock of black hair sticking out in all directions. She was such a happy little creature, always gurgling with laughter at her brothers, all of whom constantly wanted to hold her and stroke her.

It had taken us two very uncomfortable hours to get to the house, with all our worldly possessions digging into us as we drove through the deserted city streets, and by the time we arrived I was desperate for *istikan chai* (a glass of tea).

'I will show you the shelters where we have to go when the time comes,' Hilall said after we had slaked our thirst. Azziz and I followed him outside. 'It's quite a walk,' he warned us, 'but they have made it as easy as possible.'

He led us towards the next door building, and then walked straight through it. The owners of every building in the area had been told to leave their doors open so that when the bombs came the people could run through to the shelters as quickly as possible. He led us down tiny dark alleys and through gates and doors that you could barely see until you were upon them.

'I will never remember all these twists and turns,' I complained.

'Don't worry,' Hilall laughed, 'I will be with you.'

The shelters were colossal underground halls, built beneath several feet of reinforced concrete. 'This one is ours,' Hilall explained when we got there, waving to the guards who waved back and came over to talk. He seemed to know everyone in the area and to be well liked, which was reassuring. The guards were concerned to see that I was foreign, and seemed worried about my safety amongst everyone else once the attacks were under way. There might well be some strong anti-British sentiment once the bombs were falling.

'We will find you a room of your own for your family,' they said, and led us to a room where the guns were kept. 'Here, you will come here, where it is a little private.' It was a poky little room, but I could imagine that a bit of privacy might be worth making some sacrifices for when the time came, and I was duly grateful. The sight of these shelters was quite encouraging. They looked strong and they looked big, as long as they were empty of people. The three main halls were beautifully constructed rooms, with lavatories and washing facilities standing ready for the people.

'How many people will there be down here?' I asked.

'It was meant to house 150 people,' Hilall told me, 'but there will be many more than that. It will be cramped.'

'Where do people sleep?'

'Anywhere they can. There were mattresses provided, but they have been stolen. There was also food and bottles of drinking water, but they have all gone too. We will have to bring bedding and food with us when the time comes.'

I felt better after seeing the shelters. They were not as bad as I had expected. Perhaps we would survive the coming onslaught after all, I told myself as we walked home, planning what things we should prepare to take with us when the emergency came. Or perhaps it would never come and the Americans had been bluffing. Or perhaps Saddam had been bluffing and he was starting to withdraw from Kuwait already. We chewed over every possibility, but in the pit of my stomach I knew that life would never be the same again. Even if Azziz and I survived what was coming, there might be little of the country left. I felt like crying all the time, but I had to stay cheerful for the children. Azziz was very grave, and he and Hilall and other local men talked all the time about the best things to do to protect their families.

We put the children to bed and went on talking until late, then Hilall and April went off to their bedroom. Azziz and I were bedding down on the floor in the sitting room. We were both dead tired and I was confident that we would be able to get to sleep despite the worries which kept buzzing round and round in our minds. Before we settled down we prepared some bags with essentials and folded some blankets and mattresses by the door, ready for an emergency.

'I hope they don't come tonight,' I whispered to Azziz once the lights were out and everything was quiet, but he had already gone off to sleep. I was soon following him, exhausted by the worry and exertions of the last few days.

The next thing I knew it felt like the world had ended. It was impossible to tell which sounds were which, the bombs and aircraft fire in the sky mingled with the boom of the guns on the ground to create one earth-shattering, ear-splitting, nerve-tearing roar. Above it all was that most terrible noise of all – the sirens – making my blood run cold and my skin prickle with fear. The electricity had gone off immediately but the explosions had turned night into day, illuminating the streams of screaming, running people who were suddenly filling the streets outside in their panic. No one had imagined that it would be as ferocious and deafening as this. The guns sent stitches of red fire across the sky, a delicate lightshow to accompany such a terrible noise. The children were catapulted awake, screaming with terror. We scooped them up from their beds, and clutched them to us, but nothing would stop their cries.

In between the explosions it was pitch black as we stumbled with the children, the mattresses and provisions along the same route we had walked earlier. It seemed like miles; everywhere there were people running and screaming and cursing the powers that had brought this down upon our heads. In the dark it was impossible to follow the route Hilall had shown us, we kept making wrong turns, or getting into alleys which were so packed with people that we couldn't get through. Hilall kept moving, dodging and diving and shouting at us to stay with him. He no longer seemed confident that he could get us there. Many people were shoeless and still in their nightclothes. Women were clutching their children to them, the babies wide-eyed with horror and incomprehension at the bedlam which surrounded them. Old people hobbled to keep up with their families, many of them jostled aside in the terrible rush to survive. After what seemed like an age we found the shelter.

At the entrance the guards were trying to herd people in as quickly as possible, shouting at them to move along, pushing the slow ones in, causing some of them to stumble and knock over their neighbours. Once inside, people were slowing down and blocking the entrances, so others were piling up behind, shrieking to be let in and forcing the crowd further down underground with sheer weight of numbers. Everyone was shouting and panicking and pushing and the smell of bodies and fear hit us as we came in. It was like descending into hell. About 250 people had been told to seek refuge in that shelter and no one knew what to do. Everyone was milling around, jabbering and crying.

Some people were on their knees, praying wildly for help that couldn't possibly come, others were crouched in corners, clutching their loved ones to them, paralysed with fear. The bombing continued outside making the place rock and the doors of the toilets bang to and fro. The very earth itself seemed to be being blown apart by the explosions. The halls which had looked so big and strong earlier that evening now seemed as weak and vulnerable as the houses and flats above ground. It seemed that there was going to be nowhere we could go to escape from the attacks which felt as if they were encompassing our whole world.

There were some advantages to being underground; at least the lights were working there. We were able to see to fight our way through the crowds to our designated room and found that no one else was planning to challenge us for it. Once we were safely inside April and I spread our mattresses out and sat down, hugging the children to us, singing familiar songs to try to calm their trembling and take their minds off what was happening all around. The men talked to everyone they could find, trying to work out what was going on and to get news of any sort from above ground. This was to be the pattern of our lives for the next forty-three days.

Day by day the inadequacies of the shelters began to become apparent. The power was soon switched off for all but a few hours a day, and we had to manage with whatever candles we could find, mostly pathetic, twisted pieces of wax with bits of string threaded through them, which were sold in the *souks* at extortionate prices. They cast an eerie flickering light on the walls of our subterranean caverns, filling the place with shadows, and would gutter and die when you least expected it. The ventilation did not work, even when the power was on, and condensation built up on the walls and ceilings, dripping down onto the people below, turning the place into a damp swamp. There was always water on the floors, however often you tried to mop it up, which meant that the mattresses and blankets were always wet. The old and the young began to contract pneumonia, their pathetic coughs punctuating any silences that might fall between the bombing raids.

The water supplies also went off within the first week, which meant that none of the toilets would flush and there was nowhere to wash. Every few days the army would arrive with water tanks and we would all queue up to fill whatever containers we had, knowing that those supplies might have to last us for drinking, cooking and washing for several days. The duty guards would then come in with hoses to try to unblock the toilets and clean up the floors, but it was a hopeless task and the smell of raw sewage filled the air, making many people sick. Within a few days of the start of the bombing the shelters had become dark, damp, stinking holes in the ground, even more frightening for the children than the inferno raging above our heads and shaking us about like a thousand peas in a child's rattle.

The boys didn't like to come too far into the shelter, they preferred to huddle close to the doors where at least the air was fresher, even with the constant smell of burning, and there was some light, either from the sun during the day or from the explosions at night. Little Sabha clung to her mother all the time, her eyes still wide, but with fear now rather than wonder. She no longer laughed or smiled, in fact she barely made any sound at all, she just trembled and made little whimpering noises. She would doze on and off in her mother's arms, but as soon as April tried to put her down her eyes would spring open again and she would scream to be picked up, her little fingers closing onto April's neck like steel traps.

All I kept thinking was, 'Why do the children have to be made to suffer like this?' I don't think my babies will ever recover from the terror of those forty-five days of bombings. They will always wake screaming in the night, and they will always tremble uncontrollably at the sound of gunfire or an approaching aircraft engine. I know that I am still suffering exactly those symptoms, even though I am now living in a safe country. They were a hundred times more terrified than I during those terrible attacks.

People were dying all around us and the children grew used to the sight. They died from flying bullets, bombs and debris, and they died from lack of proper food or clean water. Many people seemed to be dying simply because they had given up on life. Who could blame them? Why did any of us want to go on struggling to survive in such a hell? If we hadn't had the children to care for I don't know that I would have clung so hard to life.

One of the shelters in the area had been turned into a hospital, but there was no way that they could cope with the level of casualties pouring in. When I contracted pneumonia I went along there myself, but as soon as the woman at the door saw that I was English she turned and walked away. I shouted after her, 'I'm a person too. I'm down here with you. I need treatment.' A passing doctor took pity on me and gave me some drugs, and I was able to continue looking after the others.

As well as worrying about my family around me, I was also desperate to know what was happening to my other children and their families, but there was no way of finding out. We heard rumours about which areas of Baghdad were being destroyed and which were being spared, but there was no way of telling truth from propaganda, fact from wishful thinking. We also heard stories about how the Iraqi army was being systematically destroyed. All those poor, unarmed boys were being wiped out by the most sophisticated fighting force that had ever been assembled – and two of them were my sons. In the darkest hours of the night I was sure that they were all dead and I would never see any of them again. At those moments I just wanted to die myself, so that I wouldn't have to live through the pain of discovering the truth. Sometimes I resented the fact that Hilall was with us and my two boys weren't. However much I liked him, his constantly smiling face was a reminder that John and Peter might well be dead already, or suffering some terrible hell on the front lines. I wasn't always as kind to him as I should have been, and I was never completely sure why he was not being called into the forces because he wasn't able to talk about his work. He said it was secret and it was for the government and we had to be content with that.

I had a radio at the house, which we were able to listen to occasionally, to try to find out what was happening. We heard about the Scud missiles being launched against Israel and Saudi Arabia, and we no longer cared about the possible repercussions – how could anything be worse than this?

'Let them get a taste of what we are suffering,' was how most people felt. 'Let them see how it feels to be under attack and in fear of your life day and night.'

The planes came over almost constantly, twenty-four hours a day. If there was a brief let-up in the attacks April or I would go back to the house to try to cook some soup or make something hot for the children to drink or eat, and the men would go in search of extra supplies. Sometimes they would drive out into the country in search of fuel and food, potatoes or anything which we could make a meal of. Often the bombing raids would restart before they were able to get back to the shelters, leaving April and me to worry about what might have happened to them, all for the sake of a few bits of wood which we could burn to heat water. We learnt to cook dock leaves, cutting them up fine and boiling them with onions and dried black-eyed peas. I made spaghetti for the children, without meat, seasoned and loaded with tomato paste. It filled their stomachs and they seemed to like it, begging for more. Occasionally the men even came back with pieces of meat, which we would turn into a sort of pancake with sliced onions, greenery, flour and curry powder. It is extraordinary how inventive you become when you are limited for choice.

Often I would just get back to the house, light the stove and start cooking when the sirens would go off again and I would have to abandon everything and head back to the shelters with that dreadful noise ringing in my ears, driving my legs to run faster and faster. One day, returning to the shelters in daylight with a group of neighbours we heard the planes arriving. We looked up into the sky in time to see one of them writing us a message:

'Al-maut lakum – Death to you all.'

I can't explain how chilling it is to know that someone deliberately wants to end your life and the lives of your family and friends. We had grown accustomed to the idea that although we might get killed in the fall-out, the bombs were not actually aimed at us, but at targets of military and economic importance. Civilians were merely being caught in the cross-fire. But this message seemed to be directed solely at us, and we took it to mean that today they were planning to attack the shelters.

In a mass panic everyone tried to get out from under ground. It suddenly seemed safer to be in our houses than trapped in places which had become military targets. We felt so exposed in those houses, with all the doors and windows left ajar to try to lessen the chances of the glass blowing in. However unpleasant the shelters were, they felt a great deal more solid than the buildings above. As the day passed and the message faded from the sky we began to drift back to the shelters simply because we were too frightened to stay outside.

My main worry was how to acquire bread because we had so little flour. Each day I would ration out enough from our store to make twenty or thirty small buns, hoping it would be sufficient for all of us for the day, but it never was. Other people's children were always there and always hungry. As soon as the children outside smelt the bread baking they would gaze in at the window, waiting for me to open the oven door. It was impossible for us to eat the buns with these wide, hungry eyes watching us. I often had to start baking again the moment I finished because the buns had simply disappeared into the out-stretched hands of the neighbourhood children.

The authorities would give us half a sack of flour every few weeks and we would have to borrow or buy black market flour to eke out our supplies. People became very supportive of one another. During the quiet hours, when we would all emerge and return to our houses, the doorbell would often ring and there would be a neighbour with a handful of flat *hubbas* hoping to exchange them for a cup of powdered baby milk or rice. Families would send over a plate of food that they had managed to get from somewhere to share with us, and we would do the same. All the adults were doing their best to ensure that the children got enough to eat, even if it meant they had to go without themselves. On one particularly bad day, when the bombs were falling constantly, an elderly man walked all the way into the centre of Baghdad to bring back salt, flour and other supplies from his family home, which he carried back on his shoulders to share with everyone.

It was always in our minds that should we need to flee further from the fighting, we could head north-east out to the countryside, but that would mean crossing the River Euphrates. The Allied bombers were constantly attacking the bridges in their attempts to cut Baghdad off from the outside world, and we talked endlessly about what we should do if they succeeded. Whenever there was news of an attack on the bridges Azziz and Hilall would hare off to try to assess the damage, so that we could make alternative plans. In the end only one old iron bridge was still standing. In one attempt to destroy it a British pilot aimed a rocket at it, missed and scored a direct hit on a neighbouring *souk* full of innocent people out looking for food. Hundreds of men, women and children were killed. The news of this disaster had us all in tears. Had the rocket been a few hundred metres further out it would have demolished a Red Cross hospital filled with children.

We had been under constant bombardment for forty-three days and nights when Azziz told us that we were going to have to leave the shelter.

'Why do we have to leave?' I wanted to know.

'The director of the shelter has had a letter from the Revolutionary Council telling him to evacuate,' was the explanation. 'They say there are going to be chemical attacks on the shelters.'

'If there are going to be chemical attacks on the area we must get away,' I said, feeling the familiar sense of panic at this new threat.

'Yes,' Azziz agreed, 'but where can we go?'

SIXTEEN

NO ONE knew what to make of this news. Did it mean the Americans were deliberately going to start attacking innocent civilians, or was it the Iraqi government trying to spread propaganda? Perhaps no one was going to attack, they just wanted to empty the shelters for some other purpose. No one knew the answers, but none of us wanted to defy such a specific warning. Later we were told that the true reason was that after the bombing of the Al Amaria shelter, when hundreds of innocent people had been killed, the government had decided that none of the shelters was safe any more. To get us all out they deliberately spread the rumour of a possible chemical attack.

'Where are we going to go?' I asked, despairingly. 'We can't take the children back into the city centre now.' We knew from people who had tried to return to their houses over the previous few days that the whole of Baghdad had been surrounded by the army and they were no longer letting anyone in or out. For all we knew our home had been destroyed anyway. The old man who had walked back into Baghdad had told us that the bombing was especially heavy in our area. It still wasn't certain that the Allies wouldn't end the war with a nuclear attack on Baghdad. Just because they hadn't used that sort of ultimate weapon so far didn't mean that they didn't still plan to do so. For all we knew the bombs could go on falling on Baghdad for months with the same intensity as they had for the previous forty-three days. There was no way I could bring myself to take the children back to such a nightmare, even if the army did agree to let us through.

'I have met a Kurdish family,' Hilall said, 'the husband is my friend. They have a holiday home in Sulaimaniyah, and they say we would be welcome to go there. There is nothing happening up there in the mountains, it is peaceful. We could stay there until the bombing stops and then come back home.'

'No,' Azziz spoke up, 'let the mountains go to hell. I want to go back to my home in Baghdad. I would rather sit in my house and die there from a bomb than from chemicals up a mountain. If you want to go, then go, but I'm not coming with you.'

'Hilall's friend said that it is peaceful up there,' I said desperately, 'you have to come with us. We can't take the children back down to the city to be shot by soldiers on the road. You're just being selfish, Azziz. Think of the children, for God's sake. The bombing could go on in Baghdad until everyone is killed and the city is flattened. It would be madness to go back.'

'How can we believe this man?' Azziz pleaded. 'How can you believe anyone any more after all the lies we have been told? Remember what it was like up in the mountains when we went up there before? Remember how frightened you were? Remember the look in the eyes of those Kurdish mercenaries? Remember the wolves, and the cold and the attacks on the roads? Remember those boys with their throats cut? The Kurds will kill anyone to get their freedom. We are Arabs, they will turn on us.'

'Yes,' I pleaded back, 'I know all that, but remember the bombs back home. I can't take any more of these sirens and the explosions. We've stayed here long enough, we must get the children out before it is too late.'

'Come and talk to my friend some more, Baba,' Hilall tried to calm him, 'he will put your mind at rest.'

'Please, Azziz,' I begged, 'it's a chance for us to survive. Let's take it. I'm as frightened of the mountains as you are, but I'm more frightened of going back to Baghdad. At least talk to the man some more.'

'Okay,' he softened a little, 'I will listen to him, but I don't believe it is the right decision.'

Hilall's Kurdish friend was very convincing. 'Don't worry my friend,' he told Azziz. 'The Peshmerga [Kurdish soldiers] are taking over up there. There has been a circular in Sulaimaniyah from the Kurdish leaders promising not to stand with the Americans against Iraq while Saddam Hussein is fighting the Allies. The Allies are not dropping bombs on the Kurds because they believe in their cause. Up there it is peaceful. Please believe me.'

'Believe him, Azziz,' we all pleaded. 'This is our chance to get away from the war and to put some food in the children's stomachs. We can return to Baghdad as soon as the bombing stops.'

'How can you believe what the politicians promise?' Azziz was astounded. 'As soon as they can the Kurds will try to take over the north while Saddam Hussein is busy fighting the Allies. It is obvious.'

'They have said they won't.'

'Why do you believe them? Who tells the truth any more?'

I started to cry and April and Hilall pleaded with him to see the sense in heading north. Against his better judgement he weakened. 'All right,' he raised his hands in defeat, 'we will go to the Kurds.'

If only we had listened to his warnings and taken his advice. For once he was completely right, and by ignoring him I was leading the family towards horrors which we couldn't even have imagined. But the thought of going to Sulaimaniyah was wonderful, and I had no way of knowing when the Allies would let up their incessant attacks on us. Sulaimaniyah is the most beautiful town. To a European eye it looks more like somewhere in Switzerland than the Middle East, and to be anywhere where there were no bombs or guns would be like paradise. Having Hilall, who spoke fluent Kurdish, with us would also be a great help. We had often been there for holidays and visits during more peaceful times.

'It may be hard to find good accommodation,' Hilall warned, 'many other people are going up there.'

'Oh, we'll find something,' I said cheerily. 'It doesn't have to be anything great, we aren't expecting a home from home, just a roof over our heads and some peace and quiet.' I was willing to accept anything just to be away from the constant noise. If we could start by staying with a friendly family that would be the perfect answer to our problems, it would give us time to find somewhere for ourselves. 'Oh yes,' I said, 'let's go now. Do we have enough petrol?'

'No,' Azziz admitted, 'we have used too much looking for supplies. But we will try to get some tonight, at least enough to get to Kirkuk, and we should be able to get more there.'

A terrible thought suddenly hit me. 'What if they blow up the last bridge over the river tonight?'

'We had better pray they don't,' was all Azziz could say. 'We will leave first thing in the morning.'

We were not the only family to decide that it was time to move further from the centre, now that the shelters were being evacuated. Within hours of the news circulating I saw many hundreds of people begin to set out on foot. Everyone seemed to be making for the first place they could think of, loaded down with provisions, and those who had managed to store some petrol were revving their engines ready to go. By the evening the area looked deserted and I began to worry that we were leaving it too late, but by then the men had disappeared in search of fuel. What I didn't know then was that many families who had no idea where to go had simply locked their doors and stayed in their houses. If only we had chosen to do the same our ordeal would have been over in a matter of days (yet another 'if only' to add to the growing list), but I assumed the buildings were likely to collapse like card houses any day, and I didn't want my family to be under the rubble. So we were on the verge of plunging from one hell into an even worse one.

In the early hours of the next morning the black skies were quiet as we emerged from our final night in the shelter and made our way back to April's house. A biting cold wind was sweeping around the buildings as we loaded up the cars. It had been a heavy night's bombing, but the men had still managed to get out and find us some black market petrol, at a cost of hundreds of dinars. I didn't care how much we had to pay, I just wanted to be mobile and travelling away from Baghdad.

'Go quickly,' the guards at the shelter had advised us, 'we are expecting another attack just after daybreak.' We didn't need a second urging. We tied our bedding on top of all the things we had packed the night before, filled some thermos flasks with tea and set off at four in the morning. The children went back to sleep on top of the provisions.

We were driving in convoy: Azziz and I in our car with Majid and Ali; April and Hilall following behind in their car with little Hosni and Sabha. In front of us were the kind Kurdish couple who were offering us their hospitality. They also had two small children. The roads were already crowded as we approached the river, and I heaved a sigh of relief to see that the bridge was still intact. If only it had been blown to pieces that night we wouldn't have been able to continue on our disastrous journey.

The trouble was that although the bridge was still standing, it was filled with cars, bumper to bumper, crawling towards outlying towns, carrying families in every direction in search of safety. We joined the queue and crept, inch by inch, up to the bridge. As we sat there, waiting our turn, I heard the approaching hum of aircraft engines.

'Oh no, Azziz,' I cried out, 'the Americans are coming! They are going to kill us! They are going to hit the bridge!' Azziz said nothing, his face grim, his eyes on the approaching lights which were becoming recognisable shapes. Ali began to scream in the back seat and I brought him over onto my lap to cuddle. He was shaking uncontrollably. Majid was white faced and trembling. I could hear his teeth chattering. All around I could see frightened faces turned up to the skies, not knowing what to do, whether to run or stay. Looking around the roadside I could see nothing to shelter us and nowhere to run to that wouldn't leave us even more exposed to their guns. We were like frightened rabbits, caught in on-coming headlights, waiting to be crushed.

The hum became a drone and then the crashing roar of their engines was right overhead. We waited for the sound of gunfire or exploding bombs, but there was nothing. They had their sights fixed on a target more important than a straggle of refugees, and they thundered past on their way to the city. Behind us, a few minutes later, we heard one last, terrific explosion and a column of fire lifted up into the sky.

'Oh, thank God we missed that one,' I said, squeezing Ali tightly.

Gradually the cars moved forward until eventually we were over the river and I felt myself relax a little. The traffic began to thin as people turned off to different towns and before long we had the open road almost to ourselves. We drove along the muddy track beside the wide and beautiful river, past shattered shopfronts and houses towards the main Mosul road. We drove through low-lying patches of fog, going as fast as the loaded cars would allow, hitting the odd pothole as we went, splashing mud up over the windows. It was still dark and within an hour we were out of the built-up areas and onto the main road leading up to the old town of Samarra, with its ancient minarets and medieval walls containing separate little villages. In any other circumstances it would have been a wonderful, scenic drive. The air seemed clearer and brighter as we moved away from the smoke and dust of the bombsites. There were no checkpoints to hold us up.

Mid-morning found us on the outskirts of Tikrit. The sunny weather had passed and it was now becoming windy and chilly again. Rainy squalls soaked our bedding on top of the car, leaving thick black marks on the blankets and sponge mattresses. This rain was filled with the black waste from the oil fires which were now raging all over Iraq and Kuwait, sending dense black clouds into the sky which were leaving the main war zone in a perpetual night. We knew nothing of this at the time, we just knew that our bedding was now not only drenched but filthy as well.

The further we travelled from the centre the less damage we saw around us. 'Couldn't we stay here?' I asked Azziz at one stage. 'It seems very quiet and safe.'

'No,' he shook his head, 'we are no safer here than we were before. To be safe we must get out into the Kurdish areas where the Allies aren't bombing. It may be quiet here now, but no one knows where the Allies will hit next.' I was relieved by his tone; he now seemed to be accepting that we had made the right decision.

As we came into the low hills outside Tikrit I began to feel safer. Now, if the Allied planes came, at least we had some shelter and places to run and hide. All the way across the windswept plains to Kirkuk we never saw another car; it seemed as if we were the only survivors of the nightmare few weeks we had been through. It was like venturing out into a virgin world all on our own with everyone else dead and gone. We felt very lonely. We crossed undamaged bridges over dry river beds full of round, white pebbles washed down from the mountains, and in the far distance we watched heavy grey rain clouds growing and hiding the peaks which we might soon be scaling.

When you are at the centre of a war it is impossible to imagine that such peace and quiet can exist, that the bombs which are falling on you are not shaking the whole world, that everyone isn't as frightened and battered as you. How can there be people sleeping soundly in their beds 50 miles away from where you feel you will never be able to sleep soundly again? It doesn't seem possible. As we travelled further into the wilderness it became harder to picture just how terrible it had felt to be underneath those bombs.

When the rain let up we stopped to allow the children out for a while. They ran along the verges picking up tiny, rain-flattened flowers. I idly picked some daisies and took them back to the car.

'Look,' I said, showing the flowers to Azziz, 'we aren't so very far from England, are we?' He squeezed my hand and smiled reassuringly, but his eyes looked grim and worried.

As we drove into Kirkuk we were once again surrounded by reminders of war and death. The railway station had been destroyed, the houses were riddled with bullet holes and many were blackened and burnt out, the glass blown from their windows. Shops were shuttered and a plume of grey smoke rose into the air from the area where the oil refinery had once been. My heart sank. For the last couple of hours my spirits had been lifting at the thought that with every mile we were getting further from danger. These sights merely reminded us that the bombs could still get to us wherever we went. However far we ran, there was no sanctuary.

'Let's get through here quickly,' I said. 'I don't think I could bear any more bombing, and the children won't be able to stand any more.'

'Okay,' Azziz agreed, 'but first let's try to find something to eat.'

We drew up in the middle of the town, outside the hospital gates, and got out to look around, try to get our bearings and find food. Hilall knew the area well and disappeared with Azziz to look for a kebab vendor he knew. He returned with flat, unleavened bread filled with kebab and charcoal-roasted chunks of meat, tomato, onion and greenery. We all tore into the food. Despite the freezing cold winds the grown-ups stood round the bonnet of one of the cars, sharing a salad which the Kurdish family had prepared earlier, and relishing Hilall's kebabs. It was wonderful to be able to stand up and stretch our legs after such a long drive. The children stayed huddled inside the cars for warmth and we passed their food in to them. I cuddled Sabha to me and tried to tempt her to take a few little scraps of food. She chewed absent-mindedly on what I gave her, but she didn't have any appetite. She jumped at every sound, staring around her on the look out for danger.

I spotted some stalls outside the hospital and wandered over to have a look at what they were selling. I found piles of smuggled Iranian biscuits and tins of cold Coke, even some lollipops for the children. The prices were fantastic, but who cared? We weren't worried about money any more, we just needed to fill our stomachs as full as possible to give us the strength to go on. We managed to buy some more petrol for the next stage of the journey, to fill our water bottles and drums from a tap in a mosque and to stock up on more cold drinks. We all knew how dangerous the mountains were, even without the war planes and helicopter gunships, and we had no wish to be stranded up there with no food or drink. If we had learnt one thing in the last few weeks it was always to stock up when the opportunity arose, because you never knew what was waiting for you round the next corner.

When we had eaten all we could find, we sat for a while by the roadside, dozing and preparing ourselves to continue, when the city's sirens woke us with a sickening wail. That noise again. Wouldn't I ever be able to escape from those sirens, were they going to pursue me for the rest of my life?

'Get back in the cars!' I shouted. 'Let's get away from here.' There was no way that I wanted to be caught in another raid now, especially in a strange city. I preferred the idea of taking our chances on the open roads. The sirens became more insistent, telling us that the planes were almost upon us as we flung ourselves into the cars, and gunned the engines. On the outskirts of the town we changed our minds. 'We must take shelter,' I said, and we stopped the cars at a sturdy-looking wall. We all ran behind it, finding ourselves in a graveyard, so full of graves that they seemed to be toppling over one another on the steep hill behind us and threatening to slide down on top of us.

We waited, breathless and frightened, for the inevitable explosions from the city centre, but nothing happened and we began to feel foolish. After a few minutes we climbed back into the cars and set out to cross a wide bridge leading onto the main Sulaimaniyah highway. The streets were still full of people, all going about their daily lives, taking no notice of the sirens. Passers-by stared at our loaded cars, many an up-turned hand gestured to us, as much as to say 'What is this? Where are you going? Why are you here?' If they had only known what we had been through, and what they themselves would soon be going through, they too would have been running for their lives.

Edging our way through this conglomeration of people we managed eventually to get out onto the open road again. We were now a hundred kilometres away from our destination, heading straight up into the mountains. Life had seemed almost normal in Kirkuk, and we had at one stage considered stopping there for a while, but the sirens had convinced me that we had to keep going. Our nerves could not have taken another bombing, and I had a feeling that the nearer we were to a border the better, in case we needed to get out of the country fast. We pressed on towards Sulaimaniyah.

The idea of staying in Sulaimaniyah appealed to us. We had enjoyed many happy visits to this old world city with its modern way of life. We loved its kind people, its beautiful mountains crowding round the perimeters, the fresh honey, milk, nuts and so many of the things which we craved and needed in order to survive until the war was over and we could return to whatever was left of our former lives. In our minds Sulaimaniyah took on the shape of an earthly paradise which would give us some sanctuary after the horrors which we had been through. I began to feel optimistic once more as we left Kirkuk behind us.

We could not get up much speed because of the twists and turns of the mountain roads, and whenever we opened the windows to let some fresh air into the car we were reminded of just how bitingly cold it was outside. As we drove through the beautiful valleys we found nests of Kurdish soldiers in motley uniforms on every slope, each guarding their own hundred metres of roadway, and all suspicious of the Arab refugees heading north.

For the first time it dawned on me that we had become refugees. How could that have happened? We were a normal family with a nice home, how could we have become statistics on the road, with little or no control over our own lives or destinies? We had no idea where we would be sleeping that night, or what we would be eating tomorrow. Nothing was certain or predictable any more, and that can be frightening when there is so much danger in every direction. When people are being killed by the thousand in your country, you crave the security of your home and your 'normal life'; when there are food shortages you want to be somewhere where you know the local trades people and have contacts to help you forage. You want as many certainties as possible. We had none.

At each checkpoint I expected the ferocious looking soldiers to send us back the way we had come. We might have escaped the war with the Allies, but now we were entering a different confrontation. Here the war was between the local Kurdish population and the Baathist Party Arabs who had been sent up from Baghdad to oppress them.

'Don't say anything,' Azziz ordered me at the first stop, 'let Hilall do all the talking.'

Once Hilall and the family in the other car explained who we were the soldiers' faces changed completely, and we were welcomed with smiles. They asked the same question each time.

'Why do you want to go to Sulaimaniyah?'

'We need a break from the bombing, we need a rest, we are visiting friends.' Our answers seemed to be satisfactory and they all waved us on to our destination.

'Why are these Kurdish soldiers so friendly to us,' I wanted to know, 'don't they know we are Arabs?'

'Not all Kurds are against the Baath Party,' Azziz explained, 'some of them are fanatical supporters of Saddam Hussein. They are the ones who are in power up here at the moment.'

'I don't understand any of it,' I grumbled, choosing to cut the political complications out of my mind in order to concentrate on the business of making my family safe. I should have known by then that it is impossible in that part of the world to disentangle the two things – the politics lead directly to the lives, and often deaths, of the people.

At last we came into the outskirts of the town. A lot had changed since the last time we were there but the atmosphere was the same. There were flower beds everywhere, full of colourful blooms. Neat walls held back the encroaching mountain soil and tidy new houses had popped up everywhere amongst the gardens. It was like coming home from a nightmare journey. Anyone would be happy to live in such a beautiful place, but I felt so far from home. I was sure that passers-by were giving us suspicious glances.

'Oh well,' I said, trying to convince myself as much as anyone, 'there seem to be a lot of cars with Baghdad number plates, so I guess we will be safe here.' How terribly wrong I was.

SEVENTEEN

OUR Kurdish friends led us to their house, which they normally used only as a holiday home, and we stopped the cars outside. 'Wait here,' they told us, 'while we go inside to explain who you are.'

We waited what seemed like hours before the rest of the family came out to greet us with friendly smiles. No doubt it had taken some time to convince them that they should welcome Arabs into their home. While we had been waiting outside I just wanted to run away, but I knew we had nowhere to run. It is a terrible thing to know that you are reliant on the goodwill of others for your existence. Why should these people take us in, give us precious food and warmth which they needed for their own family? What right had we to ask it of them, except that we were desperate and we had no one else to turn to? We had to find somewhere for our babies to lay their heads for the night, we had to find somewhere to stay while we looked around for a place of our own. We had no choice but to rely on these people taking pity on us. We were lucky; they were a kind, generous family and they welcomed us.

It was a comfortable home, ruled over by an elderly aunt, but conditions were primitive. The Baathists had switched off the power and there was no water, so we couldn't wash properly, which was one of the things I had most been looking forward to. I wanted to wash the damp, musty smell of the bomb shelter right away. We were asked to remove our shoes at the main door as we entered the hall, loaded down with babies and bags. What heaven it seemed – a warm room with two oil stoves burning and hot tea on the fire. I was ushered to a comfortable armchair and sank into it, letting all the Kurdish chatter go on around me, too tired even to pretend to understand any of it, cuddling little Sabha on my knee and drinking glass after glass of sweet tea. The old woman kept exclaiming in wonderment as she filled my glass up yet again.

They served up a hot meal on a nylon sheet spread on the Persian carpet, and as the daylight dimmed outside they lit candles. Our hosts gave us a sitting room to ourselves which they warmed for us with an oil heater, on top of which they put a kettle for me to make yet more tea should I need it. They covered the floor with mattresses and beautifully clean bedding from a pile which reached almost to the ceiling, and we settled the children down to sleep. A sense of peace and sadness settled over us as we sat talking by the light of a single candle. It was the first time we had been away from the sound of bombs in a long time, and the silence outside the house rang in our ears.

Every so often in the coming days sirens would go off to warn of passing planes. To start with we all felt the old panic rising inside us, especially me, and the children would scream and hide themselves under the furniture or cling to us in terror, but our hosts explained that the planes always went past.

'You will be safe here,' our host told us, 'the Americans have no argument with the Kurds, they won't drop their bombs on us. They want our help in beating Saddam Hussein.' I felt Azziz looking at me as the man spoke these words, but I avoided his gaze. I didn't want even to consider what the consequences would be if he had been right about the Kurds being prepared to launch an attack to regain their kingdom from Saddam Hussein.

For two days we stayed in the house, cleaning up the children and drinking tea with the old aunt, but it became obvious that we were a burden to the family. They were short of food and felt honour-bound to offer a share to us because we were their guests. Although we gave them what we could in exchange, I still felt we were impinging too far on their hospitality.

'We must find somewhere of our own,' I said to Azziz on the third night.

'Yes, I know,' he agreed. 'Tomorrow Hilall and I will go looking.'

None of us had any idea how hard it would be to find somewhere of our own to live. Even after our experience in Khanaqin we still weren't prepared, because we had imagined that Sulaimaniyah was so much bigger that it was bound to have more choice of accommodation. There were so many Arabs taking refuge here now that absolutely everything had been let. The men spent two days searching, until eventually Azziz came back with reports of success. 'We have found somewhere,' he said, but I could tell from the grim look on his face that it was not going to be anything too comfortable.

'What is it like?' I asked.

'It's okay,' he said, avoiding my eyes.

We packed our things, bade farewell to our friends and climbed back into the cars. We drove a little way out of the town, up a muddy track into the base of the mountains. It was raining again and gullies of rainwater were chasing the stones and mud down the cracks in the roadway. We drew up in front of a row of houses and a nervous looking Kurdish man came out to greet us, his wife and children watching from the door and windows.

'They look a nice family,' I said hopefully, and Azziz nodded.

'Yes, they are very nice.'

The man's name was Othman, and he was a technician with no job. When I first saw him I thought he was in his fifties, but he turned out to be only in his late thirties. He had been prematurely aged by the strain of living on the edge of a perpetual war zone. His hair was grey and his thin face drawn and lined and he walked with a stoop. He was kind to us but looked permanently worried about the safety of his family. I just wanted to mother him and make all his problems disappear.

The family was desperate for money and so they were willing to take the risk of letting some Arabs stay in their home. Instead of leading us up to the front door as I expected, he took us round the house and down to a small metal doorway leading into an underground room. Once again we were going to have to live beneath the surface of the earth in a damp, dark underworld.

'During the war with Iran,' Othman explained in a mixture of broken English and Arabic, 'we were in the front line. All the time the bombs fell on us. So I built this shelter for my family. Now you are very welcome to use it.'

All the time he talked his eyes were dancing around as if he was

141

trying to see who might be watching our arrival. He was taking us in because he was a kind man and because they desperately needed the money which we were willing to pay, but the idea of having Arabs in his house made him very nervous. I was gradually beginning to realise how tense the situation was between the Kurds and Arabs, and how close to exploding. Was there nowhere we could be free of politics? Was it possible that Azziz had been right and we were walking into a powder keg that was about to ignite?

As I bent down to go through the door my heart sank. Inside it was nothing but a concrete cell. There was no furniture and there were no proper windows. It was cold and damp. The kitchen area was outside the room in a square metre of concrete, roofed with galvanised metal sheeting. It was open to all the elements but at least it had a sink and a tap, even if the sink was drained by a rubber hose which tended to flood the floor. The cooker was a paraffin heater which was always belching black smoke. Everything was too high up for me to reach, so we had to find a concrete block for me to stand on just to cook.

'We can't stay here,' I said to Azziz in despair, 'we'll all die of pneumonia. Is this the best you can do?'

'There is nowhere else in town,' he replied, 'but I promise we will keep looking and move on as soon as possible.'

Othman and his wife were proud of their house and they did their best to make us comfortable. They loaned us a ginger-coloured mat and some sacking to keep the mountain mud from coming in under the door during the rain storms. They produced one rickety chair which I sank gratefully down into the moment they had gone. With an ear shattering crack the chair disintegrated and I hit the concrete floor with my full weight. They found a coffee table to keep the crockery off the floor and we used our suitcase as another table.

We borrowed a powerful paraffin heater from a neighbour to dry out the damp floors and to air our wet bedding, and we made our beds over sheets of cardboard and nylon. I didn't sleep that night. I lay in the strange surroundings, feeling the damp bedding and the cold eating into my bones, listening to the rain crashing down on the makeshift roof outside, and I cried.

The next morning I crept from the soaked bedding, chilled and worried about the children's health. Everyone else was sleeping. I made my way out to the toilet next to the kitchen, which I already knew was just a hole in the ground, with a pitcher of water to do the job of a bidet. As I squatted down I felt something move underneath me. A sleek black rat the size of a domestic cat popped out of the hole and slid over my feet to the door. My whole body lifted off the ground in a spasm of horror and I didn't stop screaming until the men were wakened and came running out to help me. From then on we kept the hole covered to ensure that nothing else got in there. The rat waged a constant vendetta against us, stealing any food that we left unguarded.

As I set about making breakfast tea that first morning some of our new neighbours arrived with a metre-high pile of white, crispy discs of bread which they had baked freshly for us. It was a wonderful sort of food which you could keep for ages on a dry straw mat, covered with a thick cloth. You just had to sprinkle water over it and in a few minutes it had softened enough to eat. We dipped it in our hot, sweet tea, which is what most Kurdish families do for their breakfast.

After breakfast the sun came out and we were able to spread the bedding all over the neighbours' walls to try to dry it out in the bright, chilly wind. I began to feel better about the situation, although I still hoped we would be able to find somewhere more comfortable before long. I wanted to stay in Sulaimaniyah at least a couple of months in order to give the children time to play and forget their awful ordeal in the bomb shelter, but I didn't relish the thought of spending the time in this cell.

Although we didn't find out until later in the day, that night had been the last of the Allied bombing. The Americans and their allies had decided that they had done their job, having sent the Iraqi troops back from Kuwait. The people of Iraq were relieved in one way, and horrified in another.

'Why have they stopped?' they wanted to know.

'Why haven't they finished the job?'

'Why haven't they killed Saddam Hussein so that we can all live in peace?'

'They have killed all those boys, but he is still alive, and now they give up?'

The whole campaign had lasted just forty-five days, but to us who had been at the centre of it, it had felt like an eternity. If only we had known that we only had two more days to endure, we could have stayed in Hilall and April's house, and been ready to go back to Baghdad as soon as the army allowed it. While the rest of the world was rejoicing at what they believed to be the humiliating defeat of Saddam Hussein, we were just thankful to have escaped with our lives. Everyone in Iraq knew that Saddam Hussein was very far from defeated. He may have lost Kuwait, but he still had absolute power and control in his own country. The losses which he had sustained were not drastic and, with the cessation of hostilities with the Allies, he could concentrate his still considerable military power against other, weaker enemies, like the Kurds and the Shi'ites. If we had stayed in Baghdad as Azziz had wanted, the worst of our ordeal would have been over. As it was we were now even further from home, living in great discomfort and unsure what was going to happen to us next.

'It will take him some months to recover from the Allied attack,' I said hopefully, 'he won't worry about anything that is going on up here yet. We are safe for a while, and then we can go home.'

'Perhaps we should go back to Baghdad now,' he suggested.

'Oh no, please, no more travelling yet,' I begged. 'We don't know what state the house will be in, or if there is any food in the city. It may be bad up here, but perhaps it is worse there. Let's rest here and try to build the children up before going back.' Azziz nodded and hugged me to him, but he wasn't smiling. I could tell that he didn't share my rather feeble optimism. He believed that we were about to get into very bad trouble indeed, and he was right.

Just a week after we arrived in Sulaimaniyah the city was to be submerged in the most ferocious battle we had yet been part of. Over the years I had learnt a great deal about the history of the area from listening to the Iraqi men talking politics. Now I was to hear the Kurdish side of the story from all our new-found friends and neighbours.

The Kurdish guerrillas who were planning to free Kurdistan from the Arabs are known as the Peshmerga. They are a ferocious fighting force, determined to oust the Arabs from Kurdistan and to reclaim a state of their own.

After the First World War the Americans intended to create a Kurdish homeland from the ruins of the Ottoman Empire, but that was all forgotten when the British started to divide up the area and turned southern Kurdistan into the country which was to become Iraq. If Kurdistan were to gain its independence now it would cover a large amount of Turkey and Syria as well as Iraq and Iran. As a result none of these people want to encourage Kurdish independence, but the Kurds continue to fight for it, relying on the ferocious mountain terrain and climate to act as their protector against their many enemies.

Saddam Hussein had proved to be by far their most terrible and treacherous foe. Determined to crush all resistance in the area he had imposed several reigns of terror, including chemical bombing attacks on towns in the region which resulted in the deaths of whole populations – men, women and children. A great deal of propaganda has been disseminated by both sides in order to win the sympathies of the outside world, but the truth is that it is a war in which neither side has shown any mercy to its enemies. It is a battle between two absolutes. It is a question of kill or be killed. We had heard many of the frightful stories, and we certainly believed most of them. But in the coming weeks we were to witness horrors which we had never dreamt of.

Everyone in Iraq was aware of what had been happening to the Kurds in the mountains to some extent, but as in any other country with troubles, ordinary people just did their best to continue their lives as the war raged on in other parts of the country. For most people with families, their own survival is their first priority, and political interests come a long way down the list. That was certainly how it had been, and still is, in our family. We might all talk about politics a great deal, but living in Baghdad we had not been particularly touched by the problems of Kurdistan, any more than the average English family is greatly affected by what happens in Northern Ireland. We all hear about these things, but unless one of our own is killed in the fighting we continue with our lives. It doesn't mean that we didn't care about what was happening to the Kurds, but it did mean that we had had neither the time, nor the energy nor the resources to do anything about it.

We had heard that many Kurdish villages had been destroyed by the government, and tens of thousands of people had been killed. But when you are not actually involved in a war, even when you are only a few hours' drive away, you sleep peacefully in your bed at night. Like so many people all over the world, we had listened to the stories, expressed our horror and then got on with our own lives. That was a luxury we were no longer going to be allowed. When you are hearing the stories first hand from the people who suffered them, they take on a horrible and inescapable reality.

'War up here is not just between armies,' Othman told us one evening. 'When the government attacks us up here it attacks the civilians, because it knows where to find us and we are easy targets. They are not merciful. It has been going on all my life, all the time. I will tell you something: in 1969 they attacked a village called Dukan. The women and children of the village managed to escape up into the mountains and hid in a cave to get away from the guns and bombs.

'As they shivered in their dark hiding place, the government soldiers, who were mostly mercenaries, burnt their village to the ground. They then went up to the mouth of the cave. They built bonfires of wood around the entrance, and sprinkled them with petrol.' I felt the tears welling up into my eyes as he paused to clear his throat, which had become clogged with emotion. I could so easily imagine how those women must have felt, hugging their children to them, hearing what was happening outside and being unable to do anything about it. 'They lit the fires,' Othman continued, 'and began shooting at the entrance so that no one could come out. People heard the screams of those women and children for miles around as they were slowly roasted. There were sixty-seven of them.' He paused to get his breath back; we waited silently for him to continue. There were tears in his sad, bloodshot eyes. He wiped them away with the back of his hand.

'In 1975 Saddam Hussein decided to impose his "final solution" upon us. He attacked sixty-five of our villages with chemicals, killing 5,000 people, and sending 100,000 more fleeing towards Turkey and Iran. The men and women who were captured were divided up. The women were sent to detention camps and the men disappeared, never to be seen again. Within a year there were 250,000 Kurdish refugees in Turkey and Iran, and as many again had been forced into concentration camps.'

He stopped talking again to recover his composure, but none of us interrupted. There was complete silence in that underground room, apart from the sounds of the rain outside. It was horrifying to think that these killings had been done by our government, in our name. It made my blood freeze to think that we had brought our babies to this place and now we were as vulnerable as the Kurds.

'In 1987,' Othman continued, 'when Iraq was at war with Iran, the Iraqi government feared that we would collaborate with the Iranians if they advanced into the country. They used mustard gas, cyanide and Tabun nerve agent against twenty of our villages and towns. In Halabja they killed 7,000 people and injured 10,000 more in one attack. The Iranians saw the clouds of chemicals in the sky above Halabja and as soon as they had dispersed they sent in television cameras to record the damage for propaganda, to warn their people what sort of adversary they were facing. Most of the dead were women and children. There were pictures of whole families of children lying in heaps, frozen where they had been playing when the cloud appeared, even the animals were dead. You could see young women clutching their babies and infants to them, trying to shelter them from the gas, but they all died where they stood.

'By the end of the war in 1988 over half of our villages had been destroyed and many of the towns, and half a million of us were placed in settlements or in concentration camps in the desert. Once you have been taken prisoner by the government, you never know when you will be killed. Upon one order they executed 8,000 prisoners who had been captured in 1983.'

Despite all these atrocities, or perhaps because of them, the Kurds continued to fight with extraordinary courage, and now they felt that they had a chance of success. The Allied attack on Iraq had given the Peshmerga a renewed confidence that now would be the best possible time to stake their claim to their ancient cities, starting with Sulai-maniyah. Whereas up till then the outside world had chosen to turn a blind eye to everything the Kurds had suffered, the media spotlight was now turned onto Iraq and the activities of its leader. He couldn't afford, they reasoned, to be seen to be murdering whole towns any more. We had lived under his rule from the beginning, and we believed that his ruthlessness had grown with every atrocity. Now he was even more desperate than before the war to maintain his powerbase. It was likely that any deeds that had been committed in his name in the past would pale into insignificance when compared with what was to come. But we didn't want to add to Othman's worries, so we listened in silence.

EIGHTEEN

GRADUALLY, as the days unfolded, we learnt enough of what was going on from Othman to be deeply frightened of what was coming, but we still didn't have any real idea of how terrible it was going to be or how quickly it would come. He would tell us how excited the Kurds were becoming, how they felt that their chance of regaining their birthright was finally upon them, and that the outside world was fighting on their side. Azziz and I had a horrible feeling that the outside world, in the shape of the Allies, would drop the Kurdish cause as quickly as it had picked it up once the initial danger in Kuwait was forgotten. That was always what had happened to the Kurds in the past. But we listened to Othman's stories and shared his excitement as best we could.

Throughout our first week in our new home there was no electricity at all. To give ourselves some light we would half fill bottles with paraffin, cut a piece of cloth to an inch width to act as a wick, and plug it into the tops of the bottles with a mixture of dates and grease. These lamps, with their noxious fumes, were the only form of lighting we had. We would leave one burning all night in the toilet to let the Peshmerga soldiers, who patrolled the area constantly, know that the house was still inhabited. From time to time we managed to buy home-made candles in the local shops. These shops were run from narrow front rooms cut into the thick walls of the owners' houses and lined with rough shelving. Most of the sellers were small children trying to make a little extra money to help feed their families for another day; everybody was trying to scrape a living from nothing. When there simply isn't enough food or water to go round in a city, the inhabitants spend their whole time foraging, trying to find sources of goods and then trying to find the money to pay for them. Any activity beyond keeping warm and dry, and fending off hunger, becomes an unheard of luxury.

I would buy things like packets of smuggled Iranian biscuits, and on one occasion a few trays of eggs, one of which we gave to Othman and his family. They couldn't believe such luck. I never knew where the eggs came from, but they made a wonderful change to the children's diet. I made them last for weeks, mixing them with onions and tomatoes if I could find any, and adding water to make the mixture go further. I would then fry them into a sort of hash and make the result into sandwiches using the local bread. We had trouble storing the bread in the room because the damp made it mildewed, so we would have to break off the mould before we could eat.

After a few days I was able to acquire a large, heavy, metal safe which had been used by the army for their accounts and now made a perfect larder for me, as well as a dry place to keep the children's clothes. We also acquired a desk which had been stolen from a deserted barracks. It was burned black but had a serviceable table top which I could use to store our household effects, mainly the teapot and a few mugs, tea, sugar, spoons and a thermos flask for the babies' hot water.

Other goods kept coming from the same source, including drums for storing water and our greatest blessing, a metal bed. The springs of the bed were all broken, but Azziz managed to mend them. It made a good seat during the day time and at night the two bigger children slept in it, end to end. Each day we put the bedding out for the short periods when the sun was shining, and gradually it grew drier. I lined the floors with cardboard and newspapers and we burned a paraffin heater day and night to keep the damp at bay.

Most of the time during that week it rained, a steady, relentless downpour, making us stay huddled inside. Whenever the sun broke through we would joyfully head outside, scraping up all the mud from the entrance, wiping the kitchen and toilet floors up and then sitting outside the neighbours' gate, gossiping and drinking hot cups of tea. The local women would all come to jabber at me and I kept nodding my head, even though I had very little idea what they were telling me.

Othman's wife, Rina, was a sweet, bird-like little woman, and we managed to converse through her few words of English and Arabic. She always seemed anxious about her husband's health, clucking round him like a little hen, trying to make him relax. When she was near him he relaxed and smiled much more, but as soon as she was out of his sight he would become anxious again.

Rina was very keen that I should wear a local costume, perhaps in the hope that I would be less conspicuous that way, although how she thought I would melt into the background with my pale skin and blonde hair I don't know. On one of the sunnier days Othman decided that we should all go up into the mountains for a picnic, and Rina made me promise to wear her best costume. This valuable outfit consisted of a heavy coat of gold sequins, which went over some lilac pantaloons, a lilac sequinned overdress and a waistcoat, and there was a pillar-box hat to match. It was a gorgeous outfit, but very heavy and hot. Because we were their guests, and because they were so poor, we were expected to provide the food for the outing, which meant I had to cook in these unfamiliar clothes, balanced on the side of a mountain.

The weather was perfect as we climbed away from the house and looked down onto the city. We had a paraffin stove to heat the food and I was terrified I was going to spill something on the clothes as I crouched down, holding them out of the mud with one hand while I cooked soup and spaghetti with the other. The men made a cup of tea for us all, and they were so hungry they licked the pans clean, which thankfully meant less washing up for me afterwards. It was a wonderful afternoon and a welcome break in our gloomy lives.

Water was a constant problem to us, despite the fact that it was pouring out of the sky almost non-stop. It would generally come through the taps once a day for a few minutes, and we would all dash out to fill as many containers as possible before it stopped again. We used to leave the taps open so that the moment the water started to flow the children could alert us. Most times we would just be able to collect enough for cooking and washing up before it dried up again.

The situation was further complicated by the fact that the Peshmerga were aware that the Iraqi army was trying to poison the water supplies. Every few days they would come round to the house and tell us not to use the water until it had been tested. They would come back a couple of days later to say that it was now running clean, but we must dispose of any supplies we had built up because they were tainted.

Even with these precautions a lot of bad water got through to the people and sickness and dysentery were quite common complaints.

As the weeks wore on Othman became more and more worried about the situation. He would come down to sit with us in the evening, drinking tea and talking about his fears.

'There will be the most terrible bloodbath,' he warned. 'The Peshmerga are ready to take over Sulaimaniyah, but the Baathists will not give up without a struggle. You should stay out of sight as much as possible.'

Azziz, April, Hilall and I didn't know what to do for the best. We talked endlessly about the possibilities of going back to Baghdad, or of going on to somewhere more remote. But now that we knew how hard it was to find shelter we were reluctant to give up our current home without somewhere else to go to, however uncomfortable it might be, and however great the dangers brewing outside.

On 4 March all Othman's worst predictions came true. In the mountains just above our house was an Iraqi army camp. The Baathists in the city used the army to help them maintain power over the people, so that they could interrogate, rape and torture the locals at their various different prisons without fear of retribution. The Peshmerga chose to start their campaign at the army camp, although it was the security forces that they thought of as their real enemies, not the regular army. It was the security forces who had been terrorising and torturing them.

If we had thought the noise was bad during the Allied bombings, it was nothing compared to the bombardment of that camp. The Kurds had been assembling guns and rockets in the mountains for many months, and they turned them all on their target simultaneously. At the same time, they swept down on every side of the city. For hour after hour the ground shook with the vibrations from the big guns and the sounds of machine guns rattled through the air. The army surrendered almost immediately, since their hearts were not in the job they had been sent to do, and the Kurds were able to turn their attack onto the security forces in the city. The security forces did not have the option of surrendering, because they knew that the Kurds were bent on revenge and would kill them whatever happened. Their only chance of survival lay in fighting back.

Day after day for nearly a week there was no let-up and we huddled inside, terrified of the bullets which were flying everywhere. Many of the Peshmerga were very young and excitable, and they would fire their weapons off at anyone or anything they saw. If they had seen some Arabs wandering the streets they would have shot us first and asked questions later. Stray bullets frequently hit the walls and doors of the room, and rattled down on the kitchen and toilet roofs. When they came close we would cuddle right at the back of the room, holding the shaking children to us. We were half expecting the door to be kicked in at any time and a stream of bullets to follow.

Many of the Peshmerga fighters knew about our presence there, but it seems they had other, more important people to deal with. As long as we didn't go outside it seemed we might survive the attack. I found an old milk tin which we could use as a urinal, because it was too dangerous for the children to go even as far as the door. Several times when I did make it to the toilet, I was sent scuttling back in by a hail of bullets on the metal roof. In the evenings there would sometimes be a lull and I would try to cook something outside, with a curtain nailed up at the opening to keep the light inside. Twice I nearly set the curtain alight with the spluttering candles.

'For God's sake, Mama,' April would shout at me, 'leave it and come back inside. Why are you risking your life like this?'

'The children have to eat!' I snapped back. Tempers were becoming very frayed under the pressure.

Othman continued to come down to bring us news. Upstairs he was listening to the Peshmerga radio station which was now broadcasting from inside the border of Iraq for the first time. There had always been Kurdish stations broadcasting from Syria and Jordan, but now they were feeling confident enough actually to work inside the country. The news on this station was all very optimistic, telling of how the Arabs were being driven back by the victorious Kurds. Othman would become very excited at the thought of what his people were achieving. Azziz, Hilall, April and I would try to listen to the BBC news on our own portable radio, although the mountains blocked the reception so much it was barely audible. What we could hear through the distortions and the static did not sound good. We heard enough, however, to tell us that the Peshmerga message was largely propaganda. They were trying to encourage the Kurdish people as a whole to rise up and back them, and also trying to allay their fears about the repercussions once Saddam Hussein had regrouped his forces.

'There is no way he is going to let the Kurds get away with this,' I voiced all our fears. 'Sooner or later he is going to hit back at them, and it will be devastating. How can they fight against an army with tanks and helicopter gunships?'

'Of course,' Azziz spread his hands wide. There was nothing I could say to him. Wasn't this exactly what he had predicted?

Knowing that yet again we were trapped in a city which would soon be a direct target for attack, and knowing just how ruthless the Iraqi forces always were against the Kurds, brought our spirits to the lowest they had yet reached. It seemed that we had deliberately chosen to join one of the most persecuted races in the world, at one of the most dangerous times in their terrible history. How could we have made such a mistake?

So now we were between two potential dangers: we had the Arabs approaching in the south with all their terrible war machinery, and the Kurds right on our doorstep. We couldn't go back now or we would walk straight into the approaching army which was killing everyone it came across, but we were afraid to stay put. But the prospect of going further into the threatening mountains was equally frightening. We knew that we were only being tolerated by local Kurds on the orders of their superiors who were anxious that they should acquire a reputation for mercy in the eyes of the outside world, flimsy orders which could have been broken any day by one of the trigger-happy Peshmerga walking the hilly streets. We were their enemy just as much as the army waiting on their doorstep.

We also knew that all of us, including the children, were in constant danger of being kidnapped by the wandering bands of Peshmerga who were in opposition to the two main leaders, Talabani and Barzani. We were always hearing tales of foreigners disappearing in this fashion, never to be seen again. At times I didn't even trust Othman and Rina, despite their seeming kindness to us. I felt that they resented having us in their house for money. I wondered what our chances would have been if we hadn't been able to pay for our shelter. Each day Othman would have to go off somewhere to report on our daily activities, so we knew we were under careful scrutiny. I was constantly in fear of my life and always kept a knife close at hand in the house. When we went out for walks I always carried a pair of scissors or a knife about me, without telling Azziz. My faith in the human race was now non-existent.

'I have got to get out for some fresh air,' I said one evening when the rain and the bullets had let up. 'Azziz, let's take the two boys for a walk.'

'Okay,' Azziz agreed, and we left the babies with Hilall and April.

We walked a little way up the mountain and looked down over the blackened city. It was all quiet. It is hard to describe just how wonderful quietness can be for people who have been subjected to so much noise. None of us spoke, we just stared down. For a moment I thought I was seeing a mirage.

'Azziz,' I said cautiously, 'is that a streetlight going on?'

'It can't be, it must be a lamp or torch,' he answered. But as we watched lights all over the centre of Sulaimaniyah started to come on. At first it was just a few here and there, glowing dimly, and then more joined them and grew in strength. I felt the most enormous surge of joy as I looked down on the city. I didn't know what was happening, but just to see light once more seemed like an enormous step forward. Then all hell was let loose again, with guns being fired everywhere, and the sky lit up with streams of tracers. Fearful for the children we raced back down to the house and found Othman talking to the others.

'We are celebrating,' he explained, almost jumping for joy. 'We are victorious. We have taken the city and now we have restored the power.'

NINETEEN

TWO days later they managed to get electricity out to our house and even our little room seemed to look more homely in the glow of an electric light bulb. Then the water came, a trickle at first and finally a permanent, icy flood, so cold it hurt your teeth to drink it. With the return of the streetlights the people came back out of their houses. We were able to walk around and we saw children playing at street corners, with the Peshmerga, their guns slung over their shoulders and strings of bullets criss-crossing their bodies, watching at every junction. Some of the soldiers looked little older than the urchins playing in the mud. Their eyes followed us everywhere and they didn't look friendly, but none of them made any attempt to harm us. Now they talked openly about Kurdistan and we knew that we were unwelcome guests, both as Arabs and myself as an English woman.

Othman was very frightened for us, and for the trouble which we might bring back to his family. 'Please don't go too far from the house,' he pleaded, 'you are still in great danger.' We listened to his dire warnings and we made sure the children understood just how danger-ous it would be to run off without us, but we couldn't stay imprisoned in that room forever. Over the last few weeks we had learnt to savour every moment of freedom that came our way, to be pleased by small things like being able to walk in the sunshine for an hour or two, or sleep soundly on a quiet night. Like shy animals we gradually emerged from our underground burrow for longer and longer periods, venturing a little further from the door each day.

Over the following weeks we came to learn more of what had been happening outside our little cell during the battle for Sulaimaniyah. The shooting and jubilation continued for several days as the Kurds rejoiced in the overthrow of their oppressors, and hunted out any of their enemies who had managed to slip through the net and hide around the city. The bodies of the Baathist security forces, many of them with their heads and legs cut off, were left in the streets for all to see, and the body of their leader was hoisted up on a post in the town square. There were corpses in the gutters and corpses in the middle of the roads, with the cars driving round them and nobody moving them. Some of them lay in exactly the poses they had died. One was leaning against a gate, another was slumped half way down a door as he tried to force his way in to escape his attackers. Many had had live anti-aircraft bullets forced up their nostrils as a sign of revenge. It was no longer shocking for us to be confronted with death in the course of our every-day lives, but that didn't make it any less disturbing. No doubt when they were alive many of those whose bodies we saw had done terrible things to the Kurdish people, but to us, who had not known them alive, they were just more people, like us, and we couldn't help but wonder how long it would be before we would end up in a gutter somewhere, perhaps clutching our dead babies to us.

The Peshmerga were far more merciful to the soldiers from the army camps than the Iraqi government would ever be to them. The survivors from the camp above our house had been relieved of their guns and boots and were allowed to wander around the city in rags, begging and sleeping in the mosques. While it was a generous gesture of the Kurds to let them live – a gesture that would not have been made to them in the opposite circumstances, it was pitiful to see these poor, ragged boys so far from home with nowhere to go. They could so easily have been our sons. There was no chance that they could go back to their homes in the south now that they had been defeated, unless they wanted to be shot by their own leaders on their return.

It was several days before Azziz and I plucked up the courage to go outside the immediate neighbourhood of the house, but as nothing had happened to us we gradually grew more confident and moved further and further from our home base.

'Let's walk down to the centre of the town,' I suggested one afternoon when we thought we were going to go mad with boredom. Azziz agreed. He was as curious as I was to see what remained of the city after the fighting. The walk took about an hour and the air was pleasantly fresh. We were both, I think, trying to hide our nervousness and to give the other the impression that everything was going to be all right. The damage which the battle had brought down on the town could be seen everywhere, and the Peshmerga were in evidence on every street. The atmosphere appeared lighter than before and no one took much notice of us, although an Arab walking with a fair-haired foreign woman was bound to draw some curious stares, even if they weren't actively hostile. A group of schoolboys kicked their football over a school wall and it landed at my feet. I kicked it back with a satisfying thump and it landed just where I aimed it. The boys whooped with laughter and gave me a cheer. I took a bow as Azziz hurried me on.

'Don't draw attention to yourself,' he warned, 'we are not in Baghdad now.'

'Okay,' I said, 'I'm sorry.' But I felt better for having had even that small contact with the boys. It is a horrible feeling to know that you are living amongst people who hate you because of what you are. I was desperate to tell everyone that I wanted to be their friend, that I rejoiced with them in their victory, and that I feared for what would happen to them next. I wanted to be part of the life going on around us, but it wasn't possible.

We passed along the street which housed the Baathist security headquarters and the adjoining prison. Othman had told us many stories about this place; about how hundreds of Kurds had disappeared inside never to be seen again, and of terrible tortures and murders within its walls. The main entrance opened into what must once have been an affluent street, but which was now a mess. Most of the bodies had been cleared away in this area, but the damage was everywhere. Rockets and bullets had riddled every square inch of the walls with holes. We went closer to the doorway, which had been blown open, and from the roadway we could see into the black, smoky interior.

Crowds of Kurds were walking silently about the building, like tourists at an historic site, just looking around them without saying a word to one another, as if in religious awe. God knows what fears and memories were going through the minds of those superstitious people who had been living in dread of this building for so long.

'Do you want to see inside?' Azziz asked. I nodded my assent, although I don't know what could possibly have drawn me into such a terrible place. There is something so compelling and awful about evil, you almost have to find out just how far people are capable of going in their cruelty to one another. As we walked from one blackened room to another the heavy scent of death mingled with the smell of burning, a thick, dirty smell which filled the dark, gloomy rooms. The stench was particularly strong in one room, where the only light came in through a hole in the wall made by a rocket. Other people were carrying kerosene lamps which threw ghostly shadows on the walls. We listened to people talking around us and picked up bits and pieces. 'Sometimes there were twenty or thirty people thrown into this one tiny room and left in their own filth, with no light, no water, no food.' The walls were charred and splashed with blood and some of the prisoners had scratched their names and little messages like 'remember me' on the stone.

'I need some fresh air,' I whispered after a few moments. 'Let's go back outside.'

Azziz led me through to a courtyard and I took several deep breaths. Looking around we saw a vehicle rather like an ambulance parked on the far side, with a crowd standing silently, staring into it. We walked over to look. All we could see was women's underwear, blooded and torn, draped over the inside and the outside of the van.

'What is this thing?' I asked out loud.

'They used the van for torturing and raping the young women,' a voice in the crowd spoke up, 'when they were brought here for interrogation.'

'The girls were just brought here for the pleasure of their interrogators,' another voice added.

'They would bring a woman here whom they thought had information they wanted,' one old woman said, crying as she spoke, 'and they would gang rape her sister or her daughter or her mother in front of her eyes. They would tell her that if she didn't talk the same would happen to her. Then they would rape her too, whether she talked or not, and kill all of them afterwards.'

I imagined how frightened those poor girls must have been, completely at the mercy of their captors, separated from their friends and families by impenetrable walls, their screams heard by no one except their torturers and fellow prisoners. Girls in this part of the world lead such sheltered lives, never understanding anything about men until they find themselves married off and having to give in to their husbands' whims. To be subjected to such barbaric horrors as these must be like arriving in hell.

Through a door beside the caravan was another torture room. On the ceiling was an electric fan with the blades removed. 'They would hang the men from the fan by their feet,' we were told, 'and then spin them round. They would use electric cables on them while they hung there to give them shocks. See these,' a man showed us ferocious hooks in the walls, 'they would hang men from these by their ears or their testicles. If they did not talk they would think nothing of hacking off their hands or their feet and eventually their heads.' The spatterings of blood on the wall bore out his horrible claims.

We walked on to another building, clambering over a mass of debris and up some broken stairs to an upper level which must have been the administration building. There were dozens of small rooms, each one burnt out by the attackers, the floors strewn with torn and broken files and the papers of thousands of Kurds, all of whom were now probably dead and buried in the massive communal lime pits which were being found all over the area. People were scrabbling through the scattered papers, trying to destroy everything that might act as evidence against their people should the oppressors ever come back in search of revenge. When you live in fear of your rulers, you want as little information to exist about you as possible. The rulers, on the other hand, want to know as much about you as they can, because the more they know the more power they have over you. The more files that could be destroyed, the less tightly the oppressors could squeeze. But it seemed such a small, hopeless gesture in the face of such an enormous power.

At the end of the corridor was a big room, which must have been a barracks for the guards. The Kurds must have fire-bombed the rooms when they stormed the building, because everything was burnt away apart from the iron bedsteads, the metal lockers, and dozens of soldiers' helmets. All the bodies must have been destroyed in the inferno.

I was having trouble stifling my sobs as we walked around that terrible place, and I could see that my husband's eyes were welling up with tears. We stumbled back out into the street and the sunshine, sickened by the atrocities committed behind those walls.

'Let's go and visit our friends,' I suggested, meaning the family we had stayed with on our arrival, and thinking that a cup of tea with the old aunt would cheer us both up. Azziz nodded his agreement and we pressed on through the centre. Walking up a tree-lined street, hand in hand, we noted the bullet holes and blood slicks on the walls and gates where Arabs had tried to escape from the onslaught of the Kurdish fury. All the houses which had contained Baathists had been rocketed. Even away from the HQ building the streets were still littered with live bullets which the children were collecting up and playing with as if they were marbles.

'My brothers and I used to do that,' I mused, 'collecting up the live ammunition as if it was a harmless toy, making bonfires on the moors and throwing the bullets into the flames to make them explode.' How different war had seemed when I was a child, how much greater my fears were now that I knew more about the ways of man. Azziz smiled at me indulgently and squeezed my hand.

When we reached our friends' house they welcomed us inside and told us how the Peshmerga had used their roof and garden as a launching pad for their rockets. We told them of the horrors we had seen at the party headquarters. It was wonderful to be able to sit in a normal home and just talk and drink tea and distract ourselves from our fears and worries. I was in no hurry to go back to our little cell, but eventually we had to leave if we were to get back before dark. On the way home we passed a group of boys dragging what looked like a charred dummy around. 'What is that Azziz?' I asked, curiously. 'Is it Guy Fawkes or something?'

'I don't know.' We walked over to the group and Azziz asked an on-looker what they were doing.

'It is one of the Baathist leaders,' came the reply. 'They burnt him to death and now they are celebrating their victory.'

I thought I was going to be sick as the boys dragged the hideous corpse over to us, lumps of blackened flesh falling off the grinning skull as it bounced through the potholes. We turned away and fled back to the safety of our cell. Over the coming days the Kurds continued to hunt out government supporters who had slipped through their nets, and when they found them they took them to the public squares and invited anyone who wanted to to kill them. They didn't need formal courts to try these people, they all knew who had been perpetrating the rule of terror over them. There was no shortage of volunteers amongst the people who had lost friends and relatives in the previous years. Their lust for revenge was understandable, but where does it end? Each act of revenge requires further retribution, and each time the scale of the hatred and horror grows; it is a never ending spiral of pain and murder. We shivered with horror at these sights, but dared not show our revulsion in case passers-by mistook it for support for the dead Baathists. The fingers of the young Peshmerga fighters hovered eagerly and nervously on the triggers of their guns. It would have been easy for them to have ended our lives for no better reason than that they didn't like our faces.

We had promised to bring back food from the markets, but we returned empty handed, too shocked to think about shopping. We passed the still-burning Sulaimaniyah Hotel, gutted and blackened by shelling from heavy tank cannons. We had been told that a band of government supporters had taken shelter there, so the Kurds had burned the building down with the men inside.

Even while they were celebrating, the Peshmerga were becoming aware of the dangers of government retaliation. They would come to the houses to warn us to be careful. 'Don't all crowd down to the *souks* at once,' they said, 'because that will make you easy targets when the Arabs come.' They knew that retribution was inevitable, but they seemed to believe that they could resist it when it came.

'We must find a way back to Baghdad,' I said to the others that evening, 'there is so much danger here for everyone. We have to escape. Saddam Hussein is not going to let these people get away with their revolution for long, and when the army comes they will kill everyone they find. We must find a way out.'

'We will go to see the Peshmerga tomorrow,' Hilall and Azziz promised, 'they will tell us the best way to get back to the south.'

Increasing numbers of Peshmerga groups were patrolling our area now. One group came up to me while I was sitting by the gate talking to Othman and Rina. 'Who are you?' they asked, gesticulating with their guns, their fingers on the triggers, their eyes suspicious. 'What are you doing here?' Othman and Rina remained silent, too frightened to speak.

Hilall came out of the house to answer for me, explaining how we had come up to the mountains to escape the bombs in Baghdad. After a while their fierce expressions lightened and they smiled. 'Stay off the streets,' they advised, 'keep a low profile, and we will tell you when any changes happen.' As they left we noticed they were jotting notes in a book. It seemed that they were finding out exactly who was in the city and where they were staying.

'Will there be any more trouble in this area?' I called after them in English.

One of them, who until then had only stood back, stepped forward and spoke in clear English, 'We always expect trouble, Madam, but we will inform you should you have to make a move.'

The only move I wanted to make was back home to Baghdad. They were mounting anti-aircraft guns on the roof of the local school, which suggested that they were now expecting bombing raids. The very thought of going through that again made me shiver uncontrollably.

The children had been playing in the sunshine behind the house when they came running back to us. 'Look what we found, Nana,' they shouted, holding out packets of medicines, syringes, morphine, tablets and bandages.

'Where did you find all that?' I wanted to know.

'Pushed into a hole. It was all wet.' I took everything from them and threw it away. It seemed bullets weren't the only dangers which the children faced in the streets.

Hilall and Azziz went to the local Peshmerga headquarters to ask what the best way back to Baghdad would be. The Kurds shook their heads. 'There are no safe roads,' they said. 'There is fighting everywhere, bridges down and helicopter patrols. You would never get through, and with the children it would be too dangerous even to try. We are watching all the roads, as soon as one becomes safe we will let you know.' One of the men came after them as they left and spoke to them quietly, not wanting the others to hear. 'The Iraqi army is coming up from the south like a wall of death,' he confided. 'They are not sparing anyone, please give up any hope of getting through.' Then he went back to his colleagues. It seemed that we were trapped, with our backs against the mountains, waiting for our attackers to choose their moment, just as we had been in Baghdad a few months before.

'You were right, Azziz,' I said that night. 'We should have stayed in Baghdad. We are in far worse danger here.'

'It's too late for regrets,' Azziz spoke kindly, 'we are here now. We did what we thought was right and now we must think what we should do next.' I was so grateful to him for his understanding and his calm. I snuggled up close.

Despite the Kurdish victory, fighting was still going on in trouble spots all around the city and we didn't dare to let the children out in the streets now, even though we had been out ourselves. The boys were becoming increasingly bored and restless.

'They should have cleared the centre up a bit by now,' I said a few days later. 'Let's take the children down in the car and find them something to eat.'

'Okay,' Azziz agreed and we set off on a family outing.

As soon as we approached the centre we realised that we had made a mistake. No one had moved the bodies yet, they were being left to rot as a warning. Azziz turned the car into the less troubled areas while I tried to distract the children's attention with anything I could see, chattering on like a nervous fool. We spotted a *kebab* restaurant and drew up right outside so that we wouldn't have to walk past any unpleasant sights.

'*Shinu hai*, Nana?' (What's that, Grandma?) Ali asked as we walked across the pavement.

'*Ya Ali – ya habibi*?' (What, darling?). I turned to look where he was pointing and saw that there was a headless corpse slumped in the gutter in front of our car. 'Oh that,' I said, searching my brain for an answer while repressing my own revulsion, 'that is just some men playing at being soldiers.' On the way home the children spotted a number of other people 'playing at being soldiers', but luckily they seemed to accept the explanation, although Majid was becoming increasingly quiet, withdrawing into himself. It is horrible to watch the innocence of childhood being forced out of your babies.

'I think we had better stay round the house for a bit longer,' I said to Azziz as we drove back, and he nodded his agreement.

Each day the men would go to the headquarters of the Peshmerga for up-dates on what was happening and what chance we had of getting back to Baghdad, but each day the news grew worse.

'The fighting has spread as far as Kirkuk now,' they were told, 'and there are reports of fighting in Arbil, Mosul and Dahuk. The Kurds are on the move all over Kurdistan. None of the roads is safe for civilians.'

Every day we heard the sound of gunfire in the streets as they celebrated some new victory, but each victory made our hearts grow heavier because we knew that the more they humiliated Saddam Hussein the greater would be the retribution. They couldn't hope to defeat the government in the longrun. Every dog must have its day, as they say, and this was the day of the Kurds, but we knew it would end soon and we would be plunged into a long, dark night. Every day we expected to see the Iraqi planes and helicopters in the sky above Sulaimaniyah and to hear the sounds of bombs falling. But still nothing happened.

163

'Kirkuk has fallen to us,' the jubilant Othman told us one evening, 'we have the oil fields in our hands. The Peshmerga are announcing it on the radio.' Our international radio stations didn't tell us about any such victories, in fact they were saying the opposite. The evidence of what was really happening was all around us. Despite all Othman's stories we could see cars and lorries full of Peshmerga soldiers returning from the fighting and apparently regrouping in Sulaimaniyah, most of them with glum faces. Through the static on our radio the BBC told us that the Iraqi army had arrived in Kirkuk and rumours began to spread of the atrocities being committed there. No two people seemed to tell the same story, and each one that we heard was more frightening than the last. First we would hear that all the women and children were being raped and murdered, then someone else would have heard that they were putting out everyone's eyes, or they were lining the routes between towns with corpses as warnings to others, or they were burning down whole areas with the people still in their houses. One eye witness told us that when the Iraqis reached the hospital, which was full of wounded Kurdish fighters, they had thrown the patients from the top floor windows and shot the doctors and nurses who had been tending them. However jubilant Othman and the other Kurds might have been, it did not lighten our hearts, because we felt sure that our fate was now sealed.

TWENTY

I WAS becoming frantic with worry and taking my temper out on the men. I found that everything they did or said annoyed me. One morning I made an omelette from our dwindling store of eggs and Hilall started eating before I could make sandwiches for the children.

'You greedy pig!' I screamed, 'at least wait for the children to eat.' Azziz became angry with me for losing my temper and I turned on him. 'It's his fault we are stuck here. He brought us up here with promises of food and safety and led us from one trap to another. Now we are in more danger than ever and he is taking the little food we have from the mouths of the children.'

Of course our situation was as much my fault as Hilall's, but I couldn't contain my frustration any longer. I was beginning to hate Hilall with his permanently grinning face and jovial manner. It was very unfair because he was the kindest of men, a wonderful husband for April and a very patient son-in-law.

'Whoever's fault it is,' Azziz tried to calm me, 'we are here now and we have to find a way to live together peacefully.'

'I just can't do it any more,' I was starting to cry, the combination of fear, worry, tiredness and ill-health dragging me down into despair. 'You have got to find a way out of here for us. I want to get back to Baghdad and see my other babies, and these babies have to have some proper food soon and somewhere dry to sleep. If we don't get out of here we are all going to die.'

Azziz was obviously worried by my outburst. He was so used to being able to rely on me just to keep going and cope with whatever came up, when I became hysterical he became anxious. He put a calming hand on my arm. 'We will go down to the city and look for some food.'

'Whatever it costs we must try to get them some dried milk,' I tried to be strong and reasonable; I had no choice.

'Don't worry,' he cuddled me to him, 'we will find some tomorrow.' They disappeared for the whole day, and returned in the evening with a sack of flour, but no milk. There was none in Sulaimaniyah.

'Things are going badly in Kirkuk,' Othman admitted to us a few days later. 'The government forces are murdering the women and children, cutting their throats and putting their eyes out as a warning to the rest of the Kurds not to stand in the way of the army.' He was obviously shocked to discover that the Kurdish victory had been so transitory, and fearful for his own family. 'There have been so many atrocities. Saddam Hussein promised the Hizbollah followers a town of their own near Khanaqin,' he continued, wringing his hands as he spoke, his face a mass of nervous twitches, 'if they would help return Kirkuk to the government. So many horrors had been instigated by those Iranians. A lorry was loaded up with captured Hizbollah followers and a rocket was launched into the back of it, sending them all to paradise. They got what they deserved.' His tone was no longer jubilant, he was now as doubtful about the future as we were. Poor little Rina was crying all the time, clutching her children to her, their faces filled with fear.

We heard so many tales of revenge on all sides, and had no idea at that stage which of the rumours were true and which were propaganda or had simply become exaggerated in the telling. In the longrun we were to find out that the truth was far worse than anything we were told. We all remembered what had happened at the town of Halabja before the invasion of Kuwait, when thousands of Kurds, men, women and children, were bombed by the Iraqis with chemical weapons. It seemed certain that it would happen again, and this time we were in the middle of the target area. Any day now we might hear the sound of planes and see the clouds descending to choke us.

The Kurds, who had thought that they would receive international backing, now realised that no one outside Iraq was going to do more than talk. The Allied forces were going home, leaving them to fight on their own again. The local women were crying all the time now, and the men's faces were set grimly as they went about their business. Anti-foreigner feeling was beginning to run high once more, and children would chant insults and spit at us if we went out walking in the streets. If our boys went out they would be jostled by groups of Kurdish boys. But the children didn't alarm me as much as their parents, who stood outside their gates glaring hatefully at us when we passed by.

I was afraid of the Kurds. They are a warrior race and to have to tolerate us amongst them couldn't have been easy, whatever our story might have been. Fear, combined with bad diet and lack of sleep, was beginning to take its toll on my nervous system. I could no longer think straight or make rational decisions. Othman and the neighbours all told us tales of kidnappings that had gone wrong, and victims who were never heard of again, especially foreigners. My fears were becoming obsessions, and I began to anger Azziz and Hilall with my aggression as I blamed them for not trying hard enough to get us away from there to safety. I knew they were doing their best, but I couldn't stop myself. I would always end up having to mumble an ungracious apology for my behaviour, until the next time. I felt I had taken all I could, after living underground during the Allied bombings, hiding from rockets, always with one terrified child or another clinging to me; eight years of war with Iran, and five years of war when I was a child in England. I had had enough. We were just existing, not really living at all. When would it be my turn for some peace and tranquillity? I felt I was too old to face another struggle for survival, with violent death constantly breathing down my neck.

I was so fearful of what was going to happen to us I felt permanently sick and shaky. Being unable to eat or sleep made my condition worse. Normally my strong will was the driving force of the family, but now I was unable or unwilling to trust my own judgement. I wanted to lean on the men, but they didn't seem to want to face up to things either, preferring to crack jokes to cover up their uncertainty. They would laugh at the stupidest things. Hilall would throw up his arms, laugh and say things like, '*Sha sawi*? (What's it to me?) What do you expect me to do, go and fight their war for them?'

I would go outside to hide my nervousness from the children. Even they were getting on my nerves with their constant demands. They were always hungry or thirsty, frightened or bored, whining or crying.

It seemed impossible to make any decisions about anything with my mind so full, so we just went on surviving day after day in the hope that something would start to go right. We spent six weeks in this dreadful limbo. It is strange the things you do when you are under such pressure. I don't know why but Azziz and I decided to walk back down to the old Baathist headquarters and have another look at the sights which they were putting on display. I think we wanted to understand more clearly what it was that we were likely to be dying for. We wanted to find out as many of the facts as possible.

It was a lovely sunny morning and we found a number of people who spoke Arabic and English to answer our many questions. There was still a lot of mess but they were working on clearing it up. A crane was bringing up piles of mud and debris from the foundations of the building where they suspected they would find the bodies of Kurdish prisoners who had been thrown into the septic tanks.

'They found a Baathist security man down there,' an onlooker told us. 'During the attack on the building he must have escaped down the drains. He had been living down there for over a week.'

'What did they do with him?'

'They poured petrol down the hole and set light to him. That is justice for what he had done.'

We collected black market petrol at every chance we had, until we had managed to fill twenty litre drums of it. Although the prices were enormous our bag full of money was still holding out. Thank God we had had the foresight to collect it in the months before the war started. Most of our time was taken up with keeping the children away from the bullets which the excitable young Peshmerga boys were loosing off all the time, and trying to listen to the BBC for news of what was happening to the south of us, in the hope of hearing that things were quietening down and we could return home. We heard nothing that offered us any hope at all.

Spring was beginning to break through, although it was still bitterly cold and wet most days. Whenever the sun shone we would try to get out of the house to raise our spirits and warm our bones. On one sunny morning Hilall and April decided to take the children down to visit our friends in the centre of town, leaving Azziz and I alone.

'What shall we do?' I asked Azziz, once they had gone.

'Let's go up into the mountains for a walk,' he suggested, 'away from the people.'

We set off with the sun on our faces. In the fields between the mountains the green corn reached up to our knees as we made our way over to Surchinal, a very lovely holiday resort that we had happy memories of from the past. We passed groups of Kurdish men practising their shooting on home-made targets, but they took no notice of us. We were both in poor physical shape by then and by the time we reached the waterfall in Surchinal we were ready for a long rest. The restaurant we had been hoping to eat in was closed and the only people around were children fishing in the waters. We bought some nuts and biscuits from a pedlar and sat with our feet in the icy mountain water, absorbing the peace and quiet.

After a couple of hours we decided to start the long walk back home. On the way we took a different route into the city and passed a number of public buildings, such as schools, where there seemed to be an unusual amount of activity. There was brightly coloured washing hanging out all over the walls. As we got closer we realised that it belonged to Kurdish refugees who must have been making their way up from the other cities, trying to stay ahead of the army.

'The stories must be true,' I said, gripping Azziz's arm tightly, 'the army must be getting nearer if these people are escaping.'

As we got closer to home three shabby looking men lurched out in front of us. I didn't like the look of them and I kept close to Azziz. They looked like members of the Baathist security army. 'Be careful what you say,' I murmured as we got closer. We couldn't get past them so we stopped and for a moment nothing was said.

'What do you want?' Azziz asked eventually.

They fired a lot of questions at us in perfect Arabic, reminding me of what it had been like to be under constant surveillance in Baghdad. Azziz told them we were on holiday and waiting to get back home. We said we had got caught in the troubles and would be going as soon as we could, but they obviously didn't believe us. Eventually they stopped asking questions and grudgingly let us past. As we walked away I heard the click of a safety catch on a gun behind us.

'Don't turn round and don't run,' Azziz muttered under his breath, 'just keep walking.' The few yards to the next corner were the longest walk of my life. I was quite certain they were going to kill us, but perhaps they did not want to draw attention to their presence in the city. They were, after all, deep in enemy territory and there is no telling what the Kurds would have done to them if they had been discovered.

We weren't the only ones who were trying to escape from the danger zone before it was too late. We heard of another family who were planning to make their escape back to Baghdad. We went to see them, thinking that perhaps we could join up with them, with the Peshmerga aiding us as far as Arbil and from there on with the hope that the Iraqi army took mercy on us.

'There are helicopter gunships hovering over the whole area,' we were told, 'shooting anyone who is going in the wrong direction. They are even shooting their own soldiers if they think they are trying to desert or have been defeated.'

'We can't take a chance like that,' Azziz decided, 'not with the children.' So we returned to our room and the endless waiting for something to happen.

Over the next few days the numbers of Kurdish refugees coming into the city increased. They were filling every empty building they could find. The Peshmerga were searching out shelter for them and then coming round asking for clothing, food, anything that would help these people to survive. Many of them had run from the Iraqi army with nothing but the clothes they wore.

The *souk* area was full of families, mostly women and children, sitting on the sides of the roads and outside the mosques waiting for help. They looked so pathetically tired and hungry, the thin, ragged and shoeless children crying all the time. Just walking amongst them made me cry. I slipped money to some of the mothers and gave away packets of biscuits. I didn't dare tell Azziz what I was doing because I knew he would be angry. We needed to concentrate our efforts on the survival of our own family. Whatever I was able to do on the streets was nowhere near enough, but it was impossible to walk amongst them and do nothing.

The defeated Iraqi soldiers from the camp were also part of the sad street throng, some of them trying to earn a crust by selling a few biscuits or cigarettes. I saw Azziz giving some of them money. These soldiers had just as much cause as the Kurds – or us – to dread the arrival of the Iraqi army.

'Do you suppose John and Peter are still alive?' I asked, looking at these sad, defeated young men.

'Sure,' Azziz patted my hand comfortingly, but his eyes were brimming with tears. So many young Iraqi men must be dead by now, what chances had we that both our sons would have survived? It was a thought that haunted me all the time, particularly in the cold hours of the early morning when I could not sleep.

The desperate shortage of food and shelter in the city, and the fear that the army would soon catch up with them, was driving some of the refugees from the other Kurdish cities to keep moving up into the mountains towards the Iranian border. Sulaimaniyah had become just one more stage on their journey, one more place which could offer them no shelter, no food, no safety and no hope. But we didn't know where else to go, so we stayed on, still trying to decide what to do for the best.

'Let's go out for another walk,' I suggested to Azziz on the next sunny afternoon. 'We'll take a thermos of tea and some nuts.'

We made our way up to the top of a hill and sat down to look at the view. Once you got away from the town it was hard to believe just how bad things were. The countryside seemed so peaceful and the views were so beautiful down into the valley below. The sun was warm and I dozed on my husband's lap, to be woken up by some distant bangs.

'What's going on?' I asked, sitting up and rubbing my eyes.

'It's something down on the road,' he said, standing up and looking down the hillside.

At first all I could see were a few puffs of white smoke alongside the road, then the noise became clearer, as did the terrible sight. The refugees were no longer walking slowly northwards towards Sulaimaniyah, they were running and scrambling along the highway, spilling over onto the sides of the mountains in their haste to escape. As well as the people on foot there was now a snake of traffic containing every sort of vehicle imaginable. There were cars and lorries, horse driven carts, dust carts, cherry pickers, combine harvesters, mules, donkeys, tractors and anything else that had wheels or legs and some form of propulsion, all loaded high with baggage, children and old people, many of them still in their night clothes.

To start with we couldn't see why they were panicking, and then we spotted the helicopters. They came round the side of the mountain like angry insects, spitting out bullets and rockets into the frightened mass of humanity below them, goading them and herding them like sheep, and killing groups of them at random. A rocket would explode into a group of people and they would fall to the ground like skittles. We stood watching in horror, unable to believe what we were seeing, or to take in what it meant to us. The Iraqi army was forcing the Kurds back at a terrifying rate. Within a few days the main government forces would have reached Sulaimaniyah. We would be just a few more insignificant specks in this tide of expendable human life, fair prey for these terrible huntsmen, sitting ducks waiting for them to decide when to amuse themselves with killing us. The 'moving wall' which the Peshmerga man had warned us about was nearly upon us, crushing everything that stood in its path.

We ran back down the mountain to find April, Hilall and the children. In the city the change of mood was noticeable. The numbers of people moving through had multiplied to fill the main streets, and most of them were no longer stopping to rest or trying to find shelter. No one believed now that Sulaimaniyah was a safe haven. To be safe they had to get up into the mountains and, with luck, over the border into Iran. We could clearly hear the thump of bombs dropping nearby.

'Where are those bombs?' we asked a group of Peshmerga.

'No, no,' they protested, 'those aren't bombs, those are our anti-aircraft guns, stopping the Iraqi parachutists from landing.' But we could tell from the stern, strained looks in their eyes that they didn't believe their own words. They were such strong men, so used to the horrors of persecution that they never showed fear, no matter how bad things became. I doubt if they could see such bravery in our faces. I could no longer disguise the terror which was taking hold of my whole body and mind, making me feel like a crazed animal trying to protect her offspring in a burning forest.

We left the crowded main streets and made our way back up to the house. The rest of the family, unaware of the happenings which we had just witnessed, was sitting outside talking with a group of neighbours, the children running around playing. We sat down to join them, trying to calm ourselves. Everyone now had one thing on their minds, the coming attack and the best way in which to save their families. As we talked the children moved a little way away from us and for a few moments I didn't hear the approaching buzz of the helicopter. Suddenly the children were running towards us, screaming, the helicopter swooping down on them like a hungry hawk on grazing rabbits. It chased the children as they ran to us, then the dust was swirling around and the roar of the engines seemed to engulf us. The rockets and guns on the underside looked close enough to touch, and for a second I saw the impassive faces of the killers at the controls.

Every bad memory and suppressed fear that the children had came screaming to the surface. We scooped them up in our arms, struggling to stay upright in the swirling dust storm and ran to the house, trying desperately to calm them, and to think clearly ourselves. There was panic everywhere as people ran for shelter. We got into the house and slammed the door.

'Get into the corner,' Azziz shouted, 'cover the children.' We threw ourselves on top of the children, waiting for the inevitable explosion of a rocket coming through one of the walls, but nothing happened. After what seemed like an age the noise outside faded and we slowly recovered our breath.

This was what everyone had been fearing. The army might not have marched to Sulaimaniyah yet, but the fact that a helicopter could reach us so easily demonstrated how impossible was any hope that they could be held back. When they decided the time was right to kill us there was nothing we could do to stop them – except try to run further away. We had to escape – but where to?

TWENTY-ONE

FROM the moment the helicopter swooped down at us we did not let the children outside the house. We realised that the time for decision was upon us. It was now 27 March. At best we had two of three more days before the government troops arrived in force, at worst they could start dropping chemicals on us at any moment. But we had no idea what we were going to do to save our family. There was nowhere left to hide.

We could now hear the thump of bombs falling on the town of Baziyan in the distance, but still the Peshmerga insisted that they were successfully holding back the attackers. They assured us that victory was within their grasp, but the look in their eyes told us that they knew as well as we did that the government's mighty military machine was crushing them helplessly. The Iraqi army might have been outgunned by the Americans and their allies, but compared to the Kurds it was virtually invincible. The only reason it had taken Saddam's army so long to reach the north was that their attention had been taken up with repressing a rebellion in the south first.

'They have killed tens of thousands of Shi'ites in the south,' Hilall told me, having been talking to some of the Peshmerga men. Many of the cities are in ruins. Any rebels left alive have fled to the Iranian border or to the marshes. Now he can turn his attention on us up here.'

'But why didn't the Americans stop him killing all those people in the south?' I wanted to know.

'The Americans don't want to become involved with our internal troubles,' Hilall shrugged, 'as long as the fighting is contained within our own borders. They have freed Kuwait. They have been seen to teach the aggressor a lesson. Now they hope that we will get on with sorting ourselves out. They don't want to get involved in another Vietnam, committing troops to fight for years in unfamiliar territory, for causes that aren't theirs.'

'But surely they won't let the government just continue this genocide?' I was in despair at this news. It seemed that all the bombs and all the fear had been in vain. If anything, the ordinary people of Iraq were in more danger of being killed now than they had been before.

Hilall shrugged again. 'They will pass resolutions and they will say that the killing must stop, but what can they do to enforce it? They will impose economic sanctions, which will mean that the people get even less to eat, but it won't have any effect on the government, and so it will go on.'

Soon it was impossible for the Kurds to deny the truth of what was happening. 'The Peshmerga are retreating,' Othman told us gloomily that night. 'They are coming up the roads as fast as they can on foot, not even waiting for transport. Saddam's army must be right behind them now.'

'We've got to get back to Baghdad.' I shivered as I talked, the weather had suddenly grown cold again.

'No one can go south now,' Othman warned, 'the roads are far too dangerous. The only way out is up into the mountains.'

'I can't climb mountains at my age!' I had a vision of myself clambering up sheer rockfaces clutching my grandchildren to me. 'We wouldn't know how to live up there. I'm not like these Kurdish women who are used to the life, and can just strap their children on their backs and go.'

'Then we should wait here for the troops to come and hope they will be merciful.' I could see in Othman's face that he knew as well as I that mercy was one thing no one was likely to be shown in the coming months. 'The only reason that the Kurdish people have been able to survive the last century at all is because the mountains offer us some protection. If we didn't have them every Kurd in the area would be dead by now. They are our only hope. The best place would be Mount

Azmar, it's one of the highest peaks, but it will be covered with snow and ice. The helicopters won't want to go up there.'

'I'm not taking the babies up into the snow,' I was adamant. That was the best decision I had made so far, not so much because of the snow but because all the people who chose that route were slaughtered by the army.

'There are other places,' Othman said, 'we must think of the most suitable.'

I didn't sleep at all that night, my mind racing over every eventuality and trying to make plans for how we were going to survive the approaching holocaust. I couldn't believe that we were being deserted by the rest of the world, that there was going to be no Allied cavalry coming to our rescue. We spent all the night and the following day listening to the BBC and talking to neighbours, desperately trying to work out the wisest course to follow. The more I thought about each alternative, the worse it seemed. We were spinning a roulette wheel, with our lives and the lives of our babies riding on the drop of the ball.

The hardest thing to do in situations like this is nothing. I started to pack suitcases, choosing the most essential things to take with us should we decide to flee. I boiled some eggs and potatoes from our dwindling stock and wrapped them up as emergency rations. I was beginning to become more and more convinced that we would have to run. I understood Othman's argument about the mountains offering us some protection, at least, from the approaching helicopter gunships.

'We can't take all our winter clothing with us,' I said to Azziz, 'there won't be room in the cars. What should we do?'

'Ask the neighbours to look after it for us,' Azziz advised. 'Tell them we will be back for it.' I did as he suggested, not realising how much we were going to need the precious warmth that those extra few clothes would have afforded us. As the night of the 28th came round I was exhausted, but I still couldn't calm my mind enough to sleep.

The next day was bright and sunny again. After a breakfast of dry bread and tea I left the children with April and walked up to the highway with Azziz to see what was happening. Nothing had changed as we stood there, hand in hand, watching the horrible scene which we now knew we were going to have to join ourselves. The line of pathetic refugees stretched as far as we could see in both directions, a sea of faces etched with misery, panic and exhaustion. The Peshmerga were going round from house to house advising people to move out, that the area wasn't safe any more, finally willing to admit openly that things were going wrong.

'The Peshmerga have been here,' Othman greeted us as we got back, 'they suggest we move into the Haemolian Mountains.'

'Where are they?' I asked. 'We don't even know which road to start out on.'

'We could show you,' Othman said, 'if we came with you. Would you have room in your cars for us?'

'Of course,' we agreed. They were such a nice family and we owed them a lot for taking us in as they had, at great risk to themselves. But how, I wondered, would we manage with their four children as well as our four and a total of six adults? Our cars were not small, but they were only saloons, built to take four or five passengers at the most.

All the neighbours were now leaving their houses, dressed in mountain clothes, with sticks and thick boots and layers of coats. They carried very little luggage with them, and looked as if they knew what they were doing. The Kurdish people have been persecuted so long that they have a saying, 'We have no friends but the mountains.' The mountains may have seemed like friends to them, but to us they were a daunting prospect; we already knew how inhospitable they could be to people who were unfamiliar with their ways. We had lived in cities all our adult lives, we had no experience of surviving in rough terrain, at the mercy of the elements, foreigners amongst a potentially hostile and desperate people. The prospect was almost as frightening as what might happen to us if we stayed and waited for the government's army to arrive.

I made us an evening meal of boiled beans, using some of the eggs for the little ones to try to build up their strength, and afterwards we sat drinking tea and listening to the radio. I was itching to get on the road now. However frightening the mountains might be it would be better to be doing something than nothing. But, I told myself, I must stay calm and not panic. It was by acting rashly that we had made so many bad decisions so far – but perhaps every hour of delay increased the danger to the children – such agonising decisions to be made all the time. No, we decided, it would be more sensible to put the children to bed, at least for a few hours. Once they were asleep I went outside in the dark for some fresh air and talked to Othman and Rina for a while. By the time I got back to the cellar the men had also gone to sleep, snoring in unison. I couldn't bear sitting in the room, not knowing what was going on outside, so I went back out.

I sat on the step and listened to the heavy shelling approaching. Bright flames were lighting up the sky. It seemed that we were the only family left in the area now, all the other houses were in darkness, closed and locked up, their occupants on the road with the columns of refugees.

'I wish I could be a man,' I thought to myself, 'able to shut everything out of my mind and just go to sleep. Wouldn't it be wonderful to let someone else do all the worrying?'

At midnight I heard someone behind me and turned to see Othman's little daughter. 'What is happening?' she asked.

'I don't know,' I replied. 'Let's go and see.'

The two of us set off, hand in hand, up a steep track to the main highway. We stood watching the now familiar scene, the dark shadows of people shuffling past like ghosts, no one talking, just walking. Every now and then the lights of a lorry would sweep over them and we would see how frightened and cold and footsore they looked, their faces gaunt and determined as they hauled themselves and their families painfully away from the dangers which pursued them.

'Let's go back and find Mummy and Daddy,' I said, and she nodded obediently.

On the way back I slipped down a muddy bank in the dark, shocking myself and frightening the girl. When we got to the house, both of us breathless and shaking, Othman and Rina were standing outside with their other children and three men.

'These are Rina's brothers,' Othman explained, and I shook hands with each of the serious-faced men, 'please can they come with us?'

'Yes, of course, your family is welcome,' I said, my heart sinking. How would we fit them all in?

Rina was talking in Kurdish and Othman translated for her. 'Rina is worried about leaving without seeing her family and telling them where we are going,' he explained. 'Would it be possible for us to go over to their house and explain what is happening?'

'Oh, I don't know.' I was doubtful, I knew that Rina's family lived on the other side of town. If we went across there we would have to rejoin the queues to leave Sulaimaniyah much further back. I saw Rina's eyes, lit up in a flash of light and they looked so sad I couldn't say no. 'We must ask my husband,' was all I could think to say.

'I think we should leave now,' one of the brothers said, 'the army is only 30 kilometres away now.'

I paused for a moment before deciding he was right. It was time to give up any hope of getting back to Baghdad. The choice now was between staying where we were to wait for the attack, or being forced up into the mountains with the thousands of other refugees, in the hope of getting to the relative safety of the Iranian border. If we stayed we might well be killed, and we would certainly be terrified once again by the endless, deafening, nerve-tearing explosions which had been pursuing us for so long. I didn't think the children would be able to take any more of that – they had already withdrawn into themselves, becoming shaking little bags of nerves at the thought of being attacked again. I didn't think I would be able to stand it either. If we went into the mountains there was no telling what would happen, we would be abandoning ourselves to luck, but at least we would be doing something rather than waiting passively for the worst to happen. If we didn't go now it would be too late, the army would arrive and we would have no more choices.

I couldn't believe that we were going to have to flee from our own people. We knew that no one was coming with the intention of killing us, but in the carnage which was approaching we also knew that the chances were that everyone would perish. Chemical weapons don't choose whom they suffocate, poison, maim or blind. We would as surely become part of the corpse of Sulaimaniyah as everyone else, just like the poor families of Halabja and the dozens of other Kurdish villages and towns. I went inside and woke April, Azziz and Hilall. They were hard to rouse from the depths of their exhaustion.

'We've got to go now,' I urged them, 'or it will be too late.'

I explained to Azziz about taking Rina to see her relatives. He was as doubtful about the wisdom of the diversion as I was, but we agreed that we owed them a lot and it would be a kind thing to do. We piled everything into our two cars again, until they looked too loaded down to move. Now we had to fit in Othman and Rina's luggage, as well as that of her brothers. We strapped as much as possible onto the roofs, and pushed our belongings into every crevice we could find. There was no system or organisation, we had no idea how we would find things if we needed them on the trip. The boys were awake and wide-eyed with fear, little Sabha remained asleep in April's arms, blessedly unaware of the panic all around her.

Somehow we got everyone into the cars and Othman directed us across the blacked-out, panic-stricken city, against the tide of refugees. We seemed to be travelling miles out of our way. I could feel Azziz becoming as anxious as I was but we held our tongues, staring out of the windows at the passing parade of fear and unhappiness illuminated in our headlights.

Our destination was a smart suburb of the city, and Rina's family all seemed to be waiting outside for us. There were three enormously fat ladies, another thinner one and a group of men. There were also more children. To my horror I saw that they all had suitcases with them.

'I need to use their toilet,' I told Hilall and he translated for me. They all seemed very happy to usher me into the house, and by the time I came out I saw why. They had all clambered into the cars, chattering and shouting as they sat waiting for us to drive them away. Azziz was standing outside, watching in dismay, but none of them was taking any notice of him.

Two of the fat women had climbed into the back of our car and another into my seat in the front. Some of the children had been piled in with them and Majid and Ali were out on the road with nowhere to sit. Sabha had woken up now and was crying pitifully, crushed in her mother's arms by the weight of bodies. Hilall's car was just as bad, although April and the other two children had managed to keep their places. The older children were climbing up onto the roof-racks and making perches for themselves up there. I was aghast. In all the terror of our plight those two cars were our only sanctuary. Without them we were completely finished. We couldn't possibly have got back across the city on foot, carrying the babies and provisions, in time to escape the army.

'What's going on?' I demanded to know, my voice shaking as hysteria threatened to take over. 'We can't take all these people. We said we would take Othman and Rina's family, but we can't take all of them. We have to be able to look after ourselves.'

Azziz and Hilall started arguing with the women and ordering them around. Eventually the one in my seat agreed, under protest, to be forced into the back with her gigantic sisters, but only on the condition that I had a bulky, twelve-year-old girl on my lap in the front. Some of the men agreed to walk beside the cars to cut down the weight on the springs and to try to find other vehicles once we joined the procession. Neither Azziz nor I was happy with the arrangements, but within an hour we had at least started to move towards the lines leaving the city.

There was a total of seven people in our car and eight in Hilall's, although each of the three fat ladies was the size of two normal adults.

The girl on my lap must have weighed 60 kilos and she made no attempt to shift her weight to make me comfortable. My legs were clamped in with bags so that I couldn't move to alleviate the pain which almost immediately started to pierce my joints. I was worried, not only because the cars could now barely move under the weight, but because as the hosts we were going to have to feed all these people on the trip which lay ahead, and I knew that we had hardly anything to eat. Our paraffin stove had been dismantled and packed into the cars somewhere, but God knows where it was.

We made our way back towards the north until we met up with the road out of town. The crowds were still shuffling forwards, the cars honking their horns and trying to force their way through, the pedestrians trudging on with their heads down, their children clinging onto them. By now it was pouring with rain, and the line of traffic was barely moving. It was also freezing cold and the heater in our car was not working. The women in the back talked and talked and talked, as if they were out for a day's picnic. I could see that they were annoying Azziz as much as me. His face was lined with tiredness and he could hardly keep his eyes open.

'I can't go any further with this girl on me,' I finally spoke up and there was a further hiatus as she changed over with Ali, who was a great deal lighter and more comfortable to share with. At least now I could move my legs a little and ease the pains which were searing through my back. By the time dawn broke Azziz and I were near to screaming point, but the three ladies in the back never shut up for a moment. Both of us had violent headaches. It was still cold and wet, but at least it was light. We climbed out of the car and looked around. We could see no end to the queue, but even then we didn't realise the full extent of it. It stretched the whole 130 kilometres from Sulaimaniyah to the gates of Iran, and we were at the end of it. All through the night we had only travelled 30 kilometres and we were still in the suburbs of the city.

Othman had been walking beside the car and was surveying the scene with me. 'It's hopeless,' he said, shaking his head. 'We will never survive up in the mountains with this many people. A crowd like this is a sitting target. If they attack us now there would be nothing we could do. We should turn back.'

'You must be crazy,' I answered, 'if we turn back now we'll be dead for sure.'

'We are not mountain people,' he insisted, 'none of us knows how to survive up here. You don't have enough food to support us all; we could be up here for months. It would be better to take the chance of dying in our own house.'

I tried to dissuade him because now we had made a decision to go to the mountains I had to believe it was right, but he had made up his mind. I was so sad to see them go, feeling sure that they were heading back to certain death, and probably torture at the hands of the approaching army which would kill the children as readily as the parents. We hugged and cried and said our goodbyes, all of us certain that we would never see one another alive again, all of us fearful of the ordeals which lay in wait in both directions. They were a sorry sight as they left us, trudging bravely against the tide, pushing their way through the crowds. To be honest I had no idea which of us was acting the more wisely, and part of me wanted to run after them and go back to huddle in our underground cell until all the dangers had passed. I felt that we had lost some people who had grown to be important to us, and it made me feel lonely and exposed. If I had had a home of my own to walk back to I might have chosen like Othman, but I couldn't walk back to Baghdad. We had no choice now but to press on.

TWENTY-TWO

GOING forward was a hideous process, grinding on a few inches in first gear and then sitting, huddled together, dozing in the cramped seats, waiting for the next few inches of progress. If you left the queue to take a break on some verge or side-road you lost the chance of moving even those few inches. The road was so full of vehicles and people moving north that it was now impossible for cars to turn back. If we had decided to give up then we would have had to abandon the cars, because we would never have been able to get them through the crowds coming up behind us. We were completely trapped, all our options gone. I felt miserable from tiredness. All the time I was urging Azziz forward.

'There! There! Move over there! You see that gap, for God's sake move forward, don't miss the chance.' I must have been driving the poor man mad. The rain continued to pour down so we couldn't even get out to stretch our legs.

I was growing to hate the three women in the back and their endless, thoughtless, unintelligible chattering. They almost seemed to be enjoying themselves, thriving on the adventure of it all. They made it known, by using little Ali as a translator, that they were hungry, and asked what we had to eat. I politely asked them where their food was. Had they brought any with them? If so we wouldn't mind at all if they went ahead and ate; we would make some sandwiches and brew tea later. I could feel their anger from the back of the car like a physical force. They were our guests, they were hungry and they expected us to feed them. They certainly hadn't brought anything themselves, or if they had they were not going to tell us about it. I became angry as well. I told them the food we had was for the children, but they were welcome to take some biscuits from a packet I had. They ate that packet and then demanded another. They went on eating packet after packet with no thought of the children. I was furious and told Azziz so in English, so that they couldn't understand. The car was bristling with hate and anger.

'I can't stand these people much longer,' I said.

'Don't worry,' Azziz's face was grim, 'I will get rid of them when we get further up the road.'

'How will you do that?'

'Just wait and see.'

'I'm taking some cold potatoes for April to give to the babies,' I told him, and climbed out into the cold, wet wind to walk back to the other car. The people travelling on foot were moving faster than the vehicles, even though many of them were weighed down by their belongings, and unable to shelter from the cold and the rain. Many were begging at the car windows to be let in and given shelter. There was no way we could have fitted anyone else in.

By midday the rain had eased up and we decided to stop for a break. We all needed to relieve ourselves and to eat something. I could see that if Azziz didn't have a short sleep soon he would not be able to continue for much longer. Hilall shouted to a passing Peshmerga that we wanted to get off the main road for a while onto a side track.

'Don't go too far,' the man warned, 'the government has bombed round here recently, it is a dangerous track.' The rain had slowed to a drizzle, but the low grey clouds still hid the tops of the mountains.

'Helicopters won't be able to fly in this weather,' I said, 'we'll just go a couple of hundred metres so that we are away from the crowd.'

Once the convoy was out of sight we stopped the car, climbed out and stretched our aching limbs. Taking a blanket for the children to sit on, our family clambered down a slope to find a place to make tea. The wind was bitterly cold and too strong for us to be able to light the paraffin stove. Rina's brothers, who were travelling on foot, joined us. It was almost impossible to find all the things we needed to make a simple snack, everything had been crammed into the cars in such a haphazard fashion. Eventually I found what I wanted and made my way down the slope to join the others, but my feet felt like blocks of ice.

'I am going back to the car for my boots,' I said, 'my feet are freezing.' As I climbed back up the slope I didn't see the helicopter approaching round the side of the mountain. I opened the door of the car and bent down to get my boots from under a load of other things. I pulled them out and took off my shoes. I was balanced on one foot, pulling my boot on when I heard the men shout their warning to me, and simultaneously felt the heat from the rocket tail flames as it flew a few metres above my head. It landed in the mud 50 metres away from me and exploded, showering me with stones. The blast lifted me in the air and smashed me against the car. Everyone was screaming and running around.

I must have made a good target for that pilot in my bright red skirt. If there hadn't been so much mud, enough to swallow the rocket whole, I would certainly have been killed by the blast. The thing that worried me most was the brooch which I had been left by my grandmother and which had been torn off my overcoat and had disappeared. It was very precious to me and for a few minutes I couldn't find it in the mud. Azziz came running up to see if I was all right.

'I've lost Gran's brooch,' was all I kept saying as I hunted around on my hands and knees, too shocked to be able to think straight.

'Never mind the brooch.' He lifted me up, 'Are you all right?'

'I don't want to lose that brooch, it's my favourite,' I just wanted to keep looking. 'Help me find it, darling.'

'Okay,' Azziz realised it was the only way to calm me down and agreed to help. I finally found it inside the car, where the blast had thrown it; the metal had been completely bent by the force of the explosion. The relief of finding it seemed to clear my head. I could hear the children screaming and crying, held by the men who were comforting them. I was shaking and as I started to take stock of what had happened I realised that the inside of my sleeve was wet with blood.

'I think I've been hit in the arm,' I said. Azziz looked all over my coat, but there were no tears in the material.

'Here,' Azziz helped me to slip it off, 'let's take a look at you.' My arm began to hurt as the coat came off and looking down I saw it was a mass of cuts. 'The blast must have sent the sharp little stones straight up your sleeve,' he said, and showed me. My arm was still hurting from that blast six months later.

I clung onto Azziz for a few minutes as he stroked my hair. 'That was a near one,' I said finally, 'I thought I was finished.'

'If you had been meant to die, Susan, you would not be here now,' he answered. 'It isn't time for you yet.' The helicopter had flown off but we abandoned our makeshift picnic, desperate to escape further into the mountains, away from the approaching army which by now must have been in Sulaimaniyah. 'This is a mistake,' Azziz said as we packed the things back into the cars, 'we are going to get killed up here.'

'We can't get back now,' I said hopelessly, 'not with all the traffic on the road behind us.' The thought of going back down towards the guns and bombs and sirens was more than I could bear. I had to keep trying to get beyond their reach. I had to keep moving or I would go mad.

'We could hide,' he said. 'There were some concrete water pipes under the road a little way back. We could wait there until the army catches up, and then surrender.' We talked over the alternatives endlessly.

The shock of the rocket attack had made Azziz determined not to continue another metre with the dreadful witches in the back.

'These women must be found some more comfortable way to travel,' he insisted to their menfolk with Hilall translating, 'they need a lorry to carry them. We don't have enough food for them and they need to be amongst their own people.' The women were equally anxious to escape from the cramped conditions of our car and accepted an offer of a lift from some friends who were passing by in a lorry. They left us without a backward glance, jabbering happily to their new hosts. With relief, we climbed back into the cars and rejoined the convoy as it crept onwards and upwards.

'The car's springs would not have survived these roads and those women,' Azziz said, and I'm sure he was right. The thought of the car breaking down and leaving us even more stranded was too terrible even to contemplate. We were constantly aware that we were Arabs, which meant that we were officially the enemies of our fellow refugees. Being inside the cars separated us a little from them, and only a few of them were openly hostile towards us. Most seemed puzzled as to why we should be there sharing their pain. The cars made us feel a little safer.

Our reaction to the near escape from death had begun to take hold and we, like the rest of the crowd, were feeling panicky at the presence of the helicopters, always looking around us to see where the next rocket would be coming from, and moving along much faster. Every few yards there were Peshmerga soldiers brandishing guns, herding us forward like sheep.

'Move on! Keep going! Don't stop, it is safe up ahead!'

The Kurdish people are like one great big family, always there to help one another in a crisis, and there was no shortage of people who needed help. Othman's family were not the only ones who were finding the hardships of the mountains more frightening than returning to whatever was happening back in the city. Some of the families with small children were starting to give up and turn round, but not enough to make any difference to the speed of the queue.

Little Ali and Majid now had the back seat of our car to themselves. They had been eating their way through our store of biscuits and now they had fallen asleep. At first Ali had wanted to be with his parents and baby brother and sister, but he realised he got more space in our car, and he knew that I would always try to find him and Majid some food whenever I could. We kept jolting onwards until midnight when the traffic ground to a halt. The word was that they had closed the gates to Iran and no cars would be moving again until 4.30 a.m.

We wrapped ourselves in blankets, which were quite inadequate against the chill, and tried to sleep where we sat. I couldn't stop my mind from turning over and over as I watched Azziz, with his head resting on the steering wheel, slumped as if he had been shot in the back, dead to the world. Outside in the rain I could hear the shuffling noises of thousands of people going past, like herds moving in the dark, and the crying of the children.

Ali was stretched across my lap and I was desperate to relieve my bladder. I slid out from under the boy without waking him and let myself out of the car. The rain had drenched me within seconds. I worked my way to one side of the road, away from the crowds of people passing like wet wraiths in the blackness. I relieved myself and scurried back to the car to spend the rest of the night drenched and shivering. This was my third sleepless night in a row. My eyes felt as if someone had thrown handfuls of grit into them, but my mind wouldn't let me sleep, keeping my nerves taut and jangling.

At 4.30 a.m. the rain was still coming down when the cars started to edge forward again in jerks and starts. For the next two days we crept forward, inch by inch, heading for the town of Arbat, where we were told there was a well with fresh water. We were now on a road which was six lanes wide, but every lane was clogged with people going in one direction only. It was a steep road, slippery with mud so the people and the cars were skidding as they climbed, and the rain continued to teem down. I saw lightning strike a short distance ahead of us in the black clouds and I became fearful that the cars were as likely to be struck by a storm as by Saddam Hussein's bullets. The rain turned to hail and thundered down onto the car roof. The people outside were wading through mud, sometimes right up to their knees. All the time they were banging on the car windows, their wailing voices reaching us over the noise of the storm, begging for food or shelter for their children. More and more people were giving up and turning back, willing to face the wrath of Saddam Hussein's forces rather than continue in this hell, but anyone with a car had to keep moving forward.

Every so often I would see someone in so much trouble I would have to get out and help. One young woman with two small children was obviously very sick. We couldn't fit them into our car, but I took her round some of the nearby lorries and asked people to take her in. Eventually someone agreed and pulled her up into the dry. I passed the children up to her and they were as light as feathers, with virtually no flesh left on them. Sometimes I would try to beg food from other families for Ali and Majid; most people were willing to give when they saw the face of a hungry child looking at them.

In normal circumstances this bit of road would have taken us about half an hour to drive up, but on 1 April we were on it for eight hours before we reached the crest. Now we were on a high plateau, buffeted and battered by rain which was carried horizontally by the freezing wind. Both Ali and I wanted to relieve ourselves but the thought of getting out of the car in such conditions was unbearable, so we hung on. I found a pencil and piece of paper and scribbled down a poem to distract myself.

> We fled before day, before Dawn's
> darkest hour,
> There was no sleep for us who stayed awake,
> From fear of the unknown properties at stake
> To take all our lives.
> We were afraid, I will not lie,

We wanted so to live, not yet to die,
The booming, heavy sound of cannons
Filled our ears, and kept our trembling
Thoughts and limbs in misery aware.
Wake up babies from your sleep,
At night's dark hour we lift you up
And hastily wrap you warmly and away.
We have to leave our shelter, for the day
Will bring an army on our heads,
And if we do not run, we shall be dead.

Up the cold muddy tracks on the mountains,
    it was raining ice that day,
All my Kurdish friends and their children,
plodding miserably on our way.
There were no fires for healing,
There was no food for eating,
We had no bed for sleeping,
Most had no shoes for walking,
Few had breath for talking,
Iran was miles away.
There were no shelters for the living
On that awful mountain trail,
There were no graves for the dying
No haven for them as well.
Lonely, lonely millions,
Weeping for life, without hope,
High up towards God's glory,
Striving hard to cope.
For many long months of moving,
Slowly higher and higher,
Desperate to save the children
From the wrath of a madman's fire.
Look on us, peoples of the world,
Aren't we also part of His plan?
All we want is the hope of living
And the gift of life if we can.
We are a nation of people,
All we ask is to live quietly in
our houses,

And not to have to run like this,
Away from our homes and family
Away from our lives as Man.

In the middle of the afternoon the storm blew itself out and a watery
sun appeared through the clouds. We made our way down a hill, where
the road had narrowed to one car's width, until we reached Arbat.
Here more people were leaving their village homes in panic, their
bedding packed up and their belongings on their heads. Refugees were
milling around everywhere, looking for somewhere to sleep and for
something to eat. We stopped the car and asked for news.

'The army is on its way,' we were told. 'Arbat is going to be bombed
tonight.'

'We must stop for a while,' I said, 'before the rains come again, to
give the children a break.'

Backing the cars into the shelter of a small fir tree copse in the mud
by the side of the crowded road, we got out to stretch our legs and lit
one of the precious few cigarettes we had left. Ali and I went to relieve
ourselves amongst the trees. There was no privacy since everyone else
was intent on doing the same thing, but when you are desperate you
stop caring.

'There is a well over that wall,' Hilall told me. 'We will fetch some
water and you can boil some potatoes and eggs and make some tea.'

In the next hour or two I made dozens of cups of tea for anyone
who asked. A hot potato and glass of tea are the most welcome things
in the world when you haven't eaten properly for days. The trouble
was that the smell of the food brought so many people over, and all of
them had hungry children with them. In the end all I had myself was
half a boiled egg, everything else was given away. That was all I had
had to eat now for three days. I was feeling so weak and so tired, and
I was losing weight fast. The only sleep I had had were the odd few
minutes of dozing in the car in between being woken up by Ali's
restless movements or the noises outside.

But even that short break and small morsel of food were cheering.
We all felt deliriously, almost hysterically happy to have something
warm in our stomachs. It was a glorious picnic, free of the chattering
women and amongst family. The boys ran around the trees, glad to
stretch their legs and smell the pine needles which I crushed in my
hands for them. Little Sabha sat up, watching them and gurgling
contentedly. A combine harvester, loaded down with people, had

become stuck in the road, blocking all the traffic and forcing the people to spill over the sides of the road in order to get past. It was like watching a comedy show as the Peshmerga tried to get this gigantic escape vehicle on the move again, with everyone shouting and waving their arms and sounding their horns.

We must have seemed a curious little group amongst all the horror and misery and we attracted the attention of a young Kurdish man, called Amin. He talked to Hilall first, and then he was introduced to us. He looked suspicious and shifty to me, a swarthy, beetle-browed man whose eyes were always darting around and whose charm was too quick. He seemed well educated and spoke quite good English and Arabic.

'Amin says we should take the road to Halabja next,' Hilall explained. 'He has friends there whom we could stay with and have a bath and a meal and a bed for the night.' Just the name of this town where so many thousands had perished made me shiver.

'There is a road to Halabja which is dangerous for those who don't know it,' Amin explained. 'None of the big vehicles will be using it, but I know it well. You will be able to travel much faster if you leave the rest of the convoy.'

'We don't know that area,' I said, frightened at the thought of going to the town which had passed into folklore as the world's most tragic example of what chemical warfare can do to civilians. 'We might get lost, or have an accident.'

'Amin says he will come with us and help us. His friends have run out of petrol, so we can do him a service by towing them behind us.'

I didn't want to go with him, but Hilall insisted that he was trustworthy, and as he understood the local people I was willing to take his word for it. Our car wasn't strong enough to tow this other one, but Hilall's was, and so they were hitched up. I wasn't sure that we were doing the right thing, but I didn't understand anything that was going on and I hadn't the strength to take control, so I couldn't argue. We had room in the cars now, I reasoned, and it would be helpful for us to have someone else who spoke Kurdish. I noticed, as he was talking, that he was carrying a pistol, and I saw him storing a Kalashnikov machine gun in our boot.

'Why are you armed?' I asked.

'It is for my own safety in the mountains,' he smiled, 'you never know whom you will meet up here.' There was something about his style and self-confidence which suggested there was more to him than met the eye. He seemed like a professional killer to me, and all we had to protect ourselves was a knife. I suspected he had been told to watch us and find out what we were doing up there.

Amin and Hilall went off on an errand while Azziz, April and I rested and watched the children. I was half dozing, with Sabha in my arms, when I was woken by angry voices. A group of ferocious looking Peshmerga had gathered round us and were demanding to see my husband's papers. April and I cuddled the children to us as they fired questions at him in Kurdish which he couldn't understand. They tried some broken Arabic and English and it was obvious that they were highly suspicious and impatient with our lack of understanding. They thought we were spies and said they would be keeping the papers until they had found out more.

This was one of the worst things that could happen. Without papers to prove who we were we would never be able to get back to Baghdad. Why would the Iraqis believe our story if we couldn't prove it? We had to hang on to those documents. Azziz pleaded with the men, but they pushed him roughly aside. I was so frightened and so relieved when I saw Hilall and Amin returning. Amin was very relaxed with the men, and they too seemed to soften when he spoke to them. After a long conversation they agreed to hand back the papers and we climbed into the cars and set off. We were now in Amin's debt.

'Watch this man,' Azziz warned me when we were alone for a second, confirming my own fears, 'I don't think he would hesitate to kill us if it suited him.'

Amin guided us along prairie roads and then up more steep mountainsides. When the cars became stuck in the mud he would help to push them out, and he was skilful at getting fires going with damp, green sticks when we stopped to boil water and eggs. He was so full of kind gestures I began to doubt my own judgement of him, but still there was something about him that made me uneasy. His presence was frightening. He seemed very at home in the harsh mountains. Because we had left the main convoy we were now travelling at a reasonable speed, and he talked about the places we were passing in a mixture of Arabic and English, explaining the sights which we saw.

'What is that?' I asked pointing to a vast expanse of ground covered with thousands of jagged rocks, each one spaced out regularly from its neighbour, and casting long shadows in the evening light.

'Those are the graveyards for the villages,' Amin explained sombrely. 'When Saddam Hussein bombed them with chemicals everyone died; the small bricks are for children, the large bricks for grown-ups.'

'But where are the villages?' I asked.

'They destroyed them. When the people were gone they came with bulldozers and they flattened the buildings. Whole towns are completely gone, and now the grass has grown over them. The evidence has vanished, but it remains in our memories.' As we drove on I saw the odd remnant of a town or village, a gate post or a piece of wall, but for mile upon mile there was nothing except flat areas which had once been inhabited, and endless graveyards amongst corn fields, with the craggy mountains towering in the background. It was so quiet and beautiful, with no sounds of gunfire or shooting, I couldn't stop crying. A few cars passed us going at high speeds, and we saw more families tramping along the verges on foot, loaded with baggage and tugging their children behind them. As it grew dark hundreds of paraffin lamps and fires glowed like fireflies on the mountainsides as people tried to cook and warm themselves. Towing the other, heavy car had slowed Hilall and April down, and they were no longer in sight. We were now completely alone with Amin.

'There is a Peshmerga checkpoint coming up,' he said. 'Don't stop at the barrier, drive past and stop twenty yards further on.'

'Won't they shoot us if they see us do that?' Azziz asked, and I cuddled Ali and Majid close to me, trying to work out what was happening.

'No,' Amin laughed menacingly, 'they will see that I am one of them.'

Azziz did as he was told, and once we had stopped Amin climbed out of the car and walked back to the checkpoint. He talked for a while to the men there. We waited in the car, watching them in the mirror. After a few minutes the Peshmerga guards came up to the car and demanded to know what nationality Azziz was.

'Iraqi,' Azziz spoke up bravely.

'Where are you heading for?'

'Iran.'

They looked suspicious, but after a few more questions they walked off with Amin again and I saw him handing over his guns to them. He then came back to the car and climbed in.

'Okay, drive on,' he instructed.

'Why did they take your guns?' I asked.

'Better that they should have them than the Iranians.'

As we came closer to Halabja the rains were falling heavily again, obscuring our vision, but Amin never faltered in his directions along the narrow country lanes. The trees were tall and black on either side of the road and I became frightened. I had no idea where we were or what was going to happen to us next. We passed some villages which had been bombed but the buildings still stood, empty of life but free of the bulldozers, their windows and doors just gaping black holes staring threateningly, like eyeless sockets.

At nine in the evening we reached a village called Sayyid Sadiq, and were once more jammed into a melee of cars. The Peshmerga were doing their best to sort out the muddled traffic which was all trying to get to the mountains from the local villages, but we were trapped there until nearly midnight. The road was a mess of black, glutinous mud. Locked in the darkness inside the car, with the wind buffeting us and the driving rain obscuring our vision, we were completely dependent on Amin's instructions.

Gradually we managed to ease our way out of the line of cars and find the road for Halabja. All I could think of was how much I wanted to reach this safe house he had told us about, with the promised hot water and food. Every few metres we were halted by the Peshmerga, shadowy figures, faceless in headsquares, bristling with machine guns, belts of bullets and long knives in their trouser bands. It rained all night as we passed dark fields, the car sometimes crashing into deep, unseen puddles. Amin sat wrapped in our only decent blanket, barking out occasional orders.

'We will stop here for the night,' Amin said as we came into the outskirts of the town.

'But you said we could go to your friend's house for a bath and meal,' I protested.

'In the morning,' he snapped. 'It is too dangerous to go on now, we don't know what is waiting for us in the dark.' So we spent another freezing night in the car. I lay on the back seat with Ali and Majid, wrapping them in my coat, and the men slept under the blanket in the front. Outside another thunderstorm broke and kept me awake into the small hours, listening to the breathing of the others. Passers-by would rap at the windows and beg for help, but I didn't respond, I just lay there with my eyes shut and prayed they would pass. I was barely surviving myself; I had no resources left to help anyone else.

TWENTY-THREE

BY dawn the rain had stopped. It was cold and misty and there was the smell of woodsmoke coming from somewhere outside. I pulled the blanket off the sleeping men and wrapped the boys in it, taking my coat back and slipping out of the car. It was like waking in a ghost-town. I stepped out into the quiet of the morning and looked around.

A family was standing round a small fire, making tea by the roadside, and I went over to beg a glass for myself. I felt so cold it was as if my bones were shivering. The people were locals and explained to me that they had fled Halabja when the bombs had started to fall. They spoke Arabic and said that they had been told by Saddam Hussein that they should return to their homes in Halabja and they would find that they had all been rebuilt. Now they had returned to find that there was nothing. When I had taken a few glasses of tea they walked around with me, showing what had happened. It was nearly three years since the planes and helicopters had rained chemicals and explosives down on the town, killing everyone there and destroying everything around, and it was still a ruin.

Amin must have known what it would be like, I thought to myself, so why did he spin us such a line about a warm room waiting for us? It must have been to get us to tow his friend's car, but was that all? Or did he have some other, ulterior motive for taking us away from the main part of the convoy? It was impossible to understand what was going on around us, and just trying to make sense of it gave me a sick headache. By the time I got back to the car the others were stirring and looking around the ruins.

'We need to find some shelter where we can boil water and cook some food,' I told them, not bothering to ask Amin where the house with hot water and food might be. There was no point antagonising him when it was obvious that there was nothing to gain. 'I have seen a shop down in the main street which still has some walls standing. You men find some water and I will clean it up.'

They found a mountain stream, filled a pot with water for me and brought it to the shop site. I had pulled away the tarpaulins that covered the front and discovered a good, tiled floor which I proceeded to scrub clean and cover in cardboard. I took some canvas and tin sheets from other desolate buildings to keep the draught off the children and keep the stove from blowing out every few minutes. While we were making these arrangements Hilall and April arrived with the babies, towing the other car behind them.

'I can make tea and cook some eggs,' I said to Azziz, 'but my hands are too dirty to make rice unless we boil up some water for me to wash in.'

He agreed and another pot was filled with water and heated over the paraffin stove until it was hot enough to wash the children and April. Then Azziz carried it to a more private room in another bombed out building for me to strip down behind the blanket and scrub myself all over while he guarded me. I threw my dirtiest clothes away.

For the first time in days I felt clean and able to cook some rice for everyone. But I was so tired I was weeping all the time I was working, and April was the same. Sabha wouldn't allow her mother to put her down now, so she had to work with the baby clutched to her side, wide-eyed and silent. The men all talked in subdued voices in another corner of the room. After we had eaten we went out to walk around and met other survivors in the town. One man took us to the remains of a beautiful house where he told us about a seventeen-year-old boy who had dived down the well to escape from a chemical attack. A little later he had lifted the hatch only to meet death face on as another wave of attacks arrived. His body is still down the well.

As I walked around the town I could just imagine how it must have been that day, with the children playing, people going to the shops, and women cooking and cleaning their houses, all of them unaware that the planes and helicopters were approaching round the mountains. There would hardly have been time to panic for the ones caught in the first onslaught, they would simply have fallen where they stood, the mothers and children reaching out for one another as a cloud of death descended on them. The survivors would have tried to run as more and more chemicals were poured down on top of them. After a while I couldn't cry any more, or even bear to think about it, I had to turn my mind to more practical matters, to ensure our own survival.

'If you show me where the stream is,' I said to Azziz once we had all eaten, 'I can wash some of our clothes.'

He led me down the side of a mountain, my feet slipping and sliding out from under me as I carried the bundle of dirty washing. It was a bright day, despite the bitter cold, but in the distance I could hear a booming sound which I took to be more thunder approaching.

'It's down there,' he pointed down a crevasse to a stream of clear water.

'I can't climb down there,' I said, 'I'd never get back up and I've got clean clothes on. You'll have to do it and I'll pass the things to you.'

Azziz clambered down into the freezing water and I passed the dirty clothes down for him to wash through. The water was flowing fast and his warmest socks escaped him and were sucked down into the current, but everything else survived. We went back to our temporary camp and put the wet clothes out to dry.

'If we could find a reasonably intact building,' I said, 'we could wait it out here until it is safe to return to Sulaimaniyah, and eventually Baghdad.' I had seen a number of other people sweeping out derelict buildings and creating temporary homes from blankets and anything else they could find. 'I'm sure the Peshmerga are well in control here.' They had stopped by our little camp already a few times and they seemed reasonably friendly.

There was no sign of Amin, who had gone off to find out what was happening, and the owners of the car which Hilall had towed all the way from Arbat had also vanished. At midday we realised that the sounds I had taken for thunder were growing louder, and that they were cannon fire. The other refugees were growing agitated. Hilall went out to ask around and came back with Amin.

'We have to move on,' Amin said. 'The Iraqi army is still coming, they are not far away.'

Hilall's car had run out of petrol. Although we had had full tanks when we left Sulaimaniyah, and although we had only covered a short distance, the stopping and starting and the steep mountain roads had burnt fuel at a terrible rate. We had seen it happen to other people along the way, and the Peshmerga organising other vehicles to tow them along.

'We'll give you a tow,' I suggested.

'That won't work,' Azziz said. 'Our car is lighter than theirs; we would never get them up the mountains.'

'Then we could transfer the petrol to their tank and they can pull us.'

The men thought over the various options, but decided it would be impractical to try to continue in both cars with so little fuel. We had to find some alternative. We asked if there was any chance of buying petrol in the town. The people shrugged. 'Sometimes,' they told us, 'it is possible to buy from the black marketeers who bring petrol through to sell to the refugees.'

'When would they be there?' we asked. 'How do we make contact with such people?' Nobody knew. Amin had said that he would be able to find us petrol, but he had promised to find us a lot of things, none of which had materialised.

'I have found someone who says that they can sell us a tank of petrol,' Hilall announced after being out for a few hours, 'but they want 300 dinars' (about £600 at that time).

'If that is what it takes to get us out of here, then pay him,' I said, giving Hilall the money. All the Kurds who had been making homes around us were packing up and moving on. I didn't want us to be the only ones left there when the army arrived. The Peshmerga were rounding people up like cattle and pushing them on down the road.

'The government has taken Arbat,' they told us. 'You are not safe here.'

But we were trapped until we could get more fuel. We waited impatiently for Hilall to come back. An hour later he returned to say that the man now couldn't find the petrol after all. 'But a lorry driver has said that he will tow the car to Tuwaila, about one and a half hours walk from the Iranian border, for 300 dinars.'

'Give him the money,' I said. 'Let's get out of here.'

This seemed like our best chance. The car was hitched to the back of the lorry and we headed out of town, past the worst devastation I had ever seen, up the route leading to the mountains, along neatly laid roads which were as silent as death. Nowhere was there a complete building left standing, just miles of desolation, bombed out shells of homes, schools, hospitals, a cinema with the burned seats still standing upright, and an eight-storey hotel which had collapsed into a pile of rubble and was believed to have 850 people entombed inside. We passed blasted shops which must once have sold bread and kebabs.

'How come only 7,000 people were killed here?' I asked Amin.

'That is just the official figure,' he scoffed. 'Well over twenty thousand died here that day.'

In the middle of all the desolation I saw one building completely intact. It must have been hundreds of years old and was built of old brick about half a metre thick. It was a small place, with grass growing out of the mud on the roof and iron-barred windows. All around it rows and rows of modern dwellings were crushed, but this one had withstood it all. I felt rather like that building myself. We found an undamaged bridge over a swiftly flowing river and headed out into the countryside.

It was like arriving on top of the world. On both sides of the road, as far as the eye could see, the destruction continued. Farm equipment still lay in the fields with no one left to plough them. Tears were streaming down my face, and my poor husband was white and sad as he drove us through this sunlit scene.

'In the mountains the poisoned gas got everywhere,' Amin explained, seeing our faces, 'even the wild dogs are dead in this area. No creature escaped.'

We crossed wide open spaces on our way to the next range of mountains, great soaring blue-black peaks, miles away, towering up into the sky, so beautiful, so lonely and so majestic, topped with snow like icing sugar. On either side of the road were fields of corn and barley planted for the first time in many years with the permission of the Iraqi government who had decided to make Kurdistan the bread basket of the region, having previously forbidden the growing of crops. With the change of policy every square metre had been given over to growing. It was a waving green world, punctuated with the brilliant red heads of the poppies, small daisies and buttercups, all of it now left to rot. It was like driving through the English countryside for me, reminding me of my childhood. The roads were narrow and the hedges often burnt black by bombs. Sometimes the potholes in the road were so deep we had to get out and push the car out of them.

'You see how fertile our land is,' Amin said, 'we could provide enough food for the whole region, if we were just allowed to.'

After driving several hours we stopped on a high plateau and let the children out to run around a field of corn and poppies. The sun was shining and the guns had fallen silent behind us. For a few moments I felt relieved to be alive. It was hard to believe that such beauty could exist in the midst of such a nightmare.

On the last leg of our journey through the fields I asked Azziz to stop the car so I could relieve myself. What I really wanted to do was take a few minutes to pick some of the little mountain flowers that grew on the verges, and to breathe some fresh air.

'Look at these,' I said as I climbed back into the car, 'they are so beautiful, and they show that life is still going on regardless of what is happening to us.'

Azziz smiled and squeezed my hand, but his eyes were so sad. As we drove on in the sunshine we passed a number of broken down vehicles, and push carts which had been emptied of their loads and abandoned. There were burned out cars with their wheels gone, just bare metal skeletons sticking up into the air. Now and again another car would pass us as we dawdled along. It was hard to believe that just a few hours ago we had been in one of the saddest places on earth, and that just a few miles away that sad snake of refugees was still plodding forward. Both Azziz and I knew that this respite was only temporary, a teasing glimpse of how pleasant life on earth can be before we were plunged back into the hell which mankind had made it.

We had left behind the lorry towing Hilall and April, but we were confident they would catch us up later. I felt optimistic that we might be over the worst and nearing the end of our ordeal. We passed an empty army barracks and in the distance I saw some blue lakes.

'What are those?' I asked.

'Those lakes supply all Iraq with its water,' Amin answered. 'They are part of a network of waterways, meeting up with the Rivers Tigris and Euphrates. When we regain independence for Kurdistan we will control much of the water supply for the Middle East, as well as the oil in Kirkuk and great reserves of copper and coal,' he smiled, 'that is why they all fight us so fiercely.' How beautiful that water looked, and how desperately we would be craving it within a few days.

Away to the left there were dark clouds and flashes of lightning. The wind was getting up again, making the fields ripple and the trees bend. It was as if our allotted respite was over and the darker side of nature was returning to reclaim us. The wind carried the clouds quickly and the storm moved towards us, slicing off the sunshine as it went, and thundered overhead. We were used to this now, and at least we believed that it would keep the helicopters away. We continued driving as the rain started once more and Azziz turned on the windscreen wipers and fans to clear the windows.

'I hope nothing goes wrong for April and Hilall,' I said. 'I wouldn't want those babies stranded somewhere where I couldn't get to them.'

'Stop fussing,' Azziz said kindly. 'April is quite capable of looking after her babies.'

'I know,' I was cross with myself for fussing so much about every-thing, 'but I can't help worrying.' I couldn't forget the picture of my daughter, her beautiful face taut with fear and worry, and Sabha's tiny hands gripping her so tightly.

'A mother always worries, no matter how old her children become,' Amin smiled at me understandingly and I warmed to him a little. I wondered if his mother had any idea where he was or what he got up to in the mountains. Perhaps she was one of the thousands who had been slaughtered. I passed the next few hours in these sorts of reveries, and then we reached the beginning of our worst nightmare yet.

Our hearts sank as we saw the end of the open road, and the same trail of cars and people that we had encountered when we left Sulaimaniyah. Only now, since we had been on the back roads, the numbers had multiplied a thousandfold. Hundreds of thousands of people and tens of thousands of vehicles had joined the queue from the towns and villages of the north. Evening was drawing in. Azziz was very tired, and dozed in the driver's seat as we returned, once more, to edging forward inch by inch towards the borders of Iran. Rain continued to pelt down, turning the ground into a marsh.

The mountain range, which had looked so wonderful from the distance, was to become the blackest part of our journey. The cars were once more nose to tail from here to the Iranian border. The streams of people whom we had seen over the last few days and weeks were already here, shuffling forward with virtually no hope of ever reaching their dream of safety. The scenes were the same as those we had witnessed before, but on a grossly magnified scale. There were oceans of people every way you turned. Tiny children without coats or shoes, their soaked hair sticking to their skinny, skull-like faces, were knocking on the car windows asking for the bread which we now had, and we started handing it out. For some of them we were able to find an item of clothing like an old pair of socks which we could pass out to alleviate their suffering.

How on earth had all these travellers managed to walk so far from places like Kirkuk and Arbil in such conditions? So many small children and old people, so few young men to help them. Many of the young men from these families must have been members of the Peshmerga, which was why they were taking such good care of us all, but many more must have been dead, captured and executed in the previous three decades, leaving the women to cope on their own.

The rain did not let up and the narrow mountain roads became quagmires, the cars sliding and sticking, some toppling over the unguarded sides of the roads and crashing down the mountainsides into the ravines below, carrying their passengers with them. Most of the people had come from the plains like us and were unused to living in the mountains. They seemed more afraid of the possibility of falling to their deaths than of the helicopters which were an ever present threat behind us. The following evening many cars stopped on the side of the trail to allow the people to light fires and rest.

'Don't stop yet,' Amin said, 'we'll keep going to the bottom of this mountain.' Azziz and I decided to go along with him. We were all anxious to get to the end of this dreadful leg of the journey.

The trail was becoming narrow here and I was frightened of the steep mountain drops which fell away from the left-hand side of the car. The surface was slippery with mud, and Azziz had to fight with the steering wheel and juggle the pedals. Several times on sharp corners the back of the car slid round and seemed about to overtake the front, threatening to pull us down to our deaths.

The Peshmerga men were wonderful. Never seeming to sleep themselves, they spent every hour helping the convoy forward, pushing cars that got stuck, arranging for the ones that broke down or ran out of petrol to be towed. They worked ceaselessly to try to get their people to safety.

'Stop now,' they told us. 'Don't go on in the dark, it is too dangerous.'

'I think we can do it,' Amin said, 'keep trying.'

I clutched Ali and Majid to me, keeping well away from the left-hand side of the car and holding my door ajar so that I could jump out with them if the car began to slip over the edge. I have never been so terrified. Azziz continued to ease the slithering car along, keeping as close to the mountainside as possible. At the bottom of the slope we reached a wide, muddy area full of vehicles whose occupants had stopped for the night, deciding not to press on up the next mountain which was towering above our heads.

'That's it,' I said firmly, climbing out of the car with the boys, 'not another metre. We stop here for the night and make a fire.'

'We can't light a fire,' Azziz said gloomily, 'we only have half the stove with us, the other half with the paraffin is in Hilall's car.' So now we couldn't even heat water ourselves. We only had dry bread or whatever we could beg from other people.

'Then we will just rest, and perhaps we will find the others.'

I went round talking to everyone in English and they were all very kind. I was looking for Hilall and April and the babies, half hoping they might have found a short-cut and got there ahead of us, but there was no sign of them. I had seen so many wrecked cars along the sides of the mountain tracks, the ones which had not been able to stay on the slippery bends and had carried their occupants to oblivion, or injured them so badly that they could no longer hope to keep up, that I was very afraid of what might have happened. I knew how reckless many of the Iraqi lorry drivers were, and I didn't know how experienced the man they had found to tow them was. Amin eventually managed to get a fire going and heated some tea and eggs, by which time the boys were fast asleep on the back seat of the car.

Azziz and Amin sat watching as other cars tried to get up the next mountain, revving their engines to give them enough speed to keep going in the mud, their headlights illuminating slices of the mountain walls as they wound round the corners.

'Our car is better than those,' Azziz said eventually. 'We wouldn't have that much trouble. Perhaps we should keep going.'

'In the morning the mountains won't look so bad,' I said hopefully. I really didn't want to go on any further that night.

'In the morning the track will be crowded again and we could be here for days.' Azziz went on. 'If the rains go on like this the conditions could get worse and we will be trapped down here in the mud. If we don't get to the top with speed we will run out of petrol before we get near the border. In a crowd it would be impossible to move fast and we would run out half way up.'

'Yes,' Amin agreed, 'it would be better to keep going now, when there are fewer cars.'

'Oh no, please,' I begged them, 'let's just wait for a while, give the others a chance to catch us up.'

'If we get stuck here,' Azziz argued, 'we might miss them. They may have taken a different route to the meeting place. We should try to get there, or they may give up waiting for us.'

I could see the sense of what they were saying, and I desperately wanted to find the babies again, so we climbed back into the car and set off up the next track with me clinging to the boys. The car did seem to prefer going up to coming down, but it was still a petrifying run. As I looked down on the fluttering, smoky firelight of the camps below, there seemed to be nothing stopping us from falling to our deaths as the wheels spun and Azziz clung to the steering wheel, wrenching it back and forth as the engine shrieked in protest.

'For God's sake be careful!' I screamed, but Azziz took no notice, concentrating on the job of forcing the car to the top of the mountain as quickly as possible. The boys cuddled me tightly and I could feel them trembling.

The Peshmerga were waiting at the top and insisted that we stop before we killed ourselves going down the other side. All the other cars we had seen coming up had been stopped as well and there was hardly any space left to park on the plateau out of the way of the speeding Peshmerga vehicles that came and went all through the night. We found a space right on the edge of a precipice and wedged the wheels with stones to stop the car sliding over the edge in the night. It rocked dangerously every time one of us moved. I saw some Kurds sitting around one of the other cars in the darkness; they had a gas fire burning and water boiling.

'I'm going to ask those people for a glass of tea,' I said. 'Come on children.'

'I will talk for you,' Amin said, getting out with us.

'I need to sleep,' Azziz said, 'I'll stay here.'

'Okay, darling,' I gave him a peck on the cheek, he looked so drained and tired, poor man. The Kurds were very welcoming and made us glass after glass of tea and some boiled eggs. I took one of the eggs back to Azziz and woke him up to eat it. I also managed to get him a glass of sweet tea. The moment he finished the food he went back to sleep. I stayed talking to the Kurds, trying to find out if they knew any more than we did about what was happening up ahead, or back in the places we had left behind, until I saw Ali's head beginning to nod and I carried him back to the car, with Majid walking beside us, almost as tired.

TWENTY-FOUR

I DIDN'T sleep again that night, I just sat there worrying about my other children and grandchildren whom I'd last seen in Baghdad. I now had no idea where any of them were, I didn't even know where April and Hilall were with their babies. Anything could have happened to them, they could all be dead. I hoped that April had learnt enough from me to be able to ask strangers for food and tea as they went along, to keep the babies going. I told myself not to be so silly. I was lucky to have such a good, strong daughter; she had been the most marvellous support over the last few months. How I wished she was there that night.

Before dawn the cars which had been camped at the bottom of the mountain were crowding onto the road and beginning the long grind up. Watching them now, from the top, I was glad that the men had taken the risk of climbing it in the night. I could see one car sticking and sliding back into the others, holding everybody up, the shouting and honking of horns carrying up the side of the mountain to us. The queue at the bottom was already fanning out as the Peshmerga desperately tried to get people to wait their turn to get off the plateau onto the narrow road.

'We must get started again if we want to get a place in the line,' Azziz called to me, and I went back to the car, dreading another day of this terrible journey but hopeful that perhaps by tonight we would be reunited with the others.

This was the most perilous part of the trail, as we dived down into a black, dark valley. Azziz stayed close to the vehicle in front and managed to control the slithering car round the corners. As we got lower down we entered a thick fog and the line stopped.

'Where are the Peshmerga?' Amin complained. 'They should be keeping the line moving. I'm going to find out what's happening.' He climbed out and disappeared for several hours.

'Let's hope that's the last we see of him,' I muttered as we sat in the cold car, hunger gnawing at our insides. Neither Azziz nor I would have been able to light a fire from the wet wood lying on the verges, so we just sat still and waited for something to happen. Eventually Amin returned, without a word of explanation as to where he had been, and plumped himself back into the car, glaring at the queue ahead.

At eleven o'clock I decided I had to get out, if only to keep my circulation going. It was still foggy but I could see some fires flickering down below over the edge of the mountain. I could smell the smoke. We were perched on a narrow part of the track and no vehicle could have passed us without tumbling over the edge. People on foot were able to squeeze by, mostly weary-looking women with children in tow. A small boy pointed to his mouth and I broke off a bit of dry bread which I had in my pocket and gave him and his sisters a little piece each. It was heartbreaking to be able to do so little.

I walked along the line for a while and found some Kurds who spoke Arabic. They offered me tea and we talked about our situation and how bitter we all felt to have our lives dictated by politicians. I was shivering uncontrollably now and I was sure I was catching a chill. I no longer wanted to eat, just to sleep, but my first responsibility was to the boys and I was afraid to leave them sitting alone for long.

I went back to the car and allowed the men to wander off and see if they could glean any information, but the same story came back: the line stretched to the border and unless Iran opened its gates to those up front we wouldn't be able to move an inch.

'They say there are over a million people sitting on the borders of Iran and Turkey now,' Azziz told me, 'and we are nowhere near the front of the line.'

So we sat, sometimes only moving a few feet in an hour. The sun had broken through weakly at midday, but by the middle of the afternoon the rain was back to stay, a constant companion to our miseries. The mud began to move faster down the mountains, swirling past us and round the feet of the walkers.

I felt so guilty huddled in the shelter of the car, watching the people outside moving past like the walking dead. Sometimes someone would beg us to let their old mother or young child into the car with us, but we knew we had to say no, even if the sight of them made our hearts break. We had seen other people agreeing to such requests and opening the doors only to find whole families forcing their way into the cars and refusing to get out. We were afraid that if that happened to us the car would break under the strain. It always seemed to be the strongest and greediest ones who did this, while the weakest and most needy were left to struggle on on their own.

Sometimes I climbed out of the car to walk for a while. It was easy to get lost in the crowd because of the continual movement and often a woman would start screaming, 'My baby! I've lost my baby!' So many of the sad little children just disappeared or died by the roadside, so many of the old people just gave up the struggle to survive. Often I would see some poor, distraught woman clutching a piece of material which was all that was left of her dead or lost child, or digging a grave on the verge, watched by her other children as they waited for her to finish so they could move on. Often I would come across some old person curled up beside the road, and when I bent down to help him I would find he was dead, frozen stiff by the chill of the long nights, with no one left to bury him. We were so high up now that there was snow on the mountains around us. When the sun came through the clouds it would reflect off the dazzling white mountainsides and burn our faces. I took to wearing dark glasses much of the time, which must have looked bizarre, but gave my eyes some rest from the glare.

I was desperate to find ways to distract the children and keep their minds from dwelling on their empty stomachs. We would go bird spotting, watching the eagles soaring up above us, or we would practise their lessons from school so they didn't forget them, or we would sing songs.

'Baa, baa black sheep, have you any wool? . . .'
'Little Boy Blue, come blow your horn . . .'
'A frog he would a-courting ride, hmm, hmm,
With a sword and a pistol by his side, hmm, hmm . . .'

It was as much to keep our spirits up as theirs. We were like lunatics in an asylum, our minds no longer connected to the words which spilled from our mouths. Amongst ourselves we would talk all the time about how we would get back to Baghdad, or how we would get a fire going, or how we could find a glass of tea or a piece of bread.

If I saw a better-off family with food I would ask if I could have some – they seldom said no – and I would wrap the dry bread up in a headscarf and give it to some of the hungry ones. To begin with I was shy about begging because everyone had so little to give, but I soon lost my inhibitions. Our store of bread and biscuits had run out within hours. All we had left was dried rice, a few eggs which I hid under a pile of towels to keep for the babies in Hilall's car, and a little fat. We hadn't seen Hilall's car for a while now and I worried all the time about the state they would be in by the time I found them. As we were unable to build a fire for ourselves I would ask other families to allow us to put our teapot next to theirs. They nearly always agreed.

I came across the widest assortment of vehicles on my walks, from dustcarts full of people to a wheelchair in which an old man was completely obscured under bedding and small children. How had anyone been able to push this load over the mountains?

From the boot of our car I pulled out all the clothes which I felt sure we would never need again, a shawl, socks, anything, and wrapped them round little children being carried on the shoulders of their parents. Some of them were wearing nothing more than gaudy, chiffon dresses. I found a baby bottle and filled it with water which had been boiled and gave it to a young mother with some dry bread and we both cried together. She told me her husband had been rounded up and taken away by Saddam's army, and she had walked all the way from the south of Sulaimaniyah with three tiny children. There were so many encounters like this. I couldn't always make myself understood, but I could see what they were going through in their eyes.

On one of my walks along the mountain tracks I saw curious, deep, spoon-shaped diggings cut into the hillside and directed into Iraq. There were five of these cuttings, side by side, each one a different size. Up close they were enormous and could have been used to lay the foundations for buildings.

'Let's go and look more closely at those things,' I suggested to the boys, who were out walking with me. Further along I found a way down on a wide track which had been newly cut. The track had been layered at different levels and the slopes were covered with grass and small flowers. It was a pretty area. Many Kurds were camped out down there, but I wasn't looking for somewhere to stay, I just wanted to look more closely at the diggings. I noticed openings in the hillside with wooden doorways which, I guessed, must lead to underground shelters, but we couldn't get any closer. We clambered back up to the car and I told Azziz what I had seen.

'The Iranians used them to base rockets for firing into Iraq,' he told me, 'Amin says some of them reached as far as Baghdad.' So this was where all those rockets which used to come over our house had been launched. 'You will see plenty more of them as we get nearer the border, but don't be frightened, they are not armed any more.'

Azziz started to become nervous when I took the boys off for walks, frightened that we might get a hostile reception from Kurds. Certainly they weren't all friendly towards foreigners, and some of them shouted insults, or spat at us as we went by, but most of them could see that we were in the same boat as them, fellow sufferers.

You had to be wary of what you said to people, and how much you told them about yourself. With all the different Kurdish factions you had to find out which leader the people you were talking to supported before anything else. 'We are following Talibani,' they would say or, 'we are for Barzani,' and we would agree that their choice was the only true leader. You had to adjust your story depending on whom you were talking to, and never express any strong opinions about any particular race, religion or political party, because you could never tell who was listening to your conversation.

Our wedding anniversary dawned, 5 April, and we didn't even have the ability to make a celebratory cup of tea. What a long way we had come from that registry office in Southampton nearly forty years before. All those people who had warned me against marrying a foreigner, but none of them could have foreseen the terrible circumstances which would befall us. If that old judge was still alive and I went to tell him what had happened to me, as he had asked me to, I doubt if he would believe me. No doubt if I had taken their advice and married an Englishman I would never have been subjected to such extremes of hardship, but then I might not have had such wonderful children and grandchildren. Who knows? Sitting up there in the mountains, looking back over my life I couldn't stop myself from crying. All their faces went past me and I wanted to hug every one of them. I went back to Azziz, who was still asleep and cuddled him on my shoulder for several hours. He didn't wake up and his face looked so lined and old.

We continued like this for days, barely eating at all, our appetites gone with our strength. Sometimes I would be able to boil a teapot on someone else's fire and beg some food for little Ali and Majid, giving some to Azziz to keep his strength up. All three of them had gone down with diarrhoea, bright yellow and orange fluid which drained their strength even more, making them sore and dirty. It was happening to everyone, the sides of the road were flooded with this brightly coloured excrement. The stench was all-pervasive and made me retch continually.

'It's the chemicals,' Amin said when I mentioned it. 'They are using helicopters to poison the water supplies, to drive us back down from the mountains.'

I was frightened for Azziz and the boys and had no medicine to give them. The only place to wash their soiled clothes was in the icy cold water of the mountain streams, causing even more contamination and spreading the infection even further. We were desperate for clean water, and above us the mountains were covered in virgin snow, but any snow that we could have reached had already been trampled underfoot and used as a lavatory by a thousand people. There was no way of escaping the diseases that were infecting the entire crowd.

Many of the Kurdish travellers carried spades with them, and were able to bury their dead and their faeces, but many more didn't have the tools or the strength to do anything about it, and so the sea of filth grew larger.

Despite his weak state, Azziz decided to go on foot and try to find out what had happened to the other car.

'Stay with us, darling,' I begged, 'you aren't strong enough to walk in these conditions and you have no idea how far on they are, it could be miles.'

'I have to try to find out,' he insisted. 'They have no way of cooking either, and April has two small babies to look after. They will need our help.'

I didn't try too hard to dissuade him. I was aching to see them again, desperately frightened about what might have happened to them in the care of the rapacious lorry driver. Azziz left us parked on the side of the road, then stumbling and sliding down the mountain, he asked questions of anyone who could understand him. After two hours he found a man who explained to him that the lorry which had been towing Hilall's car would not have been able to get up this narrow road with its hairpin bends. They would have had to take a much longer route round the mountains. When he got back to us five hours later he looked so sick I thought he was going to die. I remember sitting on a rock jutting out over a mountain edge, looking down at the sheer drop below me into the valley beyond. I have always been afraid of heights, but now I no longer cared. Nothing seemed to matter any more. The next day we continued to edge forward.

That afternoon we reached a plateau called Tuwaila, where we had originally agreed to meet up with Hilall and April, and our car finally ran out of petrol. At the beginning of the evacuation this had been a checkpoint for travellers going into Iran. Now the checkpoint had disappeared and there was nothing but cars and people milling around waiting to take their place back in line for the final long pull up into the higher mountains and the gateway to Iran.

We pushed our useless car off the road, out of the way of the procession. Even if we could no longer drive it, at least we could use it as shelter from the elements, and from the more hostile people. There were no buildings or shelters, as we had been led to expect, just thousands of people in a sea of mud and diarrhoea. The stench was overpowering, making it impossible to breath without something over your mouth and impossible to swallow without a wave of nausea.

'Where is the drinking water?' I asked everyone, and eventually I was directed to the edge of a steep mountain. At the bottom was a mud pit with a brown stream rushing down from the mountains above. To get to it I had to make my way, bit by bit, down an almost sheer mountainside. Down at the bottom, in the centre of the mud was a kind of borehole with a pipe – this was the only fresh water – used for washing and drinking and everything else by all these people. There was nothing else. We had no alternative but to join in the fight to get close to it, all the women pushing and shoving to fill up bottles, petrol drums and anything else which would hold fluid. People who hadn't eaten for days struggled weakly to pull the containers back up the slippery mountainside to the slowly moving snail of cars and people.

The ground around the borehole had once been an army camp and was surrounded by a flat, muddy area made swampy with rainwater. The bright orange and yellow human faeces were everywhere. Some women were washing their laundry in the icy water, some had lit fires to boil the water first, but most just waited for a chance to hold the clothes under the pipe for a few seconds. This place stank even more strongly of raw sewage and I watched the women unconcernedly making flat bread on fires standing in diarrhoea puddles. These women could bake anywhere, in the backs of trucks, in deep mud or open sewage.

'Is there anywhere private where women can go to do their toilet?' I asked an Arabic speaking woman.

'Go downstream to the trees,' she told me, 'and then up between those hills. That is where the women's toilet is.'

It was over a mile's walk, and it was even worse than the water hole. I watched children drinking water from a stream which was being used to clean clothes stained with diarrhoea. I was exhausted and the rain had started to pour down again. The only building which I had seen in the whole area was an old workman's hut, which must have been put up as a store when they were building the road. Lights were flickering inside so I went over to see if I could shelter until the storm passed. I pushed my way in through the door, and smoke billowed out. The flickering lights had come from the fires which were burning on the floor, the smoke having no escape except through the door. About seven Kurdish families were huddled around these fires, talking in low voices, their children lying around in bundles of rags. All their faces turned to look at me as I came in.

'Can I stay here and get warm for a while?' I asked in Arabic.

There was a moment's pause and then an old woman beckoned me to come in and they all nodded their greetings to me and made a place for me on the hard, concrete floor, giving me a cup of tea. I don't know how long I sat with those people, breathing in that smoke, but it was so wonderful to be dry and warm that I never wanted to leave. Eventually, looking at those sad little children, I began to worry about the boys. The rain had lessened and so I thanked the hut dwellers and made my way back outside.

It took me over an hour to clamber back to the car from this hell, trying to find rocks large enough to take my weight as the mud slid down past me. Sometimes I would go forward a couple of metres, only to have a stone give way and make me stumble and slip ten metres back. I was going to have to repeat this journey every time I wanted water for as long as we were stranded in this place.

Kurdish families had built themselves eyries on the cliff face. They would dig out little platforms with their spades, cover them with sticks and grass and then perch there like families of eagles. I envied them their ability to be so enterprising in such terrible conditions.

Without petrol there was nothing we could do, just sit and wait for Hilall and April to reach us, or for the Peshmerga to do something to help us. Now we were sitting ducks should the helicopters come over and start firing rockets.

The next morning I decided to go down another track to see if I could find Hilall and April there. Taking poor, shaking little Ali with me, I walked for an hour and a half, making enquiries all the way. I would walk a little way and then let Ali rest. I was surprised by the number of people I came across who spoke English and Arabic, many of them professionals, doctors, lawyers and teachers. Everyone was travelling in the hope of finding the same thing, an escape to peace and quiet, away from fear. At the moment our lives were becoming worse with every hour and every kilometre we travelled. Everyone had such sad tales to tell, like the group of young university students, fleeing with their parents even though they wanted to get back to Baghdad in time for the next semester. Some of them realised that they would never be able to go back now. The best they could hope for was that they could get across to Iran and then emigrate to a safe country somewhere, and repair their wasted lives.

'You are English,' a group of young girls said to me, 'when you get out of this you must write a book about what you have suffered here, so that the world can know how bad it really is.'

'Yes,' I said, 'I promise I will.'

I realised I was tiring Ali out and it would soon be dark. There was no point going on searching, we just had to hope that they would get to us eventually. Ali and I slowly pulled ourselves back up the mountain, stopping for frequent rests, every bend an agony to reach. We were just two bends away from where we had left Azziz and Majid when we were stopped by a crowd of people who had gathered around a young couple. The woman was holding a tiny, white-faced girl in her arms, wrapped in a blanket.

'Please,' they implored me, 'are you from the UN? This child needs help, she is so sick. Do you have any medicine?'

I took the baby from her mother and gently checked her. She was completely limp, with her eyes rolling back in her head, but so pretty.

'What were her symptoms?' I asked.

'We have no water,' the woman told me, 'she was so thirsty, she drank paraffin.'

'How long ago was this?'

'Three days.'

I knew it was too late. I had nothing I could use to wash her stomach out. I asked them if they had done anything to try to make her vomit, but I could see they hadn't done anything. I knew that there was a doctor a little further up the road and I told them so, but I also knew that he had no medicines. I carefully wrapped the child up in her blanket again and just held her. As I stood there in the cold I felt her breathing stop. I gently massaged her chest and put my mouth over hers, but I couldn't breathe any life back into the tiny, poisoned body.

I passed her back to her father, and the couple began to walk up the mountain in search of the doctor, carrying the dead body of their only child, the mother beside herself with grief. Ali and I continued our struggle back to Azziz and the car, overwhelmed with despair for ourselves and everyone around us.

I think Amin was responsible for our safe passage so far into the mountains. You only had to look at Azziz to see that he was Arab and that he was not a peasant, and I think Amin deflected some of the hostility and questioning which we might otherwise have received from the Peshmerga. Still we didn't trust him. Sometimes he would disappear for hours on end.

'Where have you been?' I asked the first time he had been away for a long time.

'What's it to you?' he snarled, and walked off.

'Be careful, Susan,' Azziz counselled me, putting his hand over mine, 'don't ask him too many questions.'

'We are going to walk to the border to see if there is any food or petrol,' Azziz told me the next morning as he and Amin prepared themselves to set out.

'How long will it take to get there?' I wanted to know.

Amin shrugged, 'We will be gone most of the day.'

'Are they letting people get that close?'

'Some people,' he said enigmatically.

Late that night Azziz returned looking half dead with exhaustion. He handed me a bag of dry bread.

'Where did you get this?'

'From the Iranians.'

'How?'

'They have closed the gates to keep the people out, and then they drive through the crowds throwing out these bags of dry bread and some tins of jam. This bag hit me in the chest, it was painful,' he rubbed himself ruefully.

'What a way to distribute aid.'

'It's terrible down there, just tens of thousands of people milling around under the walls. When anything is distributed there are fights and the strongest get the supplies and the weakest are trampled. We went along the wall a little way to where there aren't any guards and crossed over. Some of Amin's friends are camped on the other side, he thought there might be some petrol over there.'

'Did the guards see you?'

'Yes, but they didn't seem to care. There is nothing on the other side, just more mountains. There was no point in my staying there, so I came back with this.'

'Was there any petrol?'

'No, none.'

TWENTY-FIVE

NOW we had been in the mountains for ten days, stuck without petrol for two of those. We were always cold, wet and tired, both day and night. Standing around a smouldering wood fire with a Kurdish family one morning I caught a glimpse of myself in their car mirror. Was that really me? I couldn't believe that I had grown so haggard and changed so much in such a short time. My face was thin and drawn and there were deep, dark lines etched into it. My hair had turned completely black and I looked so dirty. The days passed, but still no sign of our family. I was beginning to fear that the worst had happened and they were going to be amongst the ones that didn't make it. I feared the same about myself and Azziz.

I saw so many terrible sights in those days as we continued to struggle for survival, terrified that each day would be our last and that our bodies would give up on us and collapse under the strain. Once I came across the body of an old woman. She was lying in the mud and a pack of wild dogs was pulling out the insides of her stomach, making her old body jerk and rock. I let out a scream and an old man stopped to help me.

'Look at that!' I exclaimed, trying to shoo the snarling, cowering creatures away.

'They are hungry too,' he shrugged, poking at them with a stick as they snapped back at him before running off. 'If there is nothing for the people there is even less for the dogs, except our bodies. Make sure you bury your dead deep, or the dogs will dig them up.'

The suffering drove many people mad. I was standing on the track in the rain while the men were off somewhere, holding Ali in my arms, when an elderly lady came running over to us shouting. She grabbed Ali's arm and started pulling him towards her. She was screaming that he was her son. She was a frightening sight, soaking wet with no shoes and no jacket and only one sock. I tried to reason with her, telling her that Ali was my grandson, but she was demented and just kept screaming and pulling. Ali clung to me in terror. I managed to get free of her and climbed back into the car with Ali and Majid. I slammed the doors and locked them, but she continued to circle round us, peering in through the steamed up windows, crying for her lost child. When Amin came back and talked to her she seemed to calm down. I got out of the car and offered her some tea and bread but she took no notice and just went rambling away. I started to go after her.

'Leave her,' Amin told me, 'there is nothing you can do, her mind has gone.' I knew he was right. There must have been so many women up there driven mad by the grief of losing their children. We felt so helpless, so completely at the mercy of the elements.

If I had thought the journey down to the water-hole was bad the first time, it became progressively worse as the rain deepened the mud and the crowds of people grew thicker and more desperate. On the third day I didn't think that I would be able to make it back up, even if I managed to slip and slide to the bottom. I knew that I had reached the end of my physical strength. I just wanted to curl up in a ball and sleep forever.

'I can't get down there today, darling,' I said to Azziz. 'I'm sorry, I'm so cold I can't stop shivering. Perhaps tomorrow I'll be strong enough if I rest a little.'

'I'll go,' he said.

'You have less strength than me,' I tried to dissuade him. 'Rest with me today.' I knew that he had had terrible diarrhoea for five days now and had eaten nothing since it started; I couldn't believe that he would be able to make it.

'I'll be all right,' he insisted, kissing me on the forehead with cold, cracked lips, and disappearing over the side of the mountain before I could try to talk him out of it. I was so frightened that that would be the last time I would see him alive, but I didn't have the strength to call out, or even to crawl to the edge and watch him go. I just had to rest.

I waited for several hours for him to return, and my body seemed to recover a little of its strength. My mind kept going over and over all the possibilities of what could be happening to him. I felt so alone and afraid. Although I knew how long it took to climb up the rock face I couldn't wait any longer and I decided to set out to look for him. I couldn't bear the thought of him lying somewhere in the mud and sewage, waiting for death. I wanted to be with him, to see him again. Leaving Ali and Majid in the car I set off down the mountain in the rain. My feet slid out from under me almost immediately, and I expended as much effort on slowing myself down by grabbing at the jagged rocks and scrubby plants as I did on putting one foot in front of the other. I was buffeted and banged, jabbed and scraped as the mountain mud swept me on down. Eventually I arrived at the bottom, gasping for breath and wiping the water and mud from my eyes.

I looked around, searching amongst the people to try to see where Azziz could be. Everyone looked the same in their filthy, soaked state, all of us bent double with strain, tiredness, unhappiness and sickness. I must have looked just like the rest of them as I stumbled around trying to find my husband. I eventually recognised him sitting in the dirt, his head in his hands. He had the full water cans beside him, but they were too heavy for him to move any further.

'Come on, darling,' I said, 'we've got to get back up to the car, out of this rain.'

'I can't make it,' he shook his head. 'Leave me a while to gather my strength.'

'If you stay here you will die,' I pulled at him and he yielded, too exhausted to fight me, stumbling to his feet, 'I'll help you.' Pushing him ahead of me I took the two 20 litre containers and pulled them up towards the car. It seemed to take forever with my heart banging and sickness and tiredness coming over me in waves. The rivers of mud kept trying to push us back down, pulling our feet out from under us, making rocks and other footholds crumble and vanish as we trod on them, bringing us crashing painfully down on our knees or our sides as I struggled to keep hold of the cans and haul myself forward, helping Azziz at the same time. His breathing sounded painful and his eyes looked huge and glazed in his sallow, drained face. After what seemed like hours we reached the top and staggered to the car.

We had manoeuvred our car into a sheltered position under a high bank, thinking that at least it would afford us some sort of protection from the rain, and some privacy if we wanted to go to the toilet in the night. We also had a small space for lighting a fire. By constantly foraging around the sides of the roads we managed to collect enough grass and twigs to burn, although they were always damp and hard to light. Whenever Amin was with us he would complain that he was hungry and expect me to conjure food out of thin air, but I only had one pot for boiling water because the rest were in the other car. I still had three boiled eggs left, which I had cooked in Halabja.

I noticed that there were a lot of Peshmerga around and they seemed to be keeping their eye on us all the time now. Whenever I looked up I would see one of them watching us.

That evening Azziz seemed a little stronger. We made tea and talked about what we might do the next day. 'I want to go down the mountain with Amin and look for April and the babies again,' he said. 'I think I know which road they are on now.'

'Are you strong enough?' I was frightened. So many things could go wrong on a trip like that, he could get lost or injured and I would be on my own with the boys and at the mercy of Amin, whom I still didn't trust. But I was as worried as he was, so I didn't put up too much of an argument.

Before daybreak on the 9th the two men left us and walked for ten hours. I don't know how Azziz found the strength for such a trip, but thank God he did. They found April and Hilall parked by the main road on the other side of the mountain. Both babies were sick with the same brightly coloured diarrhoea.

April was frantic as she told her father what had happened to them. 'The lorry driver that we paid the money to died on the second day of the trip through lack of insulin. We had to stop so that he could be buried and that took a couple of days and we have been stuck here ever since, trying to get another lift. We have no money and no food left, and we had no idea where you were.'

'We must get the babies to your mother,' Azziz said, 'they are sick and they need nursing.'

'I know,' April agreed in despair, 'I don't know what to do for them, and I have nothing I can give them. But one of us will have to stay with the car.'

'I'll stay with the car,' Hilall volunteered. 'I'll keep trying to get another tow so that I can join you. But are you two strong enough to do that journey back with the babies?'

'We have to,' was all Azziz could say.

Amin wanted to go on searching for members of his family. So my husband and daughter, both dangerously weak from hunger and illness, set off on the journey back up the mountain with the sick babies. April carried a bag on her back and little Sabha on her arm, while Azziz carried another bag and the paraffin cylinder which we needed to make our stove work. Poor little two-year-old Hosni had to walk on his own, stopping every little while to relieve his poisoned bowel.

That night, having struggled every inch of the way, they reached us and April collapsed, sobbing, into my arms. Azziz assembled the paraffin stove for us and I quickly made tea, putting them all to rest in the car. I made a bottle for Sabha and cuddled the babies to me. I was so relieved to have them to take care of, and so frightened by the sight of them. The baby had no nappies left so I tore up a skirt of mine and a shirt of my husband's to wrap her in; it would be enough for the night. She was just a bag of bones with no weight left on her at all. Legs and arms that had been plump and smooth when we set out were now just like those of a skeleton covered in loose, dried skin. When she did open her eyes they were glazed and bloodshot, and often rolled up into her head, leaving the whites horribly exposed as she slept fitfully, whimpering in her sleep from hunger. Now that I had the paraffin I could at least cook the rice and beans which we had left to try to bind up their stomachs, but with so many mouths to feed the supplies would not last more than a couple of days.

Later that night I talked to Azziz alone. 'We have to get away from here,' I said, 'or that baby is going to die, and probably Hosni as well. We have to take our chances and head back towards Baghdad.'

'We will never make it on foot,' Azziz warned, and I knew he was right.

'Then we have to find petrol, it is our only hope.'

All of us slept together in the car that night and at times I was so uncomfortable I thought it might be better to get out and sleep underneath. I didn't; I had seen too many people die of exposure in the last few days. April and the three little children slept on the back seat while Azziz, Majid and I were in the front. Thank God Amin didn't come back that night. Eventually I gave up trying to sleep. I got out and leant on the bonnet of the car, too weary to move or even to think, standing like a zombie in the night.

As the dawn broke I pulled myself together. Before the rest of the women crowded round the water-hole, I took Sabha's dirty nappies down to the water pipe. I had borrowed a plastic bowl from a neighbouring car and I had my last two pieces of soap. The water was icy cold, but at least I had it to myself. I scrubbed frantically to finish before the crowds started to come down for their morning supplies and elbowed me aside. Back up at the car I found the others stirring and I asked Azziz to put up a string and an old stocking of mine to make a line to dry the bits and pieces of washing. It was hopeless, nothing would dry in the continuous rain.

Using some of my precious Dettol I washed my hands and set up the stove to boil the eggs which I had been saving all this time for the babies. As soon as he could my husband set out in search of petrol. He spent the whole day hunting with no chance of success. April and I were luckier with our shopping. During the morning some smugglers came round selling packets of biscuits. I bought enough packets to last us a few days and some for the family next to us who had no money.

April spent the whole day peering down the road in the hope of seeing Hilall coming, but there was no sign. We had already finished the paraffin and were back to collecting anything which might burn and give us enough heat to cook, but the rain made virtually everything unburnable. It was all so frustrating. On 11 April a group of Peshmerga came over to us to ask what we were doing up there.

'We are escaping from Saddam Hussein,' we said cautiously, trying to work out what it was that they wanted to hear. 'We want to get into Iran, to safety.'

'Everyone wants to get in,' they said, 'but they won't let all these people in. Why should you get through?'

'We can see that now,' we explained, 'but there is nothing we can do. We have run out of petrol and we are waiting until the time is right to go back to Baghdad.'

Their leader looked at us quizzically. 'Perhaps the time is right now, they are letting some Kurds go back, so why would they not let you back?'

'They are letting Kurds back?'

'There have been negotiations in Baghdad over Kirkuk. They promise there will be no repercussions if people go back to their homes now.'

We could hardly contain our excitement as the men moved on to talk to others. Go home? That was all we wanted to do, it was all we dreamt of. But we still didn't have any petrol and we had to wait for Hilall to join us.

'What if Saddam changes his mind,' I asked Azziz, 'as he has a hundred times before, and starts to kill everyone on the way back?'

'We just have to pray he doesn't. Perhaps with the eyes of the world on him he will behave honourably.' Neither of us felt confident about that, but we were grasping at straws because the alternatives were worse. We had hope again, however flimsy, where before everything had seemed completely hopeless. Perhaps we weren't finished after all, we now had a new goal to work for – we couldn't afford to doubt it.

Little Sabha was growing weaker every hour and wouldn't take her bottle any more. Diarrhoea poured out of her in a continuous stream, but she wasn't strong enough to replace the fluid in her tiny body. Hosni was now passing blood. I heard that there was a doctor working in a tent on the next mountain. Rumour had it that he had absconded from his hospital with a quantity of drugs and medicines to help his people on the mountains. I went to look for him, taking the babies with me. He was a very kind man but his supplies had run out and he had no idea how to get more. He had even been into Iran to talk to UN people, but they had refused to help. Nor was there any sign of the Red Cross working amongst these desperate people. We had truly been deserted by everyone. I boiled rice and gave the babies water to drink, but it didn't help. If we didn't go soon it was going to be too late.

It was another two days of scrounging and struggling to keep the babies alive before Hilall's car was finally spotted being towed up the mountainside by a big lorry. God knows how many hours April had spent standing at the head of the track praying for this sight, clinging onto little Sabha, desperately rocking her to and fro in the hope of soothing the emaciated little baby back to health as she scanned the horizon for her missing husband. I felt so relieved to see Hilall's smiling face, although I was shocked to see how much weight he too had lost. Because he had been so well covered before, and because I hadn't seen him for several days, the loss was even more noticeable on him than on the rest of us.

Virtually everyone had dysentery now. We had seen helicopters circling above the mountains, spraying some sort of powder out behind them. The sight of them caused panic as we all believed they had come to spray us with chemicals. But if they wanted to kill us now there was little we could do about it. There was nowhere to run and hide; it might even be better to die a quick death than to starve slowly. But the helicopters stayed up high and the clouds did not reach us.

The Peshmerga told us that that was how they put the chemicals into the water supplies, so that none of the mountain water would be safe to drink. The chemicals went into the snow and the mountain streams and then spread on down the mountainsides and into the artesian water system. Perhaps they didn't manage to get to every drop of water in the mountains, but how could anyone know which was pure and which was poisoned? There was no way of telling until it was too late, until the chemicals were inside your stomach. For some it meant a slow death by dehydration, for the rest of us it was like a living death as the body's juices ebbed away, leaving us drained and susceptible to the germs which were rife everywhere.

As a family we were now in a bad state. Sabha was vomiting back anything that I could get her to swallow so there was no goodness getting into her at all, and I had had a bad fall down the side of the mountain, leaving me in great pain. I had been pulling the water containers up when a searing pain in my chest had knocked me backwards, as if I had been struck by a lance. I had slipped and rolled for what seemed like miles on my way up from the water-hole, before crashing to a halt against some boulders, flat on my face and unable to get up. One of the families nesting on the mountainside saw my plight and sent two men down to help me. Between them they hauled me up to the top, and a woman put my water cans on her shoulders and carried them up for me. Those people were so strong. They took me to the car and found Azziz and the others sitting there, shivering. They felt so sorry for us that they went back down the mountain and fetched some hot tea for us all. I was bruised and limping and not able to carry the water drums any distance after that.

I sat in the car for the rest of the day with Sabha in my arms, just waiting for her to stop breathing and leave us.

TWENTY-SIX

HILALL seemed very strong compared to the rest of us, and his weight loss suited him. He took over the carrying of the water drums from me that evening, even though he had been out hunting for petrol all day. I was very glad to have him there. He had been so patient with me during the months in Sulaimaniyah when I had gone on at him, always ready to forgive me and never arguing back.

'On my way up I passed a place where the Peshmerga are selling black market petrol,' he told us that night over tea, 'down at the bottom of the mountain.'

My heart skipped a beat at this news. 'Will they still be there tomorrow?'

'I don't know. They are asking a lot of money. It might cost something over a thousand dinars to get enough petrol to take us back to Sulaimaniyah.'

'I don't care what it costs,' I said. 'Take the whole bag, otherwise Sabha will be dead before we can get back to civilisation.'

Early next morning Azziz and Hilall set out to find the black marketeers. It only took them an hour and a half to find them, but they then had to drag back the sixteen jerry cans which they had bought for 1,350 dinars, a slow and painful process. It was noon before they got back to us. I couldn't believe that we were actually filling the cars up with fuel. April was holding Sabha in the back of their car and the baby's little body was completely limp. She was no longer regaining consciousness, even for a few minutes. It didn't look as if there was any life left in her. If we didn't get help within the next few hours we would lose her.

'Which route back should we take?' I asked.

Azziz had been discussing this with some of the Peshmerga. 'They say the mountain road is clear now. The other route is safer but it is blocked with traffic because so many other people are starting to go back.'

Oh God, did we really have to go back over those dreadful, twisting mountain roads? Had we survived all this to be killed in some ravine on the way home? Hilall was the first to finish filling his car and he jumped in and started it up. The sound of the engine was like music to us. At last we could move. We were still packing things into the car in any way we could as they set off and we followed about half an hour later, honking the horn to clear people out of the way.

The roads which had been so full a week before were now deserted and some of the mud had dried, making them less slippery. Azziz was determined to catch up and stood on the gas pedal, throwing the car round the corners as fast as he could. I covered my eyes and prayed. We caught up with the others at a Red Cross base run by the Peshmerga half way down the mountain. Hilall and April were inside trying to persuade the doctors to help. All they could prescribe was ampicillin to be watered down with sterile water and drunk – not much use when the baby needed glucose and saline drips.

'Come on, we don't have time to mess around here,' I called to them, 'we've got to get her to a proper hospital today.'

'Just a minute,' a Peshmerga leader stepped forward. 'Where are you heading to?'

'We are going back to Sulaimaniyah,' I said. 'Don't slow us down, please, this baby is dying.'

'Sulaimaniyah, eh?' He walked slowly over to us, his gun on his shoulder. 'You are Arabs?'

'Yes, we were trapped in the mountains escaping Saddam's army, but now he has declared a truce and we are going back.'

'Then you can take some passengers,' he said, beckoning over two tired looking Kurdish men.

'Yes, of course,' I was so relieved I would have taken anyone, just to be on the road again. Our two new travelling companions climbed in the back and we set off again at top speed. None of us felt much like talking. When you have been through such an ordeal there is little you can say to other people. We just wanted to put the mountains as far behind us as possible.

Every few hundred metres we had to stop for a Peshmerga checkpoint and Hilall had to talk us through as quickly as he could. They all wanted to know what we were doing and where we were going; each stop seemed to take an age. We kept showing them Sabha and she seemed like a passport for us; everyone could see that she was only inches away from death. Each time they relented and let us pass.

At Arbat we started to encounter Arab checkpoints and Azziz took over the talking. Now our story changed and we became unfortunate Arabs who had been holidaying in the north when the Kurds started to wage war on the Iraqis. Once again the dying baby speeded our passage, but each time there were those few terrible moments as they looked through our papers in silence, seeming to turn the pages with deliberate slowness as if trying to build the tension so that we would crack and admit to some dreadful crime, before deciding to wave us on.

The journey to Sulaimaniyah, which had taken so many days when we were heading out, now took us two and a half hours. We dropped our passengers off at the outskirts and headed for the hospital. As we drew up outside my heart sank. The building was in darkness, and every window seemed to have been blown out by bullets. It looked like a shell, but we could see there were people inside. We ran in with Sabha and grabbed a nurse. 'Our baby is dying, she needs a drip.'

'We have nothing here,' the woman obviously wasn't interested in us, 'we have no electricity, no water, nothing . . .'

I saw a doctor in the distance and shouted at him, 'You need some proper trained nurses, not rubbish like this. I'm a nurse, I can help you. This baby is dying.'

The doctor came over and looked at Sabha. 'Where have you come from?'

'We have been up in the mountains for three weeks. The baby is dehydrated.'

'We'll put her on the drip now. We also need hot water, but we haven't any power.'

'Give us some water and some paraffin and we will heat it in the road outside.'

The doctor looked at me and broke into a smile. 'All right.' He started issuing orders and within a few minutes Azziz was boiling water outside on the pavement to bring in for the baby and some of the other patients.

'You need to get under cover before dark,' the doctor warned us. 'There is a curfew and there has been a lot of shooting around the hospital the last few nights.'

We all stood round Sabha's bed as they fixed up the drip. Her breathing appeared to ease and she seemed to be sleeping properly. We were all crying with relief, holding onto one another, hardly daring to speak in case something went wrong. Once we felt Sabha was resting comfortably we left April sitting beside her bed, the drip rigged up and slowly pushing life back into her tiny, drained body. They had given us some medicines for the boys and for Azziz and we drove back to Othman's house, not knowing if we would find him and his family dead or alive.

'What will we do if they have been murdered?' I asked Azziz as we drove along.

'We will try to get into the house and rest there.'

'Won't the army have taken it over?'

'I don't know,' he shook his head, 'I don't know anything any more.'

The city was completely lifeless. Not only were there no Kurdish people, there were virtually no Iraqi soldiers either. As we turned into the end of Othman's road Hilall's car gave a mighty crack and part of the engine fell out into the road. We had made it with only a few yards to go. We pushed the car the last few yards as Othman's family came out to see what the noise was about. Rina let out a scream of joy when she saw who it was, hitching up her skirts and running down the road towards us, with Othman and the children on her heels. We were laughing and crying at the same time as we met them with open arms, hugging and kissing.

'We thought you would all be dead,' I said.

'We thought the same of you,' Othman answered. 'Come quickly into the house before we attract attention.' His joy at seeing us was quickly replaced by his old caution and anxiety as he shepherded us inside. We were all asking questions at once, no one able to find any answers. They looked a great deal better than we did, and busied themselves making tea and finding some food for us. I noticed a picture of Saddam Hussein on the wall in a place where there had been a picture of one of the Kurdish leaders when we left. I mentioned this change in allegiance.

Othman smiled sheepishly. 'Well, you have to adapt to survive in times like this. They come round the house often to check on us, we tell them what they want to hear and hide our guns well, and they go away satisfied that they have suppressed us. We have been short of food, but we have not suffered in any other ways.'

'Did they bomb the city?' I asked.

'No,' he shook his head, 'there was very little resistance left by the time they got here. You can see, the streets are empty, there is hardly anyone left here.'

'Do you know if the roads to Baghdad are clear?' Azziz asked.

'They say they have pardoned all Kurds,' Othman said, 'the message has been broadcast everywhere. Sulaimaniyah and Kirkuk are back in government hands, so the roads are clear now. You should be safe travelling south.'

News of our return had spread and the only other neighbours who were in the city came round to see how we were. They were obviously shocked by the way we looked. 'You must use our sauna to get clean,' they said. 'We have enough paraffin to heat it up if you all go in together.'

'Oh no,' my modesty came flooding back, 'there is no way I am going into a bathroom with the men. I will heat some water and wash myself off in the toilet downstairs.' They tried to talk me into it, but I just couldn't have done it, even after all the indignities which we had been through. Now that it was possible I had to have my privacy. I also felt guilty that we were using up these people's precious supplies of paraffin.

That night, three weeks since we had left to go to the mountains, we were back in our underground room. It seemed like a sanctuary to us, sipping hot tea and soup, with medicines for the children. We were warm and dry and quiet and in a few days we would be going home. I was so relieved I just hugged the boys to me and wept.

TWENTY-SEVEN

SABHA was on the hospital drip for three days, and even then she still looked like a little monkey, unable to control her wobbly neck. Although they released her she still needed heavy medication. During those three days we managed to get Hilall's car fixed, at enormous expense, and on 20 April, over three months after leaving Baghdad, we set off for home.

When we reached Kirkuk we were stopped at a checkpoint. The men manning this one were not like the young soldiers we had been encountering up till now. These were Baathist secret police, men who would murder anyone without a second thought.

'Be careful what you say,' Azziz warned me, but he needn't have bothered, I was too frightened of these people to take any risks. With suspicious looks and angry words, they let us past, but we continued to be stopped every few hundred metres along the road. As soon as we had the chance, we drove fast across the wastelands between Kirkuk and Baghdad, anxious to get back into the city before evening.

'Look at these,' I had pulled my boots off for the first time since the day the rocket nearly killed me on the side of the road. The soles were completely worn through, the remains hanging away from the rest of the boot. 'I never want to see those again,' and I threw them out of the window of the speeding car. Now I am rather sad that I threw them away like that. They had been faithful friends in those terrible days. The state of them would have been a good reminder of what we had been through, although I doubt if I will ever forget any of it.

As we entered Baghdad, Hilall and April turned off towards their home. They were running very low on petrol and were afraid they would not make it all the way, so they didn't want to deviate from their route. They were right; they ran out of fuel half an hour away from their house and had to be towed by a passing tractor.

The streets of Baghdad were quiet and empty. There was evidence of bomb damage, but not as much as we had expected. Everywhere houses were boarded up and silent, their occupants dead or run away. There were no young men to be seen anywhere and most of the shops were empty or shut. Very few lights were working. The few people we did pass stared at us in wonderment – I can't imagine what we must have looked like. Because there were so few people in the city, the dogs had moved back in. There were packs of them in every street, fearless as we drove past, intent on squabbles over whatever scraps they were able to find in this lifeless place.

As we approached our street I began to feel nervous about what I would find. Supposing the house had been bombed, or ransacked? Would I find my beautiful home ruined and defiled, or just a pile of rubble? Even if nothing terrible had happened to it the fact that it had been closed up for over three months meant that it would be musty and dirty and the facilities probably wouldn't be working properly.

We reached the gates, which were securely locked from the inside. Somebody must be in there, but who? Had the house been commandeered by the Baathists who must have noticed our disappearance? I played out our family call-sign on the bell and waited nervously to see what would happen. We heard someone fumbling eagerly with the locks on the inside and then the gates flew open. John and Peter came rushing out and threw their arms around us, their wives standing in the background. The grandchildren milled around our legs, staring up in horror at the sight of their Nana and Gidu. The smaller ones obviously didn't recognise us as the same people they had seen before the war broke out. I couldn't believe that everyone, my whole family, was alive. And they all looked well.

'Baba!' John exclaimed to his father when he had got over his initial euphoria and stood back to look at the state of us, 'what have you done to Mama? She looks terrible. Come inside at once, you look so thin and sick.'

They helped us in, all the time firing questions at us. Apparently, once the bombing ended, they went out to April's house to try to find us, but no one had any idea where we had gone. They hoped we had gone to some safer sanctuary, but they had half believed that we were dead.

I couldn't believe how clean the house was as we went in. Some of the windows had been blown out and were now boarded up, but inside it was immaculate. Laila told us it had taken her a week to clear up when they first came back. 'Because the windows were gone and cats and rats had got in and the mess was terrible,' she explained, 'Mama, you would have been horrified.'

Now it was the most wonderful sight I had ever seen. Laila had just made the children their tea, the electric kettle was steaming in the corner and the table was covered in sandwiches. As we sat down to eat the doorbell started to go again and the neighbours, who had seen our car outside, came in to welcome us back. Everyone was crying and hugging one another. Only a few days before we had been stranded in hell, unsure whether we would live for another day, and now we were home.

John took charge of me. As soon as we had eaten something he took me to the bathroom and drew me a bath. The water was a nasty brown colour and very smelly, but I didn't care, at least it was hot and I could have my first soak in months. I filled it with bath salts to disguise the smell. I looked at myself in the mirror and I could see why everyone was so shocked. I had lost nearly six stone since the beginning of the Allied attack, and aged two decades. My skin was dry and gnarled and my face deeply lined. My hair, which had once been blonde, was now completely black and oily with dirt. Azziz looked as bad, his limbs like sticks and all the muscles wasted away.

I scrubbed and scrubbed myself and then went to my bed. What a wonderful feeling to descend onto a soft mattress after all those nights curled up in the car, and on the floor of the underground room and the bomb shelter before that. What utter luxury to feel your stomach full of food and to know that you are safe in your own home again. I fell into a deep, dreamless sleep.

TWENTY-EIGHT

ALL the family came with us to the bus station to see us off. I felt very weak, both physically and emotionally. Not only did I feel I was saying goodbye to my children and grandchildren, I felt I was also saying goodbye to Iraq. It had been my home for over thirty years and I had overcome many difficulties in order to stay there with the man I loved. Now I felt I had finally been defeated. Life had become intolerable. I was too battered and exhausted to go on fighting any longer. I was going to have to leave everything I had known for the majority of my life and start again.

We were all crying, and I wasn't able to control my voice enough to say all the things I wanted to say to each of them. As I sank into my seat, waving to them, I sobbed uncontrollably. As we drew out of the station Azziz put his arm round my shoulder and guided my face down onto his shoulder and I cried myself to sleep.

For the whole of the week following our return to Baghdad the house had been full of neighbours, family and friends. It was such a warm welcome, but somehow I didn't seem able to join in the happiness. I left the rituals of hospitality to the children and I would spend a lot of time in my bedroom. It was as if my body, sensing that the state of imminent danger was passed, had relaxed and allowed all the pain and sickness which had been building up inside to wash over me. I was continually breathless and nervous, bursting into tears all the time. I had diarrhoea just like Azziz and the children had had in the mountains and what I could only describe as a 'frozen foot'. One of my toes was blue and part of my right foot was numb. That numbness has still not left me, but then I couldn't even put my foot on the floor because of the pain.

'You have to see the doctor,' Azziz insisted after a few days. 'You are getting worse, not better. All these years you have been looking after all of us, carrying the whole family. Now it is our turn to look after you.'

I knew he was right and so I agreed, even though I would rather have hidden under the covers of my own bed than gone out and faced the world. The doctor was very kind. He looked at my poor, dry, crinkly skin and listened to me gasping for breath and crying.

'You are dehydrated, my dear,' he said, 'and you are having a nervous breakdown. You should be in the hospital.'

'I'm not going to that place,' I said stubbornly, 'I would die in there. Just give me some medicine. I want to be in my own house.' The thought of being back with sick and dying strangers was more than I could stand. I had seen the inside of too many hospitals in Iraq. I never wanted to leave my own house again.

The doctor tried to dissuade me, but I was adamant and I went back home, trying to keep going with my chores around the house. Over the next few days I grew worse. My son John became increasingly worried.

'I feel like I'm dying, John,' I confessed.

'You are so tired, Mama. Why don't you lie down?'

'I'm not an invalid!' I shouted at him, but the effort made me almost collapse, gasping for breath.

'You are going to hospital,' he said, lifting me bodily off the floor.

The moment I got to hospital they put me on a drip, while Azziz and John waited outside. They gave me three bottles of saline solution while I looked around the ward. The place was just as bad as I had imagined, full of the dying and filthy dirty. A young woman in one of the other beds had been napalmed and lost the skin all over her body. She was lying, just raw burnt flesh, waiting for death. 'My God,' I said to myself, 'my problems are nothing compared to that poor creature.'

As the third bottle drained into me the doctor came to see me. 'You must stay with us overnight,' he said.

'No,' I said firmly, 'I have had three bottles, that is enough. If I stay in here I will die. I want to go home.'

The doctor tried to dissuade me, showing me other people who had been up on the mountains and who were now willingly undergoing treatment at his hands, but I was determined to be out of that place as fast as possible. John and Azziz saw that I was not to be argued with and drove me home.

'You must have a break from all this,' Azziz said as we reached the house, 'we must try to get to England for a rest.'

'Yes, all right,' I agreed.

I didn't really want to go to England just then, not without my family. They all needed a rest just as much as I did, more really, but I knew that I had to get away to recover my strength. Since returning I had been listening to everyone else's stories, and each one added to my depression and agitation. John and his wife Laila had gone to her family house in the Karbala district when the Allied bombs started to drop. This is a Shi'ite area, and once the Allies had ceased firing Saddam Hussein turned his bombers onto them with the same ferocity as he had attacked the Kurds. It was said that 22,000 people were killed in the attacks, and the Baathist tanks were simply running people down in the streets. Everyone had their own horror stories to tell, and we all needed to get out of Iraq to find some decent food and peace of mind.

As soon as we returned to the house the Baathist Party members were back at the gates asking questions about where we had been and where our family had been, and shoving forms at us to fill in. I noticed that Peter became particularly frightened whenever there was someone at the gate. I kept asking him what the matter was and he kept trying to dismiss it, but eventually he broke down and told me.

'I'm frightened that they are going to kill me, Mama,' he said.

'Who?'

'The army. You see, I lost my unit early in the war and that makes me a deserter in their eyes. They are shooting deserters without asking any questions.'

'How did you lose your unit?' my heart literally felt as if it was in my mouth as I listened to this new danger.

'You remember that I was posted to the north just before the Allies attacked,' he said, 'and then I went to settle Hala in with her family?' I nodded for him to go on. 'It took a few days to arrange that. The first house we went to had fifty-eight people in it. We had to sleep the night in the car. It was hopeless, so we decided to come back to Baghdad and look for her parents. The city was so well guarded by that time I didn't think it would be that dangerous. It was hard to get back in, but we managed to find them, staying with some relatives.

'Then I went back down to Basrah to rejoin my unit. I took the train, but it was attacked by rockets and blown off the rails. I managed to get out and climb over a fence into the street. I spent the night hiding in a policeman's traffic hut in the middle of the road, while the Allies were attacking all around. I was so frightened, Mama.' He buried his head in my lap for a few minutes and I stroked his hair as I waited for him to go on. 'It was chaos down there and I had no idea where to go. I hitched a ride back up to Baghdad and went to an army office to try to find out where I should go. They ordered me back down to join my unit again. I said I didn't know how to find them now; I told them I thought they had all been killed. They got angry and told me to obey orders. I thought they were going to shoot me then.

'I found a truck going south and went back down, but it was hopeless. My unit had been completely destroyed, like all the others. Everywhere there were men wandering around not knowing what they were supposed to be doing, having seen all their comrades killed and knowing that they were in danger of being killed by their own leaders if they did the wrong thing. They had no idea what they should be doing. Eventually I came back to Baghdad, found Hala and when the bombing ended we came here to hide. There are men like me hiding all over the country, but they are bound to find us in the end.'

'Oh my poor baby.' I held him close to me and we both cried. How desperately I wanted to take all my children away from this country now, but none of them could contemplate leaving. They all had too many responsibilities. Even my little boy crying on my shoulder was a grown man with children of his own. I could listen to his troubles, but there was nothing I could do to help him. I felt horribly impotent, but for the first time ever I realised that I could actually go off with Azziz and leave my family to fend for themselves. I could leave them with the house to live in and the money and possessions which we still had, but I couldn't do much to help them by being there. In fact, if I was going to be ill, I was more likely to be a worry to them than a help. So I agreed to Azziz's plan that we should try to get away, on the condition that they would all try to join us as soon as possible.

There were a lot of rumours circulating: only people over 55 would be allowed to travel; no one would be allowed to take more than $300 with them, and no Iraqi currency. We went to the passport office to enquire, but the doors were still firmly shut. It seemed a hopeless situation, since $300 was not going to get anyone very far in the outside world. The only people who had a chance were those, like me, who might be able to get help from people in other countries. But there was still a problem since we needed to get to Jordan before we could catch a plane, and would therefore need money in Jordan to buy tickets. The Americans had stipulated that Iraqi citizens should be free to travel, so we felt that sooner or later something would have to happen, but it was hard to see what. It was so frustrating not to be able to take control of our lives, even now that the war was over.

I was finding the strain of waiting intolerable. We concentrated all our efforts on trying to buy black market dollars, no matter what the asking price might be, taking care not to buy any of the counterfeit ones which were being sold to the unwary. Eventually we managed to collect $1,500, which we hoped would be enough to buy us two cheap tickets out of Amman. Bus tickets to Amman from Baghdad were 50 dinars each.

The telephones in Baghdad weren't working, so we made contact with all our old friends by driving to their houses in the evenings, and listening to the horrifying stories of what had happened to them. Many of the houses were boarded up and the people gone. Everyone left behind was nervous and broken, no one had a good story to tell. We still looked awful and one of my best friends didn't even recognise us when he arrived on the doorstep. We were not the only ones waiting for a chance to get to England. Some of the others had sold all their possessions, meaning never to return.

In early June we heard that passports were going to be issued for those wanting to leave. Anyone wanting to get a passport had to be prepared to queue with hundreds of others for two or three days, being shunted from one official window to another, with no certainty of success at the end of it. Often you would wait for hours in one queue, only to have the official slam his window shut when you got there, having decided he was too tired and bored to continue.

Everyone was saying the same once they got their papers. 'So now we can get as far as Amman, but we'll just have to come back after a couple of days because we will run out of money, and all the hotels are full with escaping Kuwaitis.' Their fears were well founded. The Jordanians were kind to their brother Iraqis, but there was a limit to how many of us they could accommodate, and they were short of money as well. They couldn't hope to support the tens of thousands of virtual refugees who were pouring over the border.

Despite all these things, we were still determined, as were many other people, to chance our luck. If the worst came to the worst we would just end up back in Baghdad once more, but there was always a chance that we would find a way to escape. We wouldn't know unless we tried. My diarrhoea had stopped but not my asthmatic breathing or nervousness. I would look at my grandchildren and find myself crying for no particular reason. I felt as if every nerve in my body was wound so tight it was ready to snap. How could I now leave my babies behind and go to England? None of it seemed fair. But if I stayed I felt I might soon go mad.

Just before we left, Saddam Hussein appeared on television and announced an amnesty for all the soldiers accused of deserting. It seems there were many more people like Peter than even we had imagined. It was such a relief to think that we were not going to be leaving him under sentence of death, unable to leave the house for fear of being picked up and shot. But could I be sure that the amnesty was genuine? Would he simply be taken back into the army and sent somewhere else where soldiers were dying in droves? So many questions and worries all the time, and nothing I could do.

It seemed to me that the war would never be over for my children and my grandchildren. I knew it was only a matter of time before the fighting would start up again somewhere else, and they would be sent to their deaths on some new political battlefield – presuming they weren't executed as traitors in their own home city. So many millions of people being pushed and pulled around, never knowing when they will be able to lead the sort of safe, normal lives that most people take for granted in the West. Will there ever come a time when a young family man in Iraq can sleep without the fear of war drums for himself and his children? Will there ever come a time in Iraq when mothers can feel sure that their sons will outlive them? From the south of Basrah to the north of Zakho and Sulaimaniyah, so many friends have gone whom I know I will never see again. Who will speak for them?

EPILOGUE

THE bus stopped at a dozen checkpoints on the way out of the country, arriving in Amman in the early morning. We had been given the name of a hotel that was used a lot by the men doing taxi runs back and forth across the border.

Wandering out into the shopping street we bought some delicious hot bread topped with sesame seeds, and took it along to a nearby *chai khana* (tea house), where they were serving real cups of tea with milk. It was a wonderful breakfast. The sun was already rising over the mosque and the Roman ruins across the street. I squeezed my husband's hand and felt a great surge of happiness. 'I can't believe we are actually out of Iraq and sitting here on this beautiful morning, with no more bombs and no more fear.' He smiled back at me sadly, because he knew that my happiness was only fleeting. As soon as the local children began to come out into the streets to play I remembered my grandchildren and the tears started up again in my eyes.

'Happy birthday,' he said, giving me a little hug. I had completely forgotten what date it was.

The British Council were not optimistic about the chances of Azziz getting a visa. The officials whom we saw shrugged their shoulders helplessly, there was nothing they could do to help, they had no influence at the embassy. There the girl suggested I should buy one ticket to Britain for myself and arrange for a visa and ticket for Azziz once I arrived in the UK. It seemed like the only option. I felt very nervous about spending my last dollars on this gamble. What if something went wrong and I was stuck in Britain while he had to go back to Iraq? But there didn't seem to be any choice. I kept the equivalent of £15 so that I could get from the airport to London, and left my husband with the remaining pittance. As I boarded the flight I was relieved to think that I was finally heading back to Britain, but frightened by the prospect of the bureaucratic battles ahead and the possibility that I might not see Azziz for weeks or months. Now I had lost my grandchildren, children and husband, but I had not given up hope.

The next day I sent £20 to Azziz which I had borrowed from a friend, a debt that was to grow a great deal bigger in the coming weeks. I contacted the Foreign Office and the bureaucratic wheels started to turn, very slowly.

The following day I talked to Azziz himself. 'Keep your spirits up, darling, it won't be long now. I am writing letters to the Prime Minister, with photocopies of all the letters that have been sent out. I have been to see my local MP, who is being very kind and helpful and is writing to the Home Office on our behalf.'

I did all these things, and I don't know which one of them worked, but on 7 August the Amman embassy received clearance for my husband's visa. He finally flew out of Amman on 23 August and we were reunited in England.

I was at the airport hours before his plane landed, watching the doors like a hawk. My heart sank with every group of people that came through which did not include him. When I did see him he looked smaller and frailer and older than I had realised. I felt that I had already regained some of my old strength in the few weeks I had been in England and I just wanted to put him to bed and feed him until he returned to his old self. We fell into each other's arms and just stood there for minutes, clinging onto one another.

What a relief it was for both of us to be in a free country together, without any fear of being shot in the street or bombed in our beds. Even this far from Iraq my nerves are still in tatters, with any loud noises setting them jangling. I don't suppose I will ever completely recover from those terrible years, but at least I have found some peace.

Although I am back in my native country, I still feel something of a refugee, far from my family and frightened for what will happen to them next. Many more terrible things will happen in Iraq in the coming years, and some already are happening. I wish my children could be free of it all, but they are Iraqis and must spend at least part of their lives in their own country.

When I read the newspapers, and hear the politicians making their grand statements about what they are going to do to rectify this situation and that situation, I wonder how many of them stop to think about people like us, ordinary families who just want to be left to lead their lives in peace, who have no strong political views, but who are used as pawns in the big game. The politicians are free to do whatever they like to us and we just have to fight to survive in any way we can. Please God – '*in sha Allah*' – we will see an end to it one day, but I know it will not be in my lifetime.